Enjoy,

Trevor Hodgson   Nov, 2003

Contents

LANDS OF THE VIKINGS

NORWAY
Hafrsfjord
Bergen
Hull
ENGLAND
SHETLAND
FAROES
ICELAND
ATLANTIC OCEAN
GREENLAND
Nuuk
Qaqortoq
DAVIS STRAIT
L'Anse Aux Meadows
NEWFOUNDLAND
LABRADOR

© 2000 Trevor Hodgson

Chapter 1

The First Atlantic Crossing

Toward the end of the first millennium many Norsemen left their native Norway and its overbearing rulers to sail westward. They discovered new lands where they established their homes, built farms, and raised families. Their island-by-island course took them first to Shetland, then to the Faroes, and finally on to Iceland and Greenland. For a moment they stood on the edge of the American continent until they were driven off by hostile Native Americans.

Thus this inaugural Atlantic crossing was accomplished in stages, with several generations passing between the initial departures from Norway and the crunch of the first footsteps on a beach in North America. Sailing between the more easterly Viking lands was relatively easy. Shetland is just forty-eight hours' sailing from both Norway and the Faroes. The crossing on to Iceland is longer but can still be made in about five days. From there things become more difficult. The frozen eastern side of Greenland is most unwelcoming. There is no good land for houses or farms. Icebergs sweep along the coast in the grip of the East Greenland Current, while ice in the bays and inlets lies waiting to trap unwary mariners.

This next move west, perhaps the most critical link in the whole trans-Atlantic chain, was pioneered by the homicidal Erik the Red. Along with his father, he was expelled from Norway for murder. The two felons settled in Iceland where Erik eventually married and built up a successful farm. However, old habits die hard and he was hauled before the local assembly after his neighbor was killed in a dispute. Once more Erik faced banishment. He had to leave Iceland for three years, but this time no settlements beckoned to the west and he was unwelcome anywhere to the east.

Before I discovered the joys of sailing, I climbed a few modest mountains. I've always held that my more notable ascents resulted from an inability to turn back when things got difficult. So it was with Erik. Lack of alternatives drove him to explore the barren, icy, uninhabited land to the west. He sailed southwest, rounded Cape Farewell, and discovered fiords penetrating deep into Greenland's central mountains with land where cattle could graze and cereals could grow. When his three-year banishment was over, he sailed off back to Iceland with the news of his discoveries. Before long, Erik was headed west once more, this time leading a fleet of twenty-five boats crammed with Greenland's first settlers.

The Vikings established a substantial community in southwest Greenland, and soon ships sailed there routinely from Iceland and Norway. Not all of them made it. These are hazardous seas and the navigation of the time was uncertain. Of Erik's twenty-five vessels only sixteen arrived.

The colony was still young when another ship, sailing from Iceland to Erik's new farm, was blown off course by storms. When it eventually arrived in Greenland, it brought news of another land even farther to the west, a land with plentiful pasture and vast forests, both key commodities for the Viking way of life.

In Greenland the grazing land was limited to the sides of the fiords and there was no timber for houses or boats, so the prospect of plenty, conjured by this new land, was too good to pass up. It had to be explored. Erik was now too old for adventurous seafaring, and the torch passed to his son Leif Eriksson. Thus it was Leif, known as Leif the Lucky, who explored the coast of Labrador, completing the Viking Atlantic crossing and becoming the first European to stand on American soil—five hundred years before Christopher Columbus.

The Vikings had no written language to record their adventures—their only writing was simple stick-like runes. Fortunately they were great storytellers. Tales of their exploits were passed orally from generation to generation before they were laced with romance and imagination and recorded on vellum as the classic Icelandic sagas. I like to visualize family groups clustered by fires on long winter nights, listening spellbound as parents and grandparents passed on the tales of their ancestors. Generations of telling and retelling, and the poetic license of the medieval writers, produced wonderful mixtures of history and romance featuring the colorful characters from the days of Viking exploration. While every phrase cannot be treated as historic fact, the sagas provide great insight into a fascinating period of history. In particular they enable us to follow the adventures of pioneers as they made their historic journey to the west. Much of the original detail has survived, and in many cases place-names are still recognizable and locations of historic events can be identified. Guided by descriptions in the sagas, we can find our way to the spot where Erik was outlawed at the Icelandic assembly and sent on his historic journey of discovery. We can visit the Norse settlements in Greenland and stand among the ruins of Erik's farm. We can identify several landmarks noted by Leif on his momentous voyage to America.

Vikings have fascinated my wife, Lesley, and me for several years. Their character is full of surprises, deeper and more complex than the popular image of rampaging barbarians. There's no doubt they were ferocious and cruel. They attacked defenseless abbeys with lightning speed, carrying off treasure, killing men, and raping women. They swept into Europe from the mysterious north like a raging storm, and medieval church records contrast their raw paganism with the humble piety of their Christian victims. They were fierce and exotic foes. But a thousand years on, time has softened and tinted our view. We see grace in the flowing lines of the longships that packed such deadly force. We can appreciate the romance of their adventures without suffering the pain. We can admire their daring with no sword held to our throats. They were certainly rogues, but they were interesting rogues, colorful characters who pursued their goals with compelling directness and enthusiasm. Vikings were also craftsmen skilled in working with wood and metal. They were traders who carried with them advanced ideas of law and administration. They were great adventurers, exploring every land bordering the North Sea and sailing south to the Mediterranean, east to Russia, and west to Ireland.

Nevertheless, of all Viking endeavors, it is their North Atlantic voyages and the foundation of colonies in Shetland, the Faroes, Iceland, and Greenland that we most admire. We are drawn to Erik the Red, the colorful scoundrel, and his son Leif, whose image is as squeaky clean as his father's is murky. Lesley and I have long dreamed of emulating their voyages, following their route from island to island all the way from Norway to the American continent.

Such a voyage has much to offer. The first known crossing of the Atlantic Ocean must rank as one of history's great sailing routes, and following the wake of Erik and Leif promises great cruising. It links communities descended directly from original Viking settlers and includes Inuit villages and isolated anchorages far from any habitation. The route passes snow-covered mountains, volcanoes, glaciers, and some of the world's tallest sea cliffs. We anticipate skies full of gulls and gannets and comical puffins, and waters with whales, dolphins, and seals. Throughout the voyage, from the shores of Scandinavia to the edge of the New World, we'll be guided by the sagas and accompanied by the characters they portray.

Chapter 2

The North Way

It's sunny. The water sparkles. A cool northwesterly breeze, freshened by an overnight cold front, drives white cumuli gently across a blue sky. Lesley and I squat on the summit of Ytraberget, a small rocky island overlooking Hafrsfjord in southwest Norway. Our seats are fragments of a rough stone wall just high enough to prevent memorable injuries from the sharp gorse covering the outcrop. Wavelets lap gently over the small rocks thirty feet below. Terns hover over the water, fluttering their wings, twittering incessantly, and periodically diving to the surface for fish. Several islets dot the rippled water of the fiord. One is tree-covered (though it's still too early for leaves) while the others are bare. Around the undulating shoreline, houses cluster in small groups separated by areas of trees and grass. A few boathouses perched on rocks have steep slipways straight to the water. It seems a pleasant place to live, a desirable neighborhood attractively suburban and convenient to the city. The faint rumbling of car tires reminds us the highway is not far away, and we see planes climb steeply into the sky as they depart the nearby Sola airport. To the north, the City of Stavanger threatens to invade this pleasant landscape as three stark apartment blocks and several slender radio towers break the horizon. Away to the east, mountains high and snow-covered rise abruptly from the coastal plain. Mysterious and forbidding, they're split by long dark shadows that we assume are fiords. Westward, the North Sea is just visible beyond low hills.

This place was not always so peaceful. A great battle once raged across the fiord as powerful warlords fought for control of Norway. Our minds populate the scene with fighting Norsemen. The sound of clashing arms reverberates across the water. Heavy iron swords swing in abrupt arcs and plunge back into the mêlée. Thrusting weapons strike others raised in defense. Some hit wooden shields with dull thuds while others pass unimpeded through rough woolen jerkins to find soft flesh. Screams of dying men mingle with vigorous yells

from combatants and moans of the wounded. Ships crash into ships.
Wood splinters. Years of craftsmanship are reduced instantly to ruin.
Proud fleets, seemingly invincible when they entered the fiord, are
scattered and destroyed. Vikings slash and chop at other Vikings. The
vanquished splash into the water and struggle for shore. Parrying the
blows of their enemies, survivors scramble through the shallows and
stumble onto a small rocky island. Those who can, slip away into the
thick forest, heading home to wait in fear of inevitable retribution for
choosing the wrong side in the conflict.

It is the year A.D. 872 and Harold Finehair, the region's number
one Viking, is forging a kingdom by subjugating his neighbors and
appropriating their lands. For years he has confronted his enemies in
local, inconclusive skirmishes. Now he draws them to a decisive battle and eliminates all that stand between him and his ambition.
Victorious and unrelenting, he ruthlessly squashes resistance and
extends his control to the whole west coast of Scandinavia. Those
who cannot or will not accept Harold's dominion are forced to seek
refuge in foreign lands.

A nearby notice declares our rocky seats to be sparse remnants of
an ancient fort and identifies this outcrop as the spot where defeated
warriors struggled ashore more than eleven hundred years ago.

It seems much more than a week since we left our winter berth at
Hull Marina, twenty-five miles up the Humber estuary on England's
east coast. Our minds flip back a month to long days of fitting out
until exhaustion and thirst drove us to the nearby Minerva Pub for
food and refreshment. The work is mostly routine—regular preparation for a new boating season, common in boatyards everywhere. We
sand the bottom, apply antifouling paint, and replace sacrificial zincs
on the rudder and propeller. Once *Symphony* is launched and moored
in her slip, we tune the rigging, check the engine, change the oil and
fuel filters, and service all the pumps. The Abandon Ship Bag is
packed and stored at the foot of the companionway ladder.
Throughout the work, thoughts of the imminent ocean crossing
ensure even more than regular care. We install just one item of new
equipment—a diesel-fired hot-air heater—to relieve the cold of the
arctic north.

We expect our voyage to take six months. Much of the time we'll

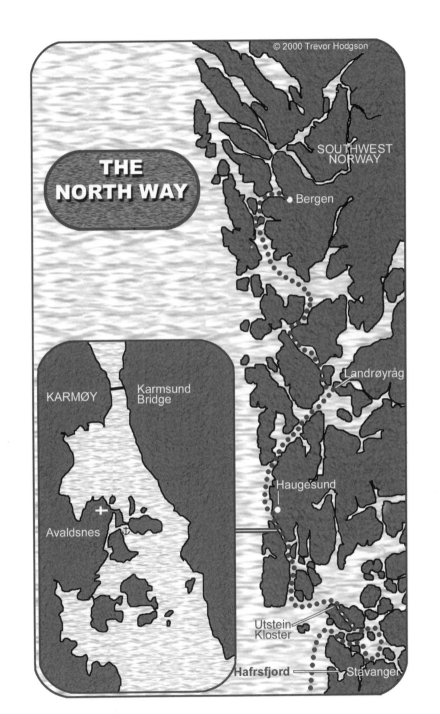

THE
NORTH WAY

© 2000 Trevor Hodgson

SOUTHWEST
NORWAY

● Bergen

Landrøyråg

Haugesund

KARMØY   Karmsund
          Bridge

Avaldsnes

Utstein
Kloster

Hafrsfjord   Stavanger

be in coastal waters and no doubt we'll find fresh provisions along the way. However, it's far from certain there'll always be a store when we need one, and we stock up with canned goods, rice, pasta, and flour for the whole voyage. A van parks nearby, and two men struggle down a sloping ramp with several large packages that soon form a huge pile on the dock. Somehow we maneuver the boxes, crates, and bags below and find a home for all the items. When the stowing is done, we have cans everywhere: in the icebox, beneath the forepeak bunk, in the bilge, and along the tops of the fuel tanks. *Symphony*'s water line sinks lower, almost disappearing under the load of equipment, fuel, stores, and spares.

While painting, inspecting, and packing, we keep one eye on a continuous stream of dark clouds rolling over the Humber. The brisk wind chills our bones. Flags over the harborside shopping center unfurl straight out from their staffs day after day. There is little incentive to abandon the sheltered marina.

The Humber drains one-fifth of England. It is a silt-laden, brown, unpleasant waterway, fast-flowing with shifting sandbars and considerable commercial traffic. It's often uncomfortable, sometimes hazardous. Despite such natural disadvantages cadres of sailors take on these challenging waters, and in summer months white sails billow against the background of oil installations and commercial waterfronts. However, it's still April. The weather is damp and somber. Visibility is poor. A few sailors visit their boats but none stay long. They check batteries, pump bilges, and pause just long enough to feel the magic of a gently rocking boat. Their nautical credentials reconfirmed, they leave to await warmer weather. It's a time when only those who have no choice set out on the river. Traditional, round-ended barges and long, flat oil carriers have the estuary to themselves.

The weather remains more suited to shopping than sailing, but by the end of April it's time to go. We must bid farewell to our neighbors of the last several months. Howard, the marina manager, drives us to the supermarket for a few last-minute items. Sue and Richard, who run the chandlery and have loaned us everything from electrical transformers to hand tools, present us with a large American flag to fly when we reach home. We talk until we absolutely must leave or miss the last "pen" (lock opening) and wait another six hours for the tide.

We have the lock between the marina basin and the river to ourselves. The large gates swing open and we motor out into short, steep waves. Les steers *Symphony* into the wind while I raise the main and set one reef. We turn down river and I hoist the stays'l and winch in the sheet. *Symphony* takes off with an irregular motion as waves buffet her starboard quarter. Water sloshes over the gunwale and along the side decks. We whisk along buoyed channels, urged by the fast-flowing ebb past ferry terminals, oil installations, and anchored freighters. A tower at the port of Grimsby is usually prominent, but today it's just a pale shadow in the clouds. By the time we approach the mouth of the estuary, we're feeling the effects of the motion and it's an easy decision to shelter behind the long, curving sand spit at Spurn Head.

We use the engine to maneuver in the basin. The anchor sets easily, but the engine refuses to stop. The cable is frozen, and I climb down to operate the lever on the side of the engine. As silence returns, I realize I'm cold and wet. The heater soon warms the cabin and banishes the dampness that settled on everything. I feel better.

For two days, easterly gales keep us at anchor. I continue the struggle to find my sea legs. The tides here are large. We anchored in ten feet, but at high tide the depth gauge shows twenty-five. Fortunately there's plenty of swinging room and we let out a lot of scope. We're in the lee of a long, curving peninsula, but the wind somehow finds its way round the promontory to stir up the water. *Symphony* sits back on a tight anchor rode. However, the day after we arrive, it's clear the fifty-five-pound plow—our main anchor—is dragging through the soft sand, and we replace it with a Danforth that seems to hold well.

In summer this is a popular anchorage. Boats race down river with the ebb, anchor for a couple of hours, and return on the flood. Now our only neighbors are the Humber pilots stationed just across the bay. Day and night throughout our stay, squat pilot-boats come and go from a small wharf. When fog reduces the visibility (despite the winds), they pass unseen and their sirens join those of anchored ships in a haunting dialogue.

Our stay, though unplanned, is an opportunity to acclimate to life aboard. We adjust some of the storage to make it more convenient, tidy everything, and complete a few last-minute repairs. Freeing the stop cable is simple enough, but by the time it is disconnected at both ends, worked loose, greased, and reinstalled, we have spent three hours twisted into unnatural positions in the bottom of the boat. I discover the stern light is not working, but this just requires remaking one connection.

Once the wind moderates and the fog clears, we haul in the anchor, which proves perversely difficult to extract, and sail for Norway. The low hills of Holderness fall below the horizon and we're alone in our private world. It feels good to be back at sea. Two huge oil platforms appear like constructor sets in a child's pool. It's a bumpy ride and I soon take two motion sickness pills.

Before long we have established a routine. Watch follows watch as the line of crosses on the chart mark our progress toward Norway. For two days we're driven east of the rhumb line by a brisk northerly breeze. The next day, Wednesday, there's little wind and we must work for every mile, tacking and adjusting sails. Finally the wind backs and we romp northward on a direct course for Stavanger.

Fog shrouds Norway for our arrival, reducing visibility below three hundred yards and hiding the rocks and islets scattered along the coast. We navigate with radar and GPS. Three unseen vessels, just blips on the radar, pass close astern. It's the early hours of Friday morning. *Symphony* speeds northward on a close reach with just the partly furled genoa. To avoid arriving at night, I roll in more headsail and slow her down. Dawn breaks and the blackness of night turns gray. Our eyes scan the thick wall of fog, straining for a varne, a small stone cairn that marks the route to the harbor. Les sees it first, just distinguishable as the highest of several rocks almost submerged by breaking waves. We turn, leaving it to port, while close to starboard, water swirls around rocks unseen below the surface. Several radio antennas appear through the fog and then, slowly, the barest outline of the coast appears. Eventually the fog condenses into a dark, misty hillside dotted with small houses. We've reached Norway.

Now, at Hafrsfjord, we're at the true beginning of our adventure. At last we're on our way, at the site of the battle that gave Norway to Harold and propelled many who opposed him on westward voyages.

We're exhilarated. Years of planning are behind us. Preparations are complete. For better or worse we've decided on the route to follow, the ports to visit, the provisions and spares to carry, and the emergency equipment to take. We feel liberated. There's no more weighing of alternatives and planning for contingencies. It's time to sail, to explore and follow the Viking trail to America.

We linger on Ytraberget, inhaling deep breaths of fresh air, reveling in our freedom, and reluctant to return to the city. Eventually we descend from our rocky perch and cross a boulder-strewn beach before striking inland. Our path lies across a playing field alive with kindergarteners wrapped in brightly colored anoraks and clustered round two teachers. The street leading to the main roads threads through a modern housing development still surrounded by fertile farmland. Small gardens are carefully tended and separated from neighbors by well-trimmed hedges of beech, hawthorn, holly, or spruce. A short incline takes us to the highway. After a ten-minute wait we speed in an almost-empty bus along the shore of Hafrsfjord. Through the window we get a brief glimpse of three massive stone swords overlooking the fiord, Norway's monument to the battle.

From the town center bus station, a walk beside a lake brings us to Stavanger's austere stone cathedral and small outdoor market. Around the corner is the *vagen*, the old harbor. Long and narrow, it's still a focal point of the city center. Ferry and steamship terminals occupy one side, while on the other the buildings are old and picturesque.

We're always relieved and happy to see *Symphony* after exploring ashore—relieved she's come to no harm and happy to admire her traditional appearance and pleasing lines. Her berth is the wall of a small boat basin separated from the rest of the *vagen* by a floating pontoon. She shares the basin with just three small power cruisers, so we have an unobstructed view of her white fiberglass hull, nicely curved between a wooden bowsprit and rounded stern. Her small ports are bronze. A varnished teak butterfly hatch along with dorade boxes, handrails, and hatch covers add a touch of warmth. The cap rails and cockpit coaming have weathered naturally to silver-gray. The sail covers and companionway dodger are blue. A stern arch supports radar and GPS antennas. It gives me much satisfaction: it looks pret-

Symphony at her berth in front of the Maritime Museum, Stavanger, Norway

ty good even though I made it from pine strips salvaged from a home remodeling project. The supports are stainless-steel dinghy davits turned vertical instead of horizontal. The arch, intended as a prototype to check feasibility and construction, works well, looks good, and was therefore never replaced with a finished version.

A notice on the dock advises that no services are available (and no fees charged) until June 15. Fortunately we're self-sufficient. *Symphony* carries a hundred gallons (U.S.) of fresh water and ninety of diesel fuel. A large holding tank enables us to live for a week without dumping waste. Everything else we need is nearby. A low building at the end of the harbor houses a fish market, while a fruit market, bank, post office, and public telephones are all within a few yards. Dumpsters intended for the use of the fish vendors provide for our trash.

The harbor walls are lined with three rows of black truck tires chained one above another. Large ships can tie up against them directly, but they're awkward for small boats as the thick black marks they leave on the hull are almost impossible to remove. We set our own fenders to keep *Symphony* off the black rubber, but these get trapped above, below, and between the tires as she rises and falls with changing tides. It's a nuisance checking and adjusting the lines several times each day.

The wharf is at the edge of a busy thoroughfare, and whenever we're aboard, visitors and residents alike stop to chat. *Symphony* is a Tayana 37, a design common in many cruising areas (over six hundred have been built) but not often seen in Europe and Scandinavia. She prompts several compliments—which, of course, serve to confirm our own favorable prejudice. Our visitors ask us many questions.

"Is she built of wood?"

"The fiberglass is molded to look like planks and can be quite misleading."

"Where was she built?"

"In Taiwan. There are lots of them, mostly built for the U.S. market."

"What's the steel fitting on the stern?"

"That's a windvane steering system."

"What's the propeller on the back?"

"A windmill to charge the batteries."
They also ask about our voyage.

"Are you heading for the fiords?"

"No, we're going first to Bergen, then to America," we reply, provoking another stream of inquiries.

"Will you go by the Azores?"

"When did you come to Europe?"

"Where else have you been?"

"Did you sail across?"

"Did you have any bad weather?"

"Did you stop on the way?"

"Would you do it again?"

When they learn we're heading north, several suggest we stay in Bergen for Norway's National Day celebrations on May 17. Several times we hear: "Everywhere there's a celebration, but in Bergen it's special."

A large motor vessel with a huge red-white-and-blue Dutch ensign moors in the main harbor just ahead of *Symphony*. She's on a summer cruise to the fiords north of Bergen. She has made this voyage before, and the owner is anxious to be helpful with directions and information. We ask him where we find Norwegian Customs, and he points to a prominent yellow building overlooking the harbor.

"It's over there, but you don't need to do it," he says in a thick accent.

"Oh, okay," I begin, "maybe that's just for European boats."

"Nobody does it anymore," my informant continues. "They've done away with all that."

Despite this advice we feel conspicuous flying the Stars and Stripes in the almost empty harbor and decide to visit the building and report our arrival. The heavy wooden door of the customshouse with its shining brass plate opens only with a determined push. With some trepidation we step into an imposing hall almost completely filled by an elegant staircase with polished wood doors accessible from side galleries. There are no signs, but a call of "Excuse me" stops a well-dressed, middle-aged woman on the stairs. She pauses, then directs us to a door on the second floor. The room behind this door is as informal as the hall is elegant. Two young men and a woman, all dressed casually, are moving their desks, computers, and filing cabinets. Books and papers are spread about. The disorder is comforting. The young woman carefully notes our names and a few particulars about *Symphony*. Two-thirds of her preprinted form is devoted to an inventory of on-board alcohol. It's not that we're heavy drinkers. We observe a strict no-drinking rule underway, but in port we enjoy a drink (or two) with dinner. However, one glass of wine a day is a significant volume over a six-month voyage. Knowing that the price of drink is prohibitive in Nordic countries, our stores include several three-liter containers.

"You have more wine than you're allowed," advises the officer matter-of-factly. "You can pay the tax now. Then when you leave, you can apply for a refund for what you have left . . . or we can seal your wine locker while you're in Norway."

"We'll have it sealed," I reply quickly, unwilling to pay cash now in the hope of recovering it later. I note she said *apply for* a refund—well short of a guarantee we'd actually see the money.

"Wait a moment. I'll find someone to come to the wharf and seal the drink cupboard," she says, disappearing briskly through the door. There's a long wait before she returns.

"We have no one able to come," she says. "You can just drink the wine." She rips off one copy of the form and hands it to us. "Enjoy your stay in Norway."

Cheered, if a little puzzled, by this abrupt change of policy, we return through the heavy door to the bustle of the streets. It seems our Dutch friend may have the right approach after all.

With about 100,000 residents, Stavanger somehow justifies the local epithet of "The Little Big City." Through its long history its fortunes have ebbed and flowed as the sea alternately brought bounty and washed it away. By the early 1600s it was big enough to have a bishop, but its decline was rapid and its commercial charter withdrawn in 1686. Later, herring arrived to restore prosperity until they disappeared late in the nineteenth century. Next came sardines. Sheds with canning plants sprang up all over the waterfront, and fifty million cans were exported in a single year. Now, sardines too have vanished, the sheds have been torn down, and all that's left is the world's only museum devoted to the process of canning fish.

Today oil drives the economy, and residents are proud of the city's modernity and affluence. Stavanger provides headquarters for several drilling companies and related service industries. Storage tanks dominate the harbor entrance, and a mammoth platform under construction dwarfs what, until recently, were regarded as tall buildings. Fortunately these monsters are distant enough to avoid dominating the city center, and Stavanger is much too nice to be dismissed as an oil town. Its long history has left many attractive buildings, including its simple twelfth-century cathedral and the largest group of wooden houses in northern Europe. The old town is a delight, with cobbled streets and white-painted wooden buildings with windows and doors in subtle shades of blue. Flowerpots decorate the windows, while rose gardens and vegetable plots squeeze into irregular gaps between the houses. The gable ends of two smart, white-clad warehouses overlook *Symphony*'s berth. Until 1920, water lapped at their doorsteps while tall square-riggers unloaded their cargoes. Now a wide roadway separates them from the harbor and they house a maritime museum.

A stone tower behind the customshouse dominates the historic buildings on the southeast side of the harbor. We first assume it's a medieval fort, only to discover it's a fire lookout tower. A broad wooden staircase winds round the inside of the thick stone walls, up past several floors to arrive at the best view of the city. We look down over the harbor and across the roofs of hundreds of surviving wooden houses crammed together along narrow streets. Many are now fashionable stores, and the area attracts many tourists. Displays on each floor of the tower show photographs of night watchmen and examples of their simple equipment, while boards describe their work and some of the calamitous fires that periodically destroyed large sections of the medieval town.

The Saturday following our arrival is Stavanger Day. We wake to find a line of railway carriages parked along the quay—apparently an exhibition promoting the national railway. A large, orange rescue boat ties up opposite, and spaces along the harbor walls fill with power cruisers. The flat roof of the fish market becomes a bandstand where a variety of performers take turns. An energetic modern group blasts out a persistent rhythm followed by a less strident female duet. It's a bright, sunny day. A large crowd saunters along the waterfront between food stalls that offer free sausage, sparkling water, fruit juice, and local specialties. Young people ride mountain bikes in a simulated course down a flight of stone steps. The rescue ship provides well-rehearsed demonstrations of recovery operations, pulling sailors or swimmers from the water. Victims in orange survival suits leap into the cold harbor to be winched back to safety. The day culminates with a waiters' race. Tuxedoed competitors, each carrying a small tray and glass, race round the head of the harbor before leaping aboard a small boat and sculling back to the starting point. A few, who dispense with the boat, make flamboyant dives into the icy water and swim to the finish, drawing loud approval from spectators.

We again board a bus for Hafrsfjord, this time to visit a reconstructed Iron Age farm. The driver willingly agrees to call us at the right stop but forgets. When it's apparent we've gone too far, I approach the front of the bus and he stops immediately, well away from any designated stop. He apologizes and then directs us on a path to the farm while an impatient truck driver honks his horn behind. The path crosses the shadow of the apartment blocks we saw from Ytraberget and we scan the stark walls in vain for some redeeming architectural feature. The top of a small hill affords a view down a grassy slope, over the roofs of some modern houses, and out over Hafrsfjord beyond. It's Sunday and several couples watch over small children scampering about on the grass with pants tucked into rubber boots and woolen hats pulled down over their ears. Below us are three long, low, grass-roofed buildings. The original houses were here well before Viking times, but they're very similar to those that came later and they occupy the classic Viking site on sloping ground back from and above the fiord.

The door of the first building is open and we stoop low to peer into the dark interior. Guides are spinning wool for a group of children. Wide benches line both long sidewalls. From the outside the houses appear to be constructed of stone, but in fact they're supported on wooden frames, with walls filled in between vertical posts. More lines of posts support the turf-covered roof. Loose stones piled outside the timber walls protect them from the weather.

We're invited into the largest house by a slim, sensitive, most un-

Viking-like young man wearing a rough-spun tunic over jeans and a sweatshirt. From a small vestibule we push aside a hide covering the inner doorway and step into a dim, smoky room. Perhaps a dozen people sit on furs and skins covering the side-benches. Silver-gray embers in a hearth down the center of the room flicker spasmodically, revealing bright red centers. Smoke curls slowly round the room before finding angled openings in the roof. Once our eyes adjust, we find seats at the end of one bench.

At the far end of the fire, a mysterious, elderly figure, frail and scholarly, occupies a simple upright chair. He talks in a quiet but guttural monotone, occasionally pausing to answer a question from one of the listeners. His strange words float through the interior with compelling authority. The unfamiliar sounds, the dim light, and the pervasive aromas of wood smoke and damp earth combine to carry us back a thousand years. The listeners' tailored pants and nylon anoraks become rough wool jerkins and leggings stuffed into leather boots. A village elder occupies the seat by the fire and describes fabulous lands discovered beyond the western seas and tells of settlers who've left Norway to begin new lives there. The atmosphere is compelling. All eyes fix on the speaker. We feel and smell the history, though we can't understand the words that pour out in a continuous stream. He's still talking as we slip quietly away through the hide-covered doorway. Outside, the sunlight seems excessively bright.

Life is comfortable in Stavanger, but it's time to explore the North Way, the coastal seaway sheltered from the North Atlantic by a string of offshore islands. It's a classic waterway, so important in days gone by that the whole country was named after it. A hundred miles north is Bergen, the largest community in western Norway. It was the main port of departure for Vikings sailing to the overseas settlements and became the hub of a vast North Atlantic empire. It's where we'll start our own transatlantic crossing. The voyage to Bergen will take two or three days with a couple of overnight stops along the way.

It's midmorning when we slip the lines and motor out though the dogleg entrance of the mooring basin. The main harbor is quiet, with ferry terminals and shipping wharves strangely empty. Outside the *vagen* we pass large oil storage tanks, slip beneath a tall bridge, and soon leave the city astern. A trawler leads the way across a wide bay bordered on each side by picturesque islands of bare red rock. Somehow a few straggling trees find enough soil to survive. No buoys mark the channel, as deep water extends right to the shoreline and the rocky bottom renders them difficult to anchor. We proceed warily, checking the GPS, lining up bearings, and plotting our position on the chart. We thread a narrow rocky gap between two islands marked "Lindøyen" and "Hellesøy" on the chart and turn to port along the three-mile-wide Horgefjorden. The sun is bright but cool, the water clear. A fresh breeze provides good sailing.

To starboard we have a spectacular view of the mountains we saw first from Hafrsfjord. Then, they were far off and indistinct, but now we see the vertical cliffs rise straight from the waters of the fiord. Above the cliffs, steep slopes, blue-gray with sprinkled snow, rise to meet the sky in a jagged ridgeline. Dark valleys, overlooked by precipitous rock faces, penetrate the mountains as far as we can see.

"How about some climbing?" suggests Les.

"They sure look challenging," I agree, as I pause to recall the exhilaration of reaching a mountain peak after a long toil to the summit.

"Trev, just look at those ridges. . . . It must be great to be up there."

"You want to go?" I ask, knowing this is just a game. "We can tie up somewhere and just head on up."

"No, let's keep going. It'd be nice to be in the hills again, though."

"Yeah, it would," I again agree. "But sailing's better. I don't have to carry a backpack and all the climbing gear."

"True. The sailing here is pretty good, too."

"It's amazing there's no other boats."

"Maybe it's busier later in the year."

We sail on, scrutinizing the mountain world of acute angles, airy ridges, and bold buttresses, nostalgic for climbing, for the sense of overcoming gravity through sheer physical effort, and for the adventures of youth. There's little horizontal ground. The few level areas where deep valleys meet the fiord are packed with tiny houses. No flat land is left unused.

To port, the low-lying coastal islands are barren, with rocks protruding from shallow scrub. Two miniature lighthouses, like red-and-white dog kennels, one low down and the other on a headland, guide us into a channel a half-mile wide. Shoreside houses stand alone or in small groups. Many have stone-built boathouses with gable ends and short slipways to the water. A few motor cruisers lie at lonely docks in small basins. One or two small fishing boats are underway, but the waterway is wide and certainly not congested. Few roads connect these communities, and residents cannot hop aboard a car or bus for a shopping trip to town. Boats are still important for transporting both people and goods. Black-hulled ferries ply continuously between the villages, emerging from one fiord and rapidly disappearing into the next.

Symphony heels in the brisk wind as we turn past an extensive fish farm into an inlet where we plan to spend the night. A cluster of buildings occupies the southwest corner, and a wooden bulkhead shelters three powerboats. Les starts the engine and brings *Symphony*'s bow to the wind. I furl the genoa on its headstay roller, drop the main, and lash it to the boom. The center of the bay is deep and we head to the northern side where the chart indicates shallower water. It's close to the beach and convenient for going ashore in the morning. Again, Les steers *Symphony* into the wind. I drop the anchor, pay out the chain, snub the rode, and wait. Will she hold? The bow whips round and *Symphony* stops. Les backs down hard to set the anchor, and we both line up rock outcrops with vertical poles on the hillside behind. We wait, but there's no sign of drifting. We both declare, "We're in." I fasten off the chain with nylon snubber lines and we settle below.

Overnight the wind rises and whistles though the shrouds. The anchor rode lifts from the water in a taut, shallow curve as *Symphony* is thrust back toward the shore. The bay is sheltered, but the thirty-knot wind generates steep, two-foot waves that roll past the hull, rise up, and break into cascades of foam just a boat-length astern. The shore seems perilously close, allowing little time to react if the anchor should give way. We anxiously repeat our routine of lining up poles and rocks, but all seems well. Were we wise to anchor so close in? Surely we're closer to the beach now than when we first anchored. Frequent checks of our sight lines show the same rock lined up with the same pole. We appear secure and decide to stay where we are. Nevertheless, we keep an anchor watch through the night, each taking four hours on and four hours at rest.

The morning is sunny, the sky clear and bright, and the anchor still secure. The strong winds have gone, leaving only a light breeze to ripple the water. We decide to walk to a nearby historic monastery. I heave the dinghy from the lazarette and inflate the chambers drum tight with a small footpump. With the camera safe in a waterproof bag, we head ashore and tie the dinghy to a projecting rock halfway up the beach. A country road curls round a rock buttress to Utstein Kloster, a group of stone buildings nestled in a copse at the head of a small lake. It's one of several places along the North Way where Harold Finehair maintained a fort or palace. This must have made a fine refuge, sheltered by low hills, nestled among trees, and fronted by a broad, sloping beach where longships could lie unseen from surrounding fiords. The monastery was built later. It became a symbol of the power of the church and is now one of Norway's most recognized medieval buildings.

By the time we're back aboard *Symphony*, there's a fair breeze. It's just a short sail to our next anchorage at Avaldsnes and we can still be there before nightfall. Turning to port from the anchorage, we continue north through a narrow waterway between two rock promontories and out into Boknafjorden. It's open to the prevailing westerly winds blowing straight from the Atlantic, and the water heaves beneath us in sympathy with the ocean swells. We sail six miles west, passing a couple of freighters, and turn north into the Karmsund. We share this waterway between the mainland and the large island of Karmoy with several ships, fishing boats, and ferries. Freighters steam past, heading for the docks at Kopervik. A Flaggruten, a sleek red-white-and-blue catamaran, cruises by at forty knots, trailing a smooth white wake, on its express passenger service between Stavanger and Bergen.

South of Haugesund, the island of Bukköy juts into the waterway leaving only a narrow passage on its eastern side. A couple of miles farther on, the North Way again narrows at a modern road bridge. We head for a small cove between Bukköy and Karmoy. A red-hulled freighter approaches from the north, but our course takes us across well ahead. However, as we reach midchannel directly in the path of the freighter, the wind disappears. Fitfully it backs and then rotates all round the compass. We follow it in a complete circle whereupon it dies altogether, leaving us drifting aimlessly. We start the engine and motor from the path of the freighter and on to the anchorage, no doubt leaving some shaking heads on the freighter's bridge. We anchor at the first attempt in the center of the small bay.

The next morning is still and sunny, the water smooth. We start with a cup of tea (Earl Grey with no milk and no sugar for me, fruit herbal for Les) while still in our bunks. Then it's bowls of porridge with sugar (but no milk) accompanied by mugs of black coffee—a traditional *Symphony* breakfast. Low rocks line all sides of the secluded bay, while Bukköy is covered with dense pinewoods. Birds are everywhere. We sit in the cockpit watching redstarts, arctic terns, eiders, herons, and grebes busy with their own breakfasts and preparing for their young families. A group of oystercatchers fly low overhead with loud cries and vivid flashes of red bills and feet.

We dinghy to shore and step onto a rocky slab covered with fragments of crab and sea urchin shells. It's clear why the cove is so rich in bird life! Across a wooden bridge to Bukköy a path leads through conifers so thick that no sun reaches the ground. The shade is cool and the air thick with an intense smell of resin. A large wooden building occupies a clearing in the wood, its roof curved like an upturned boat. Woodworking tools, wheelbarrows, and various implements lie around outside. A cycle lies on the ground beside a small tent. The building is locked and the site obviously closed. Tourist brochures describe it as a reconstructed Viking settlement, but there's no sign of activity. The tourist season is still a few weeks away.

On Karmoy, the church of Avaldsnes poses picturesquely on the brow of a hill, set off by still-leafless trees. A long, slim rock—the Virgin's Needle—inclines near the church's north wall, the tip just inches from the stonework. Tradition maintains that should the rock ever touch the wall, the end of the world is imminent. However, it's also legendary that whenever the rock appears about to make its fatal contact, a priest clambers up a ladder and removes the tip of the Needle, thus saving the world from Armageddon!

It's a steep climb to the church, and well before the top we adopt the slow methodical pace of mountaineers. From the edge of the walled churchyard we have a panoramic view down to *Symphony* lying at anchor, over Bukköy, and all along the North Way in both directions.

Avaldsnes was once a center of royal power. Needless to say, Harold Finehair had a palace here, but he was by no means the first to recognize its importance. Ancient standing stones and Bronze Age barrows, a Viking ship burial, and a large hoard of Roman coins have all been found nearby. From this hill any vessel approaching from either direction can be seen in good time to dispatch a boat to intercept it. With a few good ships a determined ruler could easily impose his will over the waterway, extracting tolls from merchants and apprehending anyone unwilling to respect his sovereignty.

Returning to *Symphony* in the dinghy, I spy a long plank of wood, about six inches wide and two inches thick, beached on a small area of exposed sand. Ever since our struggle with truck tires at Stavanger, I've been determined to get a fender board to place between our own fenders and the tires. This plank looks perfect. We tow our trophy behind the dinghy and haul it aboard. With support ropes through holes drilled at each end, it becomes an ideal fender board. Successful scavenging can be so very satisfying!

The next morning the wind, still brisk, backs to the southeast, giving a fair breeze for our short sail to Haugesund. We prepare unhurriedly, as our next mooring is only a couple of hours away. However, in midbreakfast, a loud crash shatters our composure. The whole boat shudders. Instantly we're both in the cockpit. The shore is much too close, and it's clear the anchor is dragging and the keel is scraping the rocks. I turn the ignition key and push the button. The engine starts immediately. Les already has the wheel and steers *Symphony* forward and to port toward deep water. The keel bumps again and we wince as we hear sharp rocks bite into the fiberglass. Momentarily we seem stuck, but suddenly the noise and vibration disappear as *Symphony* breaks away into clear water. We re-anchor in the middle of the bay, then collapse on the cockpit seats and look into each other's eyes. No words are necessary. We've hardly started our voyage, just two days from Stavanger. We've not left sheltered water, yet we've almost ended up on the rocks. How can we expect to reach

America if we can't navigate the North Way without running aground? I put an arm round Les.

"Well, that was lucky," I offer, not sure what to say.

"I thought the anchor was well in," Les replies.

"Me too. It must've pulled out when the wind changed."

"I guess so."

"It's a good thing we have a solid keel."

"Hmm."

"Better here than in Greenland," I add, looking for a silver lining.

"Doesn't make me feel good," Les adds.

"You're right."

We fall silent. It's not a happy moment.

In the afternoon, a following wind propels us rapidly the short distance round Bukköy, beneath the Karmsund Bridge, and on to Haugesund. The harbor's a long channel, like a river, between the mainland and the island of Risöy. It funnels the breeze into a stiff wind, and docking requires caution to avoid being blown into nearby boats. We tie up at a public wharf in the shadow of a high, steel road bridge. The quay is busy, with several power cruisers both ahead and astern and two large fishing boats just downwind. An excursion boat lies adjacent. A Flaggruten slides past close abeam and docks at its nearby wharf. Passengers disembark while others hang around the ticket office waiting to board. A chandlery, tour offices, and small restaurants line the waterfront.

The quay is a meeting place for local youth. Cars swing round with exaggerated panache to park side by side with just a hand-width between them. It must be a cool way to have conversation. The adventurous climb out—through windows, not doors—to sit on hoods or trunks. At first we're anxious, prejudiced by other youthful gatherings that became too boisterous. This time our fears are groundless. Everyone is well behaved and no one stays long. As each car leaves, another swings in to take its place. Eventually they all depart.

Just over a mile north of the center of Haugesund, a tall granite obelisk surrounded by twenty-nine smaller stones stands in a commanding position overlooking the sea. It's Haraldshaugen, Norway's monument to national unity, dedicated in 1872 on the millennium of the founding of the country. The thirteenth-century saga writer Snorri

Sturlson identified this as the place where King Harold Finehair was buried after dying of the plague.

We walk to the monument in late afternoon, first along the commercial waterfront, then through narrow back streets, and finally between large old houses and picturesque churches on the outskirts of the town. We pass a supermarket, cross a busy road intersection, and continue between modest homes. We find the monument on a small rise overlooking the sea. The northern entrance to the Karmsund is a group of small islands. Beyond them is Karmoy, green and fertile. To the west stretch the blue-gray waters of the North Sea. The monument occupies a commanding location with extensive views over a critical section of the North Way. Here, just as at Utstein Kloster and Avaldnes, Harold Finehair could meet his strategic needs in a setting of great natural beauty. It is a fitting place for him to rest.

Chapter 3

Gateway to the Atlantic

It's Wednesday morning, with three days until Norway's National Day. So many people have extolled Bergen's May 17 celebration we just can't miss it! Luckily it fits perfectly with our schedule. We should arrive there later today to find a good berth before crowds arrive for the holiday weekend.

We're anchored in Landrøyråg, a land-locked inlet off a fiord along the North Way. The high, steep-sided shores are rocky and thickly wooded. Only two buildings show through the trees, one by our anchorage and the other on the far side of the bay. Both appear empty and we assume they're summer homes. There are no other boats. The anchorage appears large enough for an entire fleet, but deep water and a rocky bottom make anchoring difficult. We find just one good place with firm holding in about thirty feet of water. The sky's cloudy, but otherwise the day's pleasant and we sit in the cockpit enjoying the tranquility while working up the energy to take on the day.

Eventually we stir ourselves and prepare to leave. The anchor comes up easily and we motor toward a very constricted exit channel. This passage needs care. A rock, right in midchannel and covered by just four feet of water, lies waiting to snag the keel of an unwary boat. There's just enough room to squeeze between the rock and the shore. Hardly daring to breathe, we edge slowly through the gap, so close to the channel edge we can reach out and run our hands along the damp rock buttress. To starboard the rock flickers menacingly in and out of view as ripples wash the surface. Once committed we quickly pass the obstructions and we're soon in deeper water. We continue between islands of rock and trees to regain the Nord Weg.

A freighter approaches from ahead as we turn toward Bergen. A stiff but fair breeze drives wavelets across the fiord and all seems set for a fine sail. Suddenly the sky darkens and the cloud base plummets. We're ready for the rain, but the squall's ferocity is a complete surprise. Wind howls through the rigging. *Symphony* heels far to star-

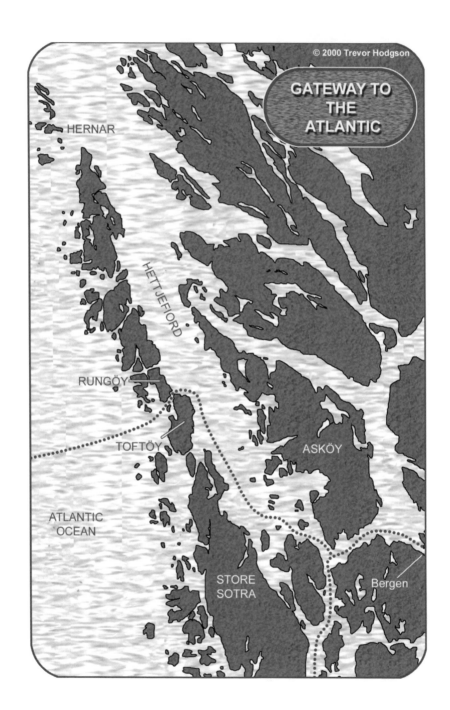

board and the gunwale disappears below the water. Blinding rain shuts out our view of the freighter, and then the mountains disappear, leaving us isolated, tossed around like clothes in a washing machine. We struggle on for a few moments, but last night's anchorage is still only ten minutes astern and it's an easy decision to turn back. The wind now blasts our faces. We turn away to shield our eyes and must twist round for a minimal view of where we're going. Once we turn toward the anchorage, *Symphony* scuds before the gale until round another corner we gain the shelter of trees. Once more we edge carefully round the hidden rock and anchor in our old spot. The bay is calm, but overhead the wind rages through the tops of the trees, whipping branches back and forth. Rain falls in torrents. We scurry below and close the companionway with a determined bang. In the short time since the squall's onset, we've gotten well and truly soaked. We each find dry clothes and settle down to wait for better weather with a second mug of coffee and a breakfast of beans on toast.

After an hour the wind dies down and the rain stops. The clouds change from thick and black to thick and gray and we set out once again. Happily we find a world that has regained its former order. We set the genoa, and a moderate southwesterly bowls us along at six knots on a broad reach. Eventually the sun comes out and drives away the remaining clouds. It's as though the squall never occurred and the whole experience was just a figment of the imagination.

For several hours we sail through a succession of broad channels between islands of reddish rock covered with small trees and scrubby bushes. Far to starboard, purple snow-sprinkled mountains meet the blue sky in a jagged line. Occasionally we pass a miniature lighthouse or a rusted metal daymark fixed to a rock. Three freighters steam past, each black-and-white, heading southward and cruising fast. They're fleeting distractions along otherwise deserted fiords. Each appears round a bend ahead, passes with a wave from the pilothouse, and quickly disappears astern. The few buildings along the waterway include World War II blockhouses set deep into rock buttresses. Slender firing slits penetrate gray concrete walls that have acquired a thin layer of lichen. Their violent purpose seems inappropriate in this pristine landscape, a shocking reminder that such a place is capable of being the scene of bitter conflict.

Late in the afternoon we see a ridge ahead, projecting toward the sea and culminating in a mountain on the starboard bow. The chart shows this overlooks the city of Bergen, but with our destination almost in sight, the breeze that's carried us briskly for several hours dies away. Soon we're motoring in complete calm. We pass beneath one high bridge, turn to starboard, and go underneath another. In the distance a gray blur appears between the fiord and the mountains. As we get closer, a modern city slowly spreads across the lower hills while higher ground is green and apparently undeveloped.

We head directly for a harbor situated in the heart of the city and called the *vagen*, like the one at Stavanger. A white cruise ship dominates the port side of the entrance. To starboard, wharves for passenger ferries are backed by office blocks and other commercial buildings. A Flaggruten lies alongside while two smaller and more conventional ships are getting underway. At the head of the harbor a short pier is crowded with people at outdoor tables with colorful umbrellas. The bulkhead around the restaurant is packed with powerboats.

The long quay forming the north side of the harbor is almost empty. A line of plain, single-story utility buildings screens the wharf from a busy highway. We select a spot midway along and tie up, arranging our fenders and new fender board to keep *Symphony* off the inevitable truck tires. It's been a long but highly satisfying day. After the squall sent us scurrying back to harbor, the weather turned out much better than we expected. We've enjoyed a great sail through some wonderful scenery. We take a stroll around the harbor and the neighboring streets, enjoy a simple spaghetti supper, and turn in with a nightcap.

The next morning, sunlight streams through the companionway hatch, bringing the sounds of the city going about its business. Cars and buses, trucks, taxis, and bicycles crowd the adjacent street, stopping in long lines at lights. Pedestrians stride purposefully along the sidewalks and dodge in and out of the traffic. It's a wonderfully cool, bright spring day. The water of the *vagen* sparkles. Patches of light and shade form contrasting patterns on the buildings opposite. Colors gleam on the painted façades of old wooden buildings. Many Bergenites seem as surprised by the weather as we are delighted and quickly point out that it's usually cloudy and rainy more than two hundred days a year.

At a tourist office on the quay we get a key to the washrooms at the rear of the restaurant on the pier. It's a good deal, just 100 Kr with 90Kr back when we return the key. That's just 10Kr ($1.50) to use the toilets, showers, and laundry for six days.

The unusual sunshine brings crowds to the streets and outdoor cafes. Tourists with cameras and leisurely gaits stream from the cruise ships, pause by the gift shops, gather in groups outside hotels, and wait for buses in long lines. Students gather at street corners and in a central pedestrian area. It's the end of the academic year and they face the climactic prospect of finals on Friday, a weekend of parties, and imminent release for the summer vacation. Many dress in brightly colored dungarees, with colors denoting different course affiliations. Blue seems to signify academic programs, and red, vocational courses.

After a morning's sightseeing and a bite of lunch, we take a few moments to relax in the cockpit. Several visitors pause on the quay to admire *Symphony*. Many shout greetings, but one voice stands out from the others.

"You have a beautiful boat," calls an unmistakably English accent. I look up to see a sun-tanned young man of about thirty with a small blonde child in a stroller.

"Oh, hi," I reply, "thanks very much."

"She looks sturdy—is she wooden?"

"No, she's fiberglass, but the molding is supposed to look like planks."

"Was she built in the States?"

"No. In Taiwan. But they're built for the American market. There aren't many in Europe."

"I'm refitting a thirty-two-footer. I'm always looking for good ideas."

"Your own boat?"

"No. It belongs to my father-in-law."

"How old's your son?"

"This is Njaal, he's three. We live just up there." He motions to white-painted houses on the hillside behind the town. "We're just out for a walk. One day I want to take off for a longer cruise."

"Would you like to come aboard?"

"Sure. But don't let me stop what you're doing."

"No problem. Let me give you a hand."

Njaal is lifted from the stroller and passed carefully down the harbor wall. The father climbs down a metal ladder and joins us in the cockpit. He extends a hand: "My name's Gerran."

We both introduce ourselves. Les bends down. "Hello, Njaal, do you like boats?" Njaal is noncommittal. "Come on down and have a look round."

Gerran examines the navigation equipment and has a quick tour of the saloon, galley, forepeak, and head. "There's more room than you'd think," he grins. "It's a lovely boat."

"You sound English," says Les.

"I was born in Cornwall."

"That's a long way from Bergen. What brings you here?"

"It's a long story. I was in the Navy."

"The Royal Navy?"

"Yes. Then I was attached to the Norwegian Navy. I met a girl here and we got married. But you're not American, are you?"

"We were both born in England—in Newark, near Nottingham. But we've lived in the States for twenty years."

Gerran cares for Njaal while his wife's at work and at the same time he's remodeling their home. Finally he gets up. "I must go. It's my wife's lunch break in ten minutes and I arranged to meet her."

He pauses by the companionway. "This weekend's a big holiday here."

"We've heard about that all the way from Stavanger."

"Will you still be here?"

"We wouldn't miss it!"

"Would you like to join us after the parade? We'll have a traditional celebration with some friends at a mountain cabin."

"Sounds great—are you sure your wife won't mind?"

"She'll love it, but . . . do you like porridge?"

A little mystified, we both assure him we like it just fine.

Gerran explains, "We have a very special porridge, a national tradition. We eat it only this one day. It's very rich. Are you sure that's okay?"

We again assure Gerran that we really do like porridge. He climbs back up the dockside ladder. I hand Njaal to his father, and Gerran, son, and stroller disappear into the crowd. Later Gerran returns with Njaal and Siri, his charming young wife, who proves as welcoming as Gerran. We talk in the saloon about life in Bergen, prices, home remodeling, and plans for sailing. Eventually Gerran and Siri rise to leave. We confirm arrangements for the mountaintop party on Saturday. We feel privileged to be sharing their celebration.

We resume our sightseeing and visit some of Bergen's popular tourist sites. Immediately behind the restaurant at the head of the harbor is the Torget, an extraordinary outdoor fish market. Open stalls are a riot of pink salmon, shrimp, crab, and lobster—all apparently larger and more succulent than any we've seen before. At home we've become accustomed to smaller fish, but here they're really large, reminiscent of the huge cod and halibut displayed on white ceramic slabs by the fishmongers of our childhood. Silver-gray, appetizing fish lie in mountains of crushed ice in long trays. A huge monkfish dominates one stall; his melancholy eyes seem to follow us as we walk by. Nearby displays of vegetables, deli items, and flowers add splashes of bright colors. We snack on sandwiches of smoked and peppered mackerel on crusty white bread while watching the tourists and locals go about their business. Individual fresh fruit tarts provide memorable desserts.

A stone castle guards the entrance to the harbor, and within its perimeter wall we find Håkon's Hall, a ceremonial meeting-place built by King Håkon Håkonsson when twelfth-century Bergen was the political hub of Norway. A long and imposing wooden staircase leads to the Hall, which is rectangular, with plain, elegant stonework relieved at one end by a rich tapestry. It's a room of simple style and dignity, a worthy setting for state dinners and formal gatherings. More modest halls, once centers of Viking social life, were common at the larger farms. There the tales of ancestors were passed on by the fireside on long winter nights. Håkon's Hall is obviously bigger and grander than most and the only example still intact. It's still the venue for grand receptions when Norway's royal family is in town.

We take a bus to Fantoft on the city outskirts to see a stave church, a peculiarly Scandinavian wooden structure. Following direc-

Lesley explores the Bryggen, medieval wooden warehouses in Bergen, Norway

tions from the driver we find the church surrounded by tall wire fencing in a small clearing in the middle of a wood. The exterior is exotic, recalling a pagoda with steep cantilevered roofs. A narrow verandah, enclosed by closely spaced vertical posts, circles the ground floor. Above, roofs rise over roofs like overlapping plates of Japanese armor, until high overhead they're crowned by a tall central spire.

An enthusiastic young woman shows us the interior and explains something of the building's history. The layout is conventional with a chancel and wooden pews in the nave, but it's smaller and more intimate than we expect. The walls are formed of vertical timbers with bases resting above ground on sills to protect them from rot. Long vertical staves (poles) rise in the body of the church to provide support for the roof. The building is new, painstakingly rebuilt after the original was gutted by an arsonist in 1992. Ironically this distressing vandalism has produced a building much more as the builders intended. Instead of a dark and venerable monument, the interior is light and its new timber fresh with the smell of pine. Once common, these curious churches are a mixture of Christian architecture and pagan images. Traditional church design is adapted to local conditions, using the abundant pine for construction, with steep roofs to avoid the buildup of snow and sides supported on sills to resist weathering. They're products of the same ingenuity, environment, and craftsmanship that created the Vikings' celebrated ships.

More extraordinary wooden buildings lie just a few yards from *Symphony*'s berth. The colorful gable ends of the Bryggen that rise over dockside warehouses are the showpiece of Bergen's travel posters. The buildings extend way back from the road and are separated by long passageways in a building tradition dating back almost nine hundred years. The passages are entered through small openings between the façades of modern ground-floor shops. They are shady, cool, and quiet. The sound of the traffic flashing past the end hardly penetrates the narrow entrances. The hush is almost audible. Overhanging gables close above our heads and shut out all but a tiny patch of sky. Wooden stairways lead to second floor galleries with some craft shops and artisans' workshops, but many rooms appear empty. Thick wooden roof beams sag under the weight of three centuries, and much of the planking has worn smooth over time. The slightly musty smell of well-seasoned timber mingles with aromas of fine sauces from the restaurants and perfumes from the roadside gift shops. The whole complex of warehouses and passages has the feel of a hollow tinderbox. It's obvious why medieval smithies, with their showers of hot sparks, were banished from this part of town.

These buildings were built in 1702 to replace earlier ones destroyed in a great fire. The passages then echoed with the sounds of industry—creaking of hoists hauling goods to upper floors, cart-wheels trundling over wooden boards, hammers striking caulking irons. Tradesmen, not tourists, filled workshops as sailmakers, coop-ers, and rope-makers, carpenters, caulkers, and riggers all went about their business. The sweet smell of wood filled the air as it does now but seasoned with pungent odors of tar, fish, rope, and paint.

When Bergen was the political and commercial hub of Norway's vast North Atlantic empire, *knarrs* (trading ships) loaded goods here for Iceland and Greenland. At the height of her influence, the city stood at the focus of trade routes stretching westward two thousand miles to Greenland and from the Arctic Circle south to Ireland, England, and the Baltic states. She was indeed "the Gateway to the Atlantic." Exotic furs, narwhal tusks, and prized falcons landed here to be shipped south to the great trading cities of Europe. These princely items shipped alongside the ubiquitous dried cod that pro-vided staple protein for much of the continent. While trade enriched the merchants of Bergen and filled the churches' coffers, it was criti-cal for the colonists' well-being. The *King's Mirror*, written by an unknown author in thirteenth-century Norway, gives a glimpse of the Greenland trade:

> In Greenland . . . everything that is needed to improve the land must be purchased abroad, both iron and all the timber used in building houses.
>
> In return for their wares the merchants bring back the following products: buckskin, or hides, sealskins, and rope which is called "leather rope" and is cut from the fish called walrus, and also the teeth of the walrus.
>
> There are also many large hawks in the land, which in other countries would be counted very precious,—white

falcons, and they are more numerous there than in any other country. . . .

For a time, trade thrived, but even before the Bryggen was built, Norway lost the enterprise and swagger that sent her sailors to explore and settle overseas. In 1349 the Black Death killed one-third of the population; the economy failed, incomes declined, and many farms were deserted. Later, Norway became subordinate to Denmark, and the Hanseatic merchants that dominated Bergen's trade had no interest in Atlantic islands. The colonies were ignored, left to survive as best they could while Europe found other, cheaper sources for its products. The empire withered. Bergen has survived as a great seaport, her harbor full of ships, but now the epithets are written by the tourist industry. Bergen has turned her back on the Atlantic islands to face inland and become "the Gateway to the Fiords."

From midmorning on Friday, the eve of the national holiday, the harbor slowly fills with boats. Power cruisers arrive one by one to swell the group of boats near the restaurant. Soon the pace quickens and vessels stream past the castle in a continuous line. When all berths at the end of the harbor are occupied, rafts grow up all along the walls. They get wider and become noticeably less straight and less secure. Before long, rafts from each side link in the middle and crews can step from one wharf and cross to the other side, moving from boat to boat.

In midafternoon an intruder interrupts the line of incoming boats. A large gray warship clears small cruisers from her path, like an elephant scattering chickens, as she steams up the harbor to a berth at the restaurant dock. *Hitra*, once a U.S. Navy patrol boat, is remembered for her role in the "Shetland Bus" operation that ferried people and equipment between Norway and Shetland during World War II. Munitions and secret agents were carried to Norway, while on the return she carried intelligence information and young Norwegians anxious to join the war effort abroad. Her exploits are still celebrated on both sides of the North Sea, and she will attract many visitors when she opens to the public tomorrow.

The profusion of gently rocking boats continues to spread. Rafts extend both ahead and astern of *Symphony*. For a time it seems no one wants to join us, maybe discouraged by the U.S. flag or the sight of a mast and sails in this world of powerboats. Eventually neighboring lines extend six or seven boats from the wharf, and it's apparent our isolation cannot last. Soon we take the lines of a twenty-five-foot motor cruiser. The ice is broken, and in no time we're the inside boat in a straggling line of seven vessels. The mooring is quite haphazard. Our neighbors set no lines ashore and few use spring lines. We worry as the line curves and wobbles but console ourselves with a forecast of calm weather and the excellent shelter inside the harbor.

Once crews have dock lines and fenders set, well-rehearsed preparations for a night of celebration go into high gear. Extra seats and cushions quickly fill the cockpits. Tables are set with white cloths, napkins, plates, cutlery, and glasses. Lamps and candles add a golden flicker to the background street lighting. Diners squeeze around the tables behind plates heaped with pink shrimp and bowls filled with salad. Glasses clink. Conversation flows freely in voices that grow more insistent as the night progresses. Festive greetings float on the night air between the boats and strollers ashore. The celebrations spill over onto the wharves and on into surrounding streets. Couples, families, and small groups stroll along, admiring the boats and eyeing the diners with a mixture of envy and amusement.

Tomorrow promises to be a long day. After the parade we'll have a two-hour walk with Gerran and Siri to the mountaintop cabin. We decide to turn in to be ready for an early start. However, our neighbors have not come to Bergen to sleep. They're here for a good time, and that means Party! Party! Party! Boats, bars, and sidewalks fuse into a single circulating throng of people. Many are spectators, content to stroll along, enjoy the balmy night air, and watch others enjoy themselves. Some, however, are dedicated participants, roving, glass in hand, from restaurants to watering holes, to boats, to watering holes. If the exorbitant price of alcohol here deters consumption, there's no sign of it tonight.

What restless creatures partygoers are! Everyone ashore craves the company of those aboard. Crews at the far end of rafts are much the most popular. However, once revelers reach their new rendezvous, there's time only to refresh their glasses before another boat becomes irresistibly tempting. Invariably this new venue is on a different raft and they must re-cross the line of boats, climb up and then down the harbor wall, and then clamber over all the boats in the other raft.

Much as we'd prefer to be a peaceful oasis in the midst of such commotion, there's no way we can escape. *Symphony* becomes as much common ground as the dock or the street nearby. Too late we recognize the advantage of delaying arrival until the rafts have formed and grabbing an outside berth. Crowds of partygoers clamber back and forth over *Symphony*'s foredeck. Their passages are neither elegant nor careful. Most slide down the harbor wall facing outward and drop the last few inches to hit the deck. A few jump with a loud thud. They're incapable of walking on deck without kicking blocks, or crossing lifelines without twanging the upper wire, or avoiding crashing into rigging. None ask to come aboard. We feel powerless in the face of a determined but unthinking invasion.

In port we sleep in the forecabin. Being the farthest from the companionway, it's usually the quietest spot aboard. Tonight it's not. No sooner are we in bed than heavy footsteps resonate on the deck above our heads. Each time we drift toward sleep, another crash jerks us back to consciousness. Occasionally the steps gather into a stampede. No five minutes pass without feet stamping or bodies crashing. As the night proceeds, footsteps get heavier and less regular and collisions more frequent. Voices become more strident and unrestrained. We feel isolated, besieged in foreign surroundings and surrounded by incomprehensible chatter. Frustrated though we are, I decide to simply ride out the storm. The revelers are high-spirited, rather rude and inconsiderate, but not threatening or really objectionable. They do no more to *Symphony* than to any of the other boats and it seems unwise to provoke a gathering of inebriated Vikings. However, after yet another display of clumsiness, my frustration boils over. I scream into the night about the need for sleep, the lateness of the hour, and the clumsiness of the visitors. There's no reply. The partygoers probably don't hear and almost certainly don't care, but at least for a while it seems quieter. I finally drop into sleep feeling modestly vindicated.

It seems just minutes before we're jolted awake by cannon fire. It may be ceremonial, but it hits us like a broadside from a ship of the line. We're tired and not at all ready for the day. Coffee is even more welcome than usual. Happily we're greeted by sunshine and blue sky.

The frantic atmosphere of last night has disappeared. Bergen is now dignified and sedate. Hundreds of people are already strolling along the quay, clearly not bound anywhere in particular. This is not about getting anywhere. It's a day for being here, for walking up and down, for watching others and for being seen. The clothes are festive. Many women wear a *bunad*, a traditional national dress with a long, colorful wool skirt, ruffled white blouse, and bodice decorated with silver or tin jewelry. Each community has its own design, resulting in almost infinite variations of deep solid colors and elaborate embroidery. A few men wear the much simpler and less flamboyant male version of the *bunad*: a three-piece knickerbocker suit with waistcoat, knee-high socks, and shoes. Most, however, prefer what my parents called their "Sunday best."

Many boat crews, who were still celebrating enthusiastically when we turned in, are still socializing. The people are the same, many now looking rather worn, but the wine and seafood have given way to black coffee and croissants. A woman on a boat astern anxiously surveys the quay for familiar faces, occasionally waving to a passerby or welcoming visitors and plying them with coffee. Soon, apéritifs replace the coffee. She's a determined hostess. Her efforts to attract visitors show no sign of flagging through breakfast, brunch, and lunch.

Another booming round of cannon fire reverberates off the buildings to announce the start of the parade, and soon a column of marchers advances along the wharf. I videotape the parade over the heads of the crowd while balancing on top of a small roadside bollard. Hundreds file past with bands playing and flags flying. Every organization in Bergen is on the move. Children pass in uneven lines. Police, fire, and ambulance organizations join military veterans in an effort to march in step. Gymnasts and dancing clubs stop in front of the Bryggen to give short displays. National flags are everywhere. Everyone waves to everyone else. The brass and drums of one band still echo from the walls of the Bryggen when the next thunders round the corner. Several vintage cars, shiny and polished, drive along slowly, wedged between doctors, nurses, and young soldiers. At the rear of the marchers are students fresh from final exams. Understandably happy, they climb from a decrepit red-painted bus and gather to sing what sound like college songs. From their responses it appears many of the spectators are alumni.

As the sound of the last band grows faint, the strollers once again reclaim the streets. There are fewer now as some return home for family celebrations. It's time for us to head for the hills.

We've arranged to meet Gerran and Siri at the upper station of a cable railway that runs up the steep mountain behind the city. It's a popular destination and we join a long line of Bergenites waiting in a tunnel that forms the station approach. Finally we're pressed up to the platform barrier and watch a train ease slowly down steep tracks to the platform. We squeeze aboard with the next load of passengers, and the car draws slowly from the dim station into dazzling sunshine and a magnificent view of the harbor and city. Gerran, Siri, and Njaal are waiting as we step from the train. Together we pause for another view of the city and harbor before passing through a gate across a road.

In an instant we go from busy city to rural woodland. The road undulates through the forest with picturesque clearings on both sides and then rises diagonally across a steep mountainside. A low crash barrier offers nominal protection from a precipitous drop to the left while a rock cliff towers above on the right. Gerran and Siri take turns pushing Njaal in his stroller. We pass several individual hikers spending their holiday away from the crowds. They're all male, all wear shorts, and all have miniature Norwegian flags projecting from their packs. With the summit in sight we leave the stroller in a small stone shelter and strike off across the hillside. The path winds past small rock outcrops, then follows an easy scramble to a low ridge which leads gently down into a shallow valley. We pass between two small lakes with crumbling concrete dams, suggesting they were once reservoirs. On the brow of another small rise a wooden cabin perches above a broad valley. Gerran digs into his backpack and produces a small Norwegian flag for each of us. We arrive at the cabin waving our flags and calling greetings to three figures who emerge and wave back. It reminds me of a scene from *The Sound of Music*!

Tindeborg occupies a most enviable position with panoramic views over woods, hills, and valleys. It has bunks for several people, a common room with an uncommon view, and a small area for cooking. There's no electricity or running water. Our hosts are Arve and Siv, with their five-year-old daughter, Heide, in her smart *bunad*, and three-year-old son, Karl. Other guests include Arve's sister, Gruve, and a friend, Paal. A table is already set up outside and we all carry plates, glasses, bowls, and cutlery from the kitchen. Everyone has brought a contribution to the meal. We've learned that in a country of ten-dollar drinks, wine is universally acceptable, so we brought one of our three-liter containers. It proves very welcome. Meats and cheeses are spread out on plates. Lettuce and tomatoes and onions go into a huge salad. All the while a large pan simmers on the stove in the kitchen. Siv pauses frequently to stir the pot with a large spoon and to sample the creamy, bubbling concoction of sour cream, whole milk, yogurt, white flour, and salt. Each time, she declares all is well with the celebrated porridge.

The meal is a wonderful, friendly, relaxed affair. Gerran explains the many combinations of smoked and seasoned meat and we try several varieties. *Spekekjøtt* is seasoned, rolled lamb. This we like and it becomes a favorite for lunch anytime we find it in a store. At last it's time for *Rømmegrøt*, the special porridge that's the feature of the meal. The large dishes all have generous portions, with toppings of cinnamon, sugar, and raisins. Gerran's right—it's different from any porridge we have had before—and we're porridge eaters. It's good—rich, thick, and creamy. Nevertheless, porridge is porridge. It fills you up, but it's difficult to make it exciting. We understand why it's eaten just once a year.

When the meal is over and the dishes cleared, we sing folk songs. There's only one copy of the music and everyone gathers behind Les and me to read the score. We don't recognize the tunes, either from the music or from the efforts of our hosts. We search vainly for meaning in Norwegian lyrics printed in mysterious gothic script. We "la la" and "da da da" along with the others, but the whole thing proves very ragged. I like to think we make up in enthusiasm for our total ignorance of both words and melody, but it's not so. It's soon apparent our hosts are not so good at singing either and we move quickly on to children's games. Adults and children dance in circles and play a Norwegian version of "The Farmer in the Dell." When the grownups sit exhausted to sip beer and wine, Heide and

Karl continue with their own game of hide-and-seek.

All too soon it's time to thank Siv and Arve and head back down the mountain. The sun is still high in the sky, but the air now takes on the feel of evening. At the station we bid farewell to Gerran and Siri and continue down on the train. When we reach the harbor, we see that our erstwhile neighbors have left. We look each way along the wharf. *Symphony* is alone at her mooring. The world has regained a sense of normality. We fall into a deep, contented sleep.

Chapter 4

The Red Square and Black Raven

Soon we must sail for Shetland, but we can hardly leave Norway without finding a real Viking ship! There are several good replicas carrying tourists on short cruises—we'll see one in Lerwick and another at Reykjavik—but we're looking for the real thing, one that has carried real Vikings over salty seas with timbers hewn by skilled craftsmen using primitive hand tools. Fortunately the Viking Ship Museum in Oslo has two authentic longships, both fully restored after spending hundreds of years buried in clay mounds that protected them from weathering and decay. The ornate *Öseberg* and the plainer, more seaworthy *Gokstad* have been pictured so often in magazines and books they've become familiar icons for the Vikings and their ships.

As the raven flies, Oslo is 165 miles from Bergen but on the opposite side of the formidable mountains of central Norway. Once, the only practical route was the long sea journey round the bulging south coast, but now a daily train service connects the two cities. It's still a long way and the train's no super-express—it takes eight hours each way! It's a long time to sit in a railway carriage, but we have only this one chance to see these ships. We have to go. It'll be interesting to see Oslo and have a close-up look at the inland mountains.

Bergen's station is an imposing, early-twentieth-century building. A high, arched roof covers the platforms and passenger concourse. We wait in line a few moments at the booking office for our turn at a small service window. A slight, balding ticket agent looks up.

"Good morning. May we speak English?" I ask.

"Of course. How can I help you?" he replies, with just a slight accent.

"We'd like to make a short visit to Oslo. I understand there are some discount fares."

"Maybe," says the agent, as though it is a privilege and requires good behavior. "When do you want to go?"

"Tomorrow, if possible," I reply hopefully.

The agent doesn't respond immediately but flips through the

pages of a book in front of him. "There's nothing tomorrow, but I have seats the day after," he says.

"Wednesday's fine," I confirm.

"How long do you want to stay?" he asks.

"Oh, just a couple of days."

"That's not long for such a big journey," he says with a slight smile as he once more searches his book. "I have seats on the overnight train on Friday. It arrives here at seven o'clock Saturday morning. After that, all seats are taken until next week."

We accept the Friday-night return. It's an ideal arrangement for us. We'll have two full days to visit the museum and see something of Oslo and be back here for the weekend. Then we'll leave for Shetland. We buy the tickets and are agreeably surprised at the modest fare.

We have a couple of days to find a new berth for *Symphony*. Maybe she'd be safe in the *vagen*, but to leave her unattended in such a public place seems unwise. Gerran recommends a marina at Elsesro, a small community about two miles north of the city, and we take a morning to travel there by bus, check out the facilities, and make a reservation. A nearby bus stop on the main highway will be convenient for our trip to the station. On Tuesday we fill the water tanks, do two loads of laundry, and in the afternoon move *Symphony* to her new berth.

Catching the Oslo train requires an early start. On a colorless morning we make our way through the boat yard and up a steep incline to the empty bus shelter. The few early commuters who share the ride appear to be as much in need of coffee as we are. We alight in the city center and cross a large city park where cyclists and joggers are getting their morning exercise. The roads round the perimeter are already busy and vehicles wait in long lines at junctions and traffic lights. At the station we have time to buy coffee and muffins before boarding the train and stowing our overnight bags. Most seats are taken and we're pleased to have ours already assigned. Almost immediately the train pulls slowly from the platform. It's 0733, right on schedule.

The station falls away behind us, and city buildings slip past the windows. Quickly these give way to industrial plants and warehouses that in turn are replaced by suburban houses. Soon the wheels adopt a determined, regular rhythm as the train begins a long, slow climb into the mountains. In places we enjoy classic views of the fiords. Small farms occupy idyllic sites beside rivers and lakes, cattle ruminate in green pasture, and rugged mountains provide picturesque backgrounds. The train is not fast, but after weeks moving at walking pace aboard *Symphony*, the images flash past the window at dazzling speed. After about an hour we stop in a high mountain valley at the small town of Myrdal, where a few tourists leave to board another train to take them down a dramatic ravine to the shores of a fiord. From there they'll return to Bergen aboard a cruise ship.

We continue through a world of inhospitable, snow-covered highlands. The summits are quite modest, rising from long, relatively shallow valleys in scenes more desolate than spectacular. The train curls round the hills. One minute we're chugging through the winter landscape, the next we're plunged into darkness as the train enters a tunnel. Each tunnel entrance has a hut-like structure to divert the snow, and where the track crosses steep slopes, it's protected by metal roofs. A dull mist hangs in the air like a cold, wet blanket. The breath of construction workers freezes into gray mist as they stand at the side of the track bundled in thick clothing. In two hours we've exchanged warm sunshine in Bergen for a chilly world of snow and ice. Winter glides past the window like a Christmas movie.

We have no real sense of "reaching the top," but eventually the carriage wheels adopt a new rhythm. The train no longer struggles to gain ground but runs freely downhill. We've crossed the central divide. Slowly, spring returns. We stop at small stations and speculate about the people living in small wooden houses, how they earn livelihoods, educate children, care for the sick, and provide the necessities of life so far from the city and so high in the clouds. The lower we go the warmer it gets, the more luxuriant the grass, and the fatter the cows. We follow a wide, meandering river past farms and towns, through forests and prairies. Finally the train clatters through suburban Oslo, threads its way between tall city buildings, and finally draws up in the station. As we step down onto the platform, sunlight filters through the high glass roof of the station. We're back from the cold. It's springtime and warm.

We need somewhere to stay, so we call first at a tourist booth inside the station building. A clerk hands us a list of hotels, but when she calls to make a reservation, most are already full. However, luck is with us. The least expensive hotel is convenient to the harbor and has a room available. We book for a couple of nights. The rate is reasonable, maybe too reasonable for an expensive city, and we wonder what we'll find as we trudge along the street, bags in one hand, map in the other. At the appointed address there's no grand entrance or doorman to greet us, just a locked steel-and-glass door, and a button to summon attention. In response to the buzzer, the lock releases with a solid click to admit us to a small foyer. The only way forward is through a folding metal gate into an antique elevator that grinds its way slowly upward. On the second floor a receptionist greets us from behind an old-fashioned office desk. We sign the register and she assigns us what turns out to be a surprisingly pleasant and functional room.

It's now late afternoon, but there's still time for sightseeing. We walk through city back-streets of dull buildings and small businesses to the Akerhus fortress, a royal castle overlooking the harbor. Several people stroll on manicured lawns beneath its high stone buttresses and enjoy a panoramic view of islands and blue water. Below the castle's guns, traditional sailing ships with wooden masts, tarred rope rigging, and well-varnished hatches share the quay with modern excursion boats, all waiting for their next complement of tourists. A small marina occupies one corner of the harbor. Two former ferry-boats have been converted into bars and restaurants, while the western side of the harbor is a long line of eating places and watering holes.

One wharf accommodates the terminals of several ferries that serve nearby coastal towns and the Viking Ship Museum on the nearby island of Bygdøy. We note the times for our visit tomorrow. Four local fishing boats moored at the quay display their catches in open crates. Buyers stand on the wharf looking down to check the quality and compare prices. The seafood looks wonderfully appetizing, but my eyes are drawn to hand-held scales the fishermen use to weigh the fish. They're straight from the pages of history books, little changed from those used by Scandinavian merchants hundreds of years ago.

At the head of the harbor, Oslo City Hall, a huge, rectangular, and rather austere building, presides over a wide-open area that is part roadway and part garden. Flowers in formal beds relieve the uniformity of the concrete with splashes of red and yellow. Cars pass the front of the building in a continuous stream, weaving between double-length trams that clatter along tracks in the roads and make frequent stops to pick up and discharge passengers. Throngs of people jam the sidewalks and stream across the streets when lights bring vehicles to a halt. A central park with thick, low trees provides a small haven from traffic. We wander rather aimlessly along a few streets, looking at store windows and watching people. After a short rest at the hotel we set out in search of Indian food for dinner. In the end we enjoy an excellent meal at L'Opéra, a French/Italian restaurant, which provides a very pleasant meal, and we return quite early to the hotel and fall instantly asleep.

The next morning we make our way to the harbor for the nine-o'clock ferry. The city is already at work. Only four passengers disembark when the boat ties up, and only two join us for the fifteen-minute ride to Bygdøy. At the landing stage where we alight, a small sign directs us along a tree-lined residential street, and, sure enough, at the second corner we find the museum. The large parking lot is almost empty.

We step through the high wooden door and blink. Right in our faces a curving prow soars from the ground to a curling stemhead way over our heads. Immediately behind, the longship's gunwale flows down to a low point amidships before rising again to an equally magnificent stern. *Öseberg* is seventy feet long (a little small for a longship) and constructed entirely of oak. She's covered in ornate decoration and was probably a ceremonial vessel, like a yacht or royal barge, and suitable for inland waters rather than for open ocean.

We work our way along the hull, examining the elaborate carving and admiring the flowing lines. We run fingers over gouges left by craftsmen's tools, our minds reaching out to the builders whose hands fashioned them so long ago. On the starboard side near the stern, the steering oar is lashed to the hull with leather thongs. Absorbed by *Öseberg*, we don't see the nearby *Gokstad* until we're almost beneath her prow. She's similar in length to *Öseberg* but plainer, with emphasis on strength and seaworthiness rather than ornamentation. She once carried a thousand square feet of woolen sail to scud along before a fair wind. When this failed or blew on the bow, her crew of thirty-two sturdy Vikings heaved on long oars to keep her moving.

Both ships appear so perfect and symmetrical it seems their construction would require elaborate plans and drawings. However, there were none. The curve of the gunwale, the turn of the bilge, the form of the hull were all shaped solely by the experienced eye and skill of the builder. The timbers, from the single massive oak beam of the keel to the delicate planking of the topmost strake, were hewn by axe. The seams were caulked with woolen cloth impregnated with tar, and the planks nailed in place. It's fortunate that timber was plentiful, as each boat consumed over one hundred trees, each three feet thick.

Gokstad and her sisters were the advanced weapons of their time. Fast under both sail and oar, they outmaneuvered adversaries in brisk winds or calm, fair or foul. They attacked with the sudden fury of *blitzkrieg*, striking quickly and moving on before effective resistance was organized. The longships' shallow draft allowed them to sail up estuaries and onto shelving beaches where attackers could deploy rapidly. No docks were needed, as men and horses just stepped over the gunwale as the ship lay over on her side.

The simple functionality of *Gokstad* appeals more to us than the rich ornamentation of *Öseberg*. Her proportions appear perfect, and her plain museum berth emphasizes her sensuous curves. She's so clean and so still, frozen in a timeless pose. With no sea lapping at her hull and all trace of the preserving blue clay scrubbed away, her timbers smell of furniture rather than the tang of the seashore. Once a much-feared instrument of terror, she has lost all function to become pure art.

Built by great craftsmen, these remarkable ships were sailed by men who went to sea as we go to school or work. They had to, as their lives did indeed depend on it. Boats were the only practical form of travel through the multitudes of islands, as rugged mountains made journeys by land impossible. Even today boats provide the best means of travel along the Norwegian coast. Ships were needed for fishing and transportation. They created wealth and symbolized honor and prestige. Power meant control of the waterways. For every

Viking boy, gaining boat-handling skills and learning seamanship were essential parts of growing up.

Both ships ended their working days by being used for ceremonial burials, and when discovered, still contained various grave goods. Inside *Öseberg*, excavators found the skeletons of two females and nearby were those of a horse and an ox. They were accompanied on their final voyage by several items, some functional and some decorative. The sailing equipment included oars, a wooden bailer, and a plaited leather strap to hold the steering oar. There were spades, forks, hoes, and many domestic items: textiles, a spindle whorl, iron scissors, needles, pins, and ladles. The most ornate items were three sleighs, a sled, a cart, and two sled shafts, each magnificently carved with striking and elaborate designs.

Consistent with her plainer design, items found with *Gokstad* are not decorative but simpler and more immediately useful at sea: a small axe, fishing hooks, a steering oar, and an oar blade. A cauldron, pothook, beds, and tent supports would all be valuable on a longer expedition. Each of sixty-four crewmen had a small circular shield. A wooden gaming board suggests a lighter side of Viking character and a need for relaxation on long voyages or during long winter nights ashore. Beside the ship were skeletons of six dogs and two horses, and (surprisingly) a peacock.

Gokstad was also accompanied by three small boats, the longest thirty feet long, the smallest fifteen, each a beautiful miniature of the mother ship. All are clinker-built in oak, with double ends, sturdy prows, and small steering oars. They're lightly constructed and probably quite fast, typical of small boat design wherever Vikings settled. It's an influence we'll find still strong in the Atlantic islands.

After *Gokstad*'s discovery it was just twelve years before the first full-size replica was constructed. *Viking* sailed to America under Captain Magnus Andersen to represent the government of Norway at the 1893 Chicago World's Fair. The voyage was intended to demonstrate that these open ships could cross the Atlantic and to bolster the Scandinavian claim to be the first Europeans to set foot in America. This was particularly pertinent, albeit brazen, as the theme of the Fair was to celebrate the four-hundredth anniversary of the voyage of Christopher Columbus. *Viking*'s voyage was the first to explicitly re-create a historic route, although she sailed from Bergen directly to New London, Connecticut, rather than taking the historic island-to-island route that we intend to follow.

Andersen made several modifications to the *Gokstad* design. *Viking* had a deep keel and a large fender of reindeer hair around the gunwale to provide buoyancy in case of swamping. She also carried additional sails. Surprisingly Norway could no longer provide a piece of solid oak big enough for her keel, and this had to be imported from Canada. She was launched near the *Gokstad* grave mound in Oslo Fiord, decked in Norwegian and American flags and the Viking emblem—a red square and black raven. She sailed first to Bergen, which she left at the end of April with a crew of twelve, two chronometers, a large selection of spares, and a thousand bottles of beer. Fully laden, she weighed over thirty tons—much more than likely for the original *Gokstad*.

Andersen was no newcomer to the North Atlantic. He'd crossed several times and served for a time as superintendent of the Scandinavian Seaman's Home in Brooklyn. He'd already made three attempts in small boats. In 1886, with one companion, he sailed in an eighteen-foot open boat. The pair reached the Newfoundland banks before winds and waves caught up with them and the boat capsized. All the equipment and food was lost. It took them thirty hours to right the boat, after which they abandoned the trip and accepted a ride home in a passing ship.

Andersen reported that *Viking* sailed remarkably well, proving fast and weatherly and easily surviving two fierce gales. She regularly logged speeds of ten knots and proved completely watertight. The hull was surprisingly flexible. The keel gave with the movement of the ship, and in a strong head sea, moved up and down three-quarters of an inch, while in heavy seas the gunwales twisted by as much as six inches. Caught in a gale, she hove to with a sea anchor for eight hours. She shipped a little water forward, but according to the skipper, there was "little cause for fear." Almost a month after setting out, the crew had their first sight of North America—a light off Newfoundland. They continued round Cape Cod, through Vineyard Sound in thick fog, and on to New London where they arrived forty-four days after leaving Bergen.

After a civic welcome, *Viking* proceeded under tow westward through Long Island Sound. Off City Island she was greeted by a naval escort, several steam excursion boats, and a fleet of private yachts all decked out with Norwegian flags and bunting. Leading the naval escort was *Miantonomah*, a double-turreted monitor, basically a floating gun battery and quite a contrast from the diminutive *Viking*. Her guns thundered over the water in welcome, and then *Viking's* crew joined the dignitaries aboard *Miantonomah* for several long speeches. The principle oration, delivered by the president of the New York Scandinavian Society, indicated no doubt regarding the true significance of the voyage. He declared:

> There is a fine appropriateness in your demonstrating in this Columbian year the feasibility of the Norse discovery of America and reminding us that Columbus, great as was his achievement, was not the first to penetrate the vast unknown wonder realm to the west and furrow the trackless seas with his keels.

The crew apparently looked as Vikings should. The *New York Times* described them as "bearded sunbrowned men with fierce mustaches and fair hair," while it portrayed Andersen himself, Viking of all Vikings, as "a stalwart specimen of Norse manhood, blond of complexion, with that red gold hair and long drooping mustache seen in the pictures of the old sea kings."

After the speeches *Viking* was escorted down the East River, round the Battery, and up the Hudson River where she anchored off 36th Street. The crew was feted by the city, the mayor, and especially by New York Scandinavians. Their engagements were reported enthusiastically in New York newspapers. However, these modern Vikings attracted trouble as easily as their rampaging ancestors. Returning to the ship after a reception, Andersen and five crewmen got into a fracas with a group of locals. The police were called, and in the ensuing scuffle, Andersen was struck on the shoulder by a police baton. When order was restored, the locals were allowed to go, while the Vikings were thrown into a Brooklyn jail on charges of intoxication and disorderly behavior. They were released on bail the next morning with a hearing set for the following Monday and went straight from the cells to a reception given by the mayor of the City of New York.

The whole city flew into indignant outrage at this affront to the "gallant visitors." Andersen protested the innocence of himself and his companions. The Vikings were victims, the *Times* reported, "defending themselves against a gang of roughs." The situation demanded a scapegoat and the newspapers chose the judge who committed the Vikings for trial. Pressured by the mayor, this unfortunate magistrate convened a special court session and dismissed the charges. Honor, always preeminent in Viking affairs, was satisfied and peace restored. Finally *Viking* sailed up the Hudson River, through the Erie Canal and the Great Lakes to Chicago, where she arrived on July 12 to another naval escort and grand civic welcome.

Several *Gokstad* replicas have been built since *Viking*. Many carry summer visitors for short excursions in harbors from Scandinavia to North America. Some have emulated *Viking*'s voyage to the New World. In 1992 *Gaia* sailed from Norway to Newfoundland. How strange it is that Scandinavians should again choose a Columbus anniversary to remind the world of Leif Eriksson's voyage. *Gaia* departed from Bergen with great ceremony on National Day, May 17. She was forced to shelter for three days from a storm on her way to Orkney. She called at Fair Isle and Shetland, and then sailed to the Faroes and the Westmann Islands off southwest Iceland. At Reykjavik she was re-registered as an Icelandic vessel. Like *Viking* she proved flexible and fast, achieving speeds in excess of nine knots. In America *Gaia* joined two other replicas, *Saga Sigla* and *Öseberg*, and together they toured cities on the East Coast on their way to the Earth Summit in Rio de Janeiro. *Saga Sigla* had already crossed the Atlantic in 1984 as the first leg of a circumnavigation. However, not even sturdy Viking longships are invincible. *Öseberg* and *Saga Sigla* both sank (fortunately with no loss of life) in a storm off the coast of Spain in 1993.

We spend a long time looking over *Gokstad* and *Öseberg*, one moment with noses pressed to some detail in the planking, the next standing back to appreciate the full sweep of the hull. At last we've examined every section of both boats and every item on display at least twice. We've returned several times for "one last look." It's time to go.

Bygdøy is a mecca for ship lovers, with three nautical museums in addition to the Viking ships that drew us here. They're all different and unlike museums elsewhere—illustrating the variety of Norwegian maritime interests. Prominent in the large first-floor hall of the Maritime Museum is a large painting depicting Leif Eriksson as he first sights America. It was commissioned for display at the 1893 Chicago World's Fair. Fifteen feet wide and ten feet high, it shows Leif at his steering oar, dressed in yellow jerkin and dark leggings with a knitted hat covering his head and the back of his neck. His arm extends toward the coast of the New World, while the crew scramble for their first view of the new land. A row of small shields lines the gunwale.

A second-floor gallery houses a large collection of boats. All show their *Gokstad* heritage with their size and details adapted for various tasks and conditions. Boats for fishing inland waters are lighter and smaller. Offshore vessels are large to accommodate more crewmen and stronger to withstand waves and weather. We examine them all and try unsuccessfully to remember their various names.

We're more than satisfied with our day, but tired by continuous walking and standing, we take the ferry back to Oslo. This time we succeed in finding our Indian restaurant—almost directly across the road from where we ate yesterday. After another pleasant dinner, we again return early to the hotel. The next morning we repack our bags and leave them in store at the hotel. Once again we take the ferry to Bygdøy.

Today is full of contrasts. In the museum of the same name we find *Kon Tiki*, a flimsy balsa raft sailed by Thor Heyerdahl across the tropical Pacific from Callao, Peru, to Tahiti. It was an evocative voyage to prove the feasibility of an historic route. We envy them the warm blue water. However, the large raft looks very fragile and difficult to sail—certainly no vessel for us! Across the road in her own museum, *Fram* is different in almost every way, a large wooden ship strongly reinforced for arctic exploration. In her huge, specially constructed boathouse we examine *Fram*'s tough, reinforced beams and massive bow to protect her from ice. We reflect on *Symphony*'s fragile fiberglass stem. Photographs in galleries alongside the ship show Norwegian explorers Nansen and Amundsen looking intrepid in frightful conditions. Some pictures are truly intimidating. We think of our own voyage. Will we meet icebergs around Cape Farewell and in Davis Strait? Will we see them at night in time to maneuver around them? The exhibit is impressive and sobering. We decide to keep as far from the ice as we can.

When we emerge from the *Fram* building, it's raining hard. We shelter under a covered walkway while the shower blows over and then walk out onto the wooden pier to wait for the Oslo ferry. Weak sunshine filters through the clouds.

I turn to Les. "So what do you want to do now?"

"I don't know," she replies. "Any ideas?"

"Well, there's a city museum in Oslo." Les is quiet, so I add, "And there's an art gallery."

"You have to be kidding," she blurts out, but I'm already laughing.

"I'm pretty much done with museums," I confess.

"We could spend more time around the harbor," Les offers with little enthusiasm.

"Hmm. . . . How about an early train back to Bergen?"

"Let's see if we can change the tickets."

We walk straight from the ferry to the hotel to collect our bags, and from there on to the station. We get seats on an earlier train with no trouble, and by midafternoon we are heading out of the city. By eleven o'clock we're back in Bergen. Unsure of late-evening bus schedules we indulge ourselves with a taxi ride back to *Symphony*.

Chapter 5

Hjaltland

Bergen remains warm and sunny throughout our visit, and despite statistics and local anecdotes, it lives in our memories as a city of sunshine-washed colors, people in summer clothes, and diners at street-side cafés. Midmorning we motor from the marina as two small gaff-rigged schooners and three yachts tack across the outer harbor into a moderate breeze. From time to time they disappear behind ferries steaming steadily to their berths. As we pass the castle at the harbor entrance, we have a final view of the *vagen* and the surrounding buildings. Slowly these now familiar landmarks fall astern.

Bergen has no immediate access to the open sea. Departing ships must first head north or south along the North Way to find a suitable passage between outlying islands. We head north, taking the shorter, traditional route and avoiding backtracking our earlier course. Once under the Askøy road bridge we make a starboard turn into Hjettsfjord, a wide waterway with strings of islands on both hands. We have the fiord to ourselves. Just a few buildings are scattered along the tree-lined shores and there's no sign of the city we left just a few moments ago. After motoring seven or eight miles we make a sharp turn to port between the islands of Toftöy and Blomöy, pass beneath a bridge and close by another small island, and on to the open sea.

As soon as we clear the outlying rocks we hoist the mains'l, unroll the genoa, and head for Lerwick. From the weather forecast we expect to sail northwest in moderate southwesterlies. Later, when the approaching warm front has passed, the wind is supposed to veer to the northwest, allowing us to come onto starboard tack and regain ground to the south. However, forecasts are just that. The actual wind is north of west and our course is southwest, close-hauled on starboard tack from the outset.

It's a beautiful day, with white clouds floating gently across a blue sky. The barometer reads 1030 Mb. Water swishes rhythmically past the bow as *Symphony* pitches gently into two-foot waves. As far as we can see—north, west, and south—the sea is empty. Only the

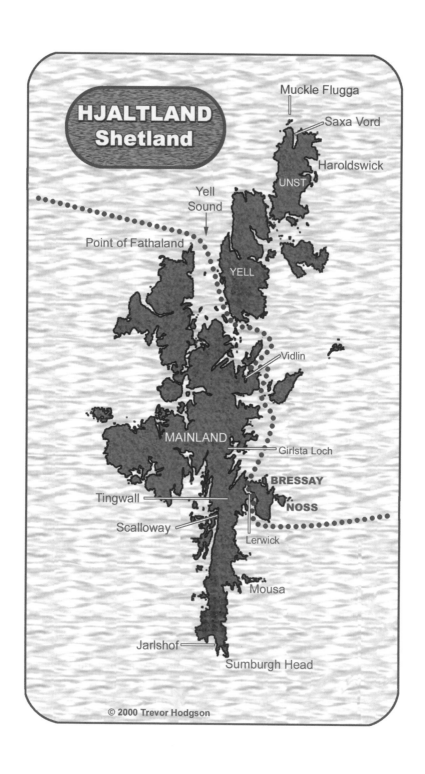

HJALTLAND
Shetland

Muckle Flugga

Saxa Vord

Haroldswick

UNST

Yell
Sound

Point of Fathaland

YELL

Vidlin

MAINLAND

Girlsta Loch

BRESSAY

Tingwall

NOSS

Scalloway

Lerwick

Mousa

Jarlshof

Sumburgh Head

© 2000 Trevor Hodgson

characteristic buzz of a helicopter disturbs the peace, and overhead
we see a miniature bug-like silhouette. The chopper heads out to sea
and is soon gone, no doubt en route to one of many offshore oil installations.

Brown rocks and green vegetation on receding coastal islands,
bright in the direct rays of the afternoon sun, contrast with the dull
purple of distant snow-sprinkled mountains. The islands extend to the
southern horizon, but ten miles northward a long ridge terminates in
a bold headland. At the foot of this mountain at the main outlet of
Hjettefjord lies the small island of Hernar, the classic point of departure for Vikings heading for Greenland. The *Icelandic Book of
Settlements* includes succinct sailing directions for the direct voyage:

> From Hernar in Norway one must sail a direct course
> west to Hvarf in Greenland, in which case one sails north of
> Shetland so that one sights land in clear weather only, then
> south of the Faeroes so that the sea looks halfway up the
> mountainsides, then south of Iceland so that one gets sight of
> birds and whales from there.

Cape Farewell at the southern tip of Greenland is on the same latitude as Hernar. The route is classic latitude-sailing with occasional
sightings of land and sea life to confirm a steady westward course.
Viking voyages along this route became quite routine, showing they
were competent latitude sailors. Until the eighteenth-century development of chronometers enabled seafarers to determine longitude, a
ship first sailed north or south to the latitude of its destination. Then
it sailed east or west, checking the course by the height of the pole
star or the midday sun. How Vikings measured the height of the sun
is problematic. Maybe sighting the sun against a stick held to the gunwale was sufficiently accurate. Fortunately distances from island to
island are not too great and measurements did not need to be exact to
see seafarers safely to their destination.

An incomplete circular disc found in Greenland has prompted the
idea that Vikings used a form of sun compass. A vertical, central pin
casts the sun's shadow onto the disc surface. It's calibrated before
departure by tracing the tip of the shadow as the sun makes its daily

Using The Bearing Dial

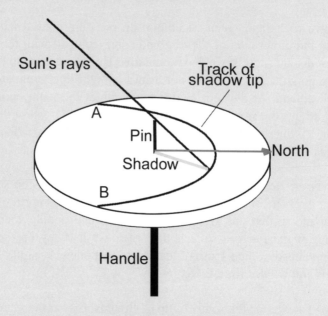

Sun's rays

Track of shadow tip

A

Pin

North

Shadow

B

Handle

Calibrating the dial:

1. Fix dial in horizontal position
2. Mark positions of shadow tip approximately each hour
   (these will follow an arc from A to B)
3. Mark the north line bisecting the arc

Route finding at sea:

1. Hold dial horizontal
2. Rotate dial until sun's shadow tip lies on the arc
3. Note direction of north from the north line

passage round the sky. At sea the dial is held horizontally and rotated until the shadow tip lies on the trace. The orientation of the dial is then the same as when the trace was made. The direction of north can be read and the course to sail noted. The shadow track varies with the sun's seasonal movement in the sky, but this has little effect for the relatively short duration of a voyage.

Before leaving home, we watched a television program of Robin Knox-Johnson testing a dial in the English Channel. He seemed to have good results, so we decided to try it ourselves in the Vikings' home waters. I made a plywood dial at home and calibrated it at our mooring in Bergen. On one of those beautiful sunny Bergen days, I propped the disk on deck, supported as horizontally as possible, and marked the tip of the shadow at intervals of about an hour. Joining the dots produced a curve approximately as expected—a wide horseshoe open to the south.

The dial is awkward to use at sea, as it's difficult to keep it horizontal while *Symphony* rolls with the waves. We take several readings. I hold the disk as level as I can while Les rotates it to line up the sun's shadow. Under the circumstances the results are better than we expect and provide a good general indication of north and so the course to Shetland. We estimate the dial's course is accurate to about ten degrees—good enough for island-hopping across the North Atlantic.

We consider covering the compass and GPS and following the Viking route using only the dial to find our way. However, continuous position displays from the GPS are too convenient to give up easily and we decide against it. I'm anxious not to lose time by straying too far from the rhumb line, as delays will reduce time for exploring along the way. However, the dial does seem to work. The Vikings could have used it . . . but did they? We don't know. Maybe there are other explanations for the dial found in Greenland. Its photographs look very similar to a circular disk in Stavanger Museum. This has a diameter of five inches and a twenty-four-point design round the circumference. It's rather curiously labeled as "a digging stick weight."

The sagas make no mention of sundials, but they do describe another, very different, way-finding technique. Floki Vilgerdarson— "a great Viking"—departed for Iceland around the year 860. Floki was devoted to Odin, and before sailing he made the appropriate prayers and sacrifices. His ship carried a full crew and a boat full of livestock, "for he planned to settle permanently." He also took three ravens, "because in those days oceangoing mariners in the Northlands had no lodestone," and so his ship became known as *Hrafna-Floki* (Ravens-Floki). His voyage was eventful. En route he lost two daughters: one drowned in Shetland, the other married in the Faroes. He arrived safely in Iceland, so the ravens must have served him well! He settled temporarily in northwest Iceland but did not stay long. He had a difficult time through the winter, as he neglected to make adequate preparations. When he surveyed the snow-covered hills and ice-choked fiord, he named the island "Iceland" and returned to Norway!

As the long afternoon draws into evening, there are signs of change in the weather. Periodically shadows cross the deck and momentarily the light dims and the air turns cool. The wind backs first west, then southwest, and we go about onto port tack. High cirrus clouds spread a thin gray veil across the sky. The cloud layer thickens and in a couple of hours low stratocumulus clouds roll first toward us and then over us. The scene darkens. Slowly the coastal islands disappear below the horizon and colors fade from the mountains. The remaining mountain humps gain dark blankets of cloud until rock and cloud fuse into a single blue-gray mass. Finally this last vestige of Norway sinks astern.

The wind freshens and we fall off a little to ease the motion. A freighter steams past close enough for us to read the name *Leng* clearly on her stern. A little later a slow-moving light tanker follows and yet another tanker hauls over the horizon to starboard and appears set to cross quite close. There's no way her watchkeeper could fail to see us: the visibility is still excellent and we're only a couple of miles apart. Nevertheless, she steams steadily on and I call her on the VHF: "Vessel heading south in approximate position sixty degrees zero three north, zero degrees one eight east, this is *Symphony*. We're the sailing vessel on your port bow, over."

There's a long silence. Just as my fingers tighten on the microphone button to repeat the message, a reply comes in with a tone of some surprise. "*Symphony, Symphony . . . Anna Knutson . . . over.*"

"*Anna Knutson . . . Symphony.* We'll cross quite close. Is it okay if we hold our course?" I ask.

There's another pause, then we hear *"Symphony,* stand by." Eventually the voice continues, "I think it's better now if we go ahead," suggesting that she'd have given way if I'd called earlier.

"Roger. This is *Symphony.* We'll slow down till you've passed. *Symphony* standing by, channel 16." We reduce speed to little more than bare steerage. *Anna Knutson* is slow coming on, and long before she crosses our track, it's clear we could have passed safely well ahead of her.

Around eight o'clock we have dinner in the saloon, taking turns to climb to the cockpit to check for shipping. As soon as the plates are cleared away, I take the first watch while Les lies down to rest. Apparently we've left the tanker route and my watch is uneventful. I slip easily into a routine of writing e-mail to the family, checking the radar, and scanning the horizon.

Around midnight Les takes over, and almost immediately the breeze moderates and then dies away. We heave to in rather unorganized waves to wait for a new wind to get established. There's little to do. Les reads while I rest. When I take over again at 0300, I listen to the BBC World Service on the SSB. The colorless dawn brings only light, fitful winds and overcast skies. Midmorning the barometer begins a long steady fall. A southwest breeze fills in and rises steadily to a brisk twenty-five knots with higher gusts. We roll up the genoa, set the stays'l, and tie a reef in the main. It is spirited sailing. *Symphony* feels alive, a thoroughbred bounding over the waves. Occasionally we're jolted as she falls off a crest and crashes into the following trough. The wind whistles through the stays at over thirty knots. I begin to feel decidedly unwell. The Frigg oil platform appears far off to port and a fishing boat to starboard. Throughout the day we make steady, if unspectacular, progress. There are no problems with gear and we encounter no more ships.

On watch the following night I see the green and white lights of a trawler ahead on the port side. She's a comfortable distance from our track and appears dead in the water. I assume she's tending her nets. However, we've learned to be wary around fishing boats, as they make frequent and erratic changes in course and speed, and I continue to watch her closely. Sure enough, as we approach, she makes a sudden move toward us and then stops. We still have crossing room and hold our course. We're safely past, when the VHF suddenly bursts into life and we're hailed in a strong Scottish accent. "D'ye think ye should have some lights on?"

I respond: "Vessel calling, this is *Symphony*, over."

The trawler skipper repeats his message and then continues. "I can only see a red, just a single red—you're not bright at all."

"This is *Symphony*. We're a sailing vessel. You should just see our port navigation light. A single red. Over."

"Well, you're not very clear," grumbles the fisherman.

"This is *Symphony* standing by, channel sixteen."

No doubt the crew was preoccupied with their gear and didn't see us approach. We decide that from now on we'll routinely radio all vessels that approach *Symphony* or that are on crossing courses.

A couple of hours after passing the trawler, the wind again dies and we spend several hours drifting with little or no progress. When the wind returns, it has finally veered to the northwest as originally forecast. By 0700 there's enough breeze for us to get underway, and in a repeat of yesterday it rises quickly to twenty-five knots. We set the stays'l and carry a single reef in the main. On this new tack, our sense of well-being returns. We're sailing well—while the motion's uncomfortable, it's purposeful. Instead of hanging around, we're steadily closing the distance to Lerwick. However, we have little time to enjoy it. Suddenly there's a harsh rip. We look up to see the mainsail split from leech to luff just above the reef points. Les grabs the helm and releases the wind-vane steering. As she turns *Symphony* into the wind, we quickly lose way. I clip my harness to a safety line and rush forward to the mast to release the main halyard. The sail flaps wildly. Les winches the topping lift taut and I haul in the second reefing line. As soon as the clew is down to the boom, I tie the line to a cleat. Les slackens the sheet, and with the tack hooked to the gooseneck, I reset the halyard. The sail, now double-reefed, is drawing again with the torn seam tied into the lazy bundle round the boom. A repair will have to wait until we reach harbor.

Symphony continues to make good progress, just a little slower but with easier motion. The tear in the sail is irritating but not too serious, as we can keep the double reef all the way to Lerwick. If necessary, we can use the trysail instead of the main. Nevertheless, it's frustrating. Last winter we sent the mains'l and genoa to a sail loft to be checked and serviced ready for the voyage. The sailmaker should have found any rotten stitching. It took only a few days of moderate wind to expose the weakness once we put to sea.

Early afternoon we arrange a crossing with a tanker over the VHF, and a little later another passes well to port heading west. From my habitual lookout position at the top of the companionway, I watch four oystercatchers fly past, their black-and-white wings beating purposefully, long red beaks outstretched ahead and red legs trailing behind. The sagas report sailors navigating by interpreting the movements of whales, seals, and birds. I wonder what our Viking predecessors would glean from the oystercatchers. They're flying directly away from the Shetlands, but if uncertain of our position, would I confidently backtrack their course to find the islands? I'm happy I have the GPS and don't have to decide.

At 1700 hours, after safely passing another large freighter, we sight a dark and distant land on the port bow. It's our first view of Hjaltland (Highland), long since anglicized as Shetland. It's over sixty hours since we left Bergen. Our many tacks and two long periods of calm have produced a very slow passage. Even now with our destination in sight, we need more tacks, as the wind continues to vary. The air feels cold, but we enjoy good visibility and encounter no further traffic. Just before midnight we pass tall cliffs to starboard and enter an open bay south of the island of Bressay. Ahead, unseen, is the largest island, Mainland. Lerwick lies up Bressay Sound, between Mainland and Bressay and directly into the wind. Unfamiliar with the approach, we heave to and wait for daylight.

The next morning we're underway at 0800. With two reefs still in the mains'l and the genoa partly furled, we tack toward Bressay Sound. One fishing boat tows another along the Mainland shore to rendezvous with a lifeboat and a police vessel. We give all four a wide berth as the tow is transferred to the lifeboat in a long and complex operation. Half an hour later as we turn into Lerwick harbor, all four boats still appear in the same positions. We drift in the channel as we hand the sails and start the engine. I dig mooring lines and fenders from the lazarette. Just inside the harbor, two people from a cruising boat catch our lines and help us tie up along a wall. We have little time to thank them as they declare their imminent departure for Norway, climb down to their own boat, and cast off.

The harbor is the focus of Lerwick and just one block from the main shopping street. The road along the waterfront is busy all day with cars, buses, and light trucks. Large freighters and fishing vessels moor in a basin to the north, small boats and yachts in another to the south. Between them a wide pier serves as parking lot and taxi stand during the day. In the evenings most parking places are vacant and the pier becomes a meeting place for the town's youth, several of whom race their cars with roaring engines and squealing tires. The mixture of high speed, parked cars, and pedestrians seems hazardous, but no one objects and the local police appear unconcerned.

We find Customs in a cramped, modern office along the main highway and complete the usual paperwork. Then it's down the street to check in at the harbor office. Compared with our free berths in Norway, twenty-two pounds (£22) for a stay of five days seems expensive, but this price includes the use of facilities at the Lerwick Boating Club. This occupies a gray stone building overlooking Bressay Sound, a hundred yards or so from the harbor. It has showers, laundry, and a bar, and provides good value for money. Each morning we parade along the waterfront with towels and toothbrushes. Later we carry bundles of clothes and coins for washing machines and dryers, and in the evenings we join local sailors in the bar.

The local newspaper, the *Shetland Times*, devotes much of its space in each issue to ships and fishing. Two days after we arrive, a large headline announces the arrival of *Andromeda III*, a spanking-new, bright-green fishing boat making her first call at her home port. Moored a few yards astern of *Symphony*, she's open to visitors. Although trawlers are regular sights at sea and often close neighbors in harbor, we've never before been invited aboard so we jump at this opportunity. We climb a long gangway to the pilothouse and join a crowd of people snacking on smoked salmon and sipping white wine from plastic cups. We squeeze between other visitors for a look at the steering and navigation areas and find an impressive array of radios, plotters, radars, and television sets that includes at least one example of every navigation device we can imagine.

One group of visitors clusters round Tina, the vivacious wife of the ship's mate, who explains that *Andromeda* is owned by a partnership of three local fishermen: the skipper, the engineer, and Tina's husband. She'll operate off the west coast of Scotland with a crew of eight and, once commissioned, will make only rare visits to Lerwick. Tina conducts us on a tour of the ship, including the complete fish-processing plant and the deck gear for handling the nets. We climb steel ladders and peer into neat cabins that have the clean, plastic smell of a new car. We inspect the fully equipped kitchen, launderette, and Jacuzzi. With spacious accommodation and every possible amenity, *Andromeda* creates an illusion of comfortable, almost luxurious, life at sea. How different she'll be, braving the wild North Atlantic in winter, rolling violently, and straining with her gear. The pristine paintwork will be caked with salt, and the stench of fish will soon overcome the sweet-smelling, new interior. A couple of days later Tina and the skipper's wife return our visit by spending some time with us aboard *Symphony*.

One task we must face before we leave Shetland is to repair the mains'l. Fortunately the weather's sunny and it's pleasant working outside. I haul the portable sewing machine from its lashings beneath the saloon table and set it on the cabin top. The sail is much too large to spread neatly in the limited space, and it heaps up in voluminous folds over the whole deck. Les makes a striking picture, enveloped in white sailcloth as she works patiently and diligently, partly by machine, partly by hand, along the long triple-stitched seam. The quay is a popular stroll for sailors, townspeople, and visitors, and many stop to talk. Les becomes adept at continuing her slow, rhythmic needlework while conducting a wide variety of conversations.

Shetland was settled early in the Viking migrations, and Scandinavians ruled here over six hundred years. A version of the Old Norse language was spoken here until the nineteenth century, and today ninety percent of all geographic names are Norse, including *voe* (bay or sound), *ness* (headland), *kirk* (church), *fell* (hill) and *bister* (farm). "Lerwick" is pure Norse, with the rather prosaic meaning of "muddy inlet." In a few places on the islands, the ruins of Viking houses, or at least the stones at the base of the walls, are visible, and artifacts in the local museum include typical Viking items such as loom weights, whorls, bowls, and lamps, all made from soft-green soapstone.

As befits island people, Shetlanders have a strong boat-building tradition. There's little demand now for traditional sixareens, the open boats that once set out in large fleets in search of herring. However, the open, double-ended design inherited from *Gokstad* is still alive. Each community hosts a summer regatta when rowing crews compete for honors in similar boats called *yoles*. Even small sailboats that decorate summer evenings in Bressay Sound have inherited some Viking character. Three of them rest on trailers by the wall of the boat basin. Well cared for with bright wood trim and polished chrome fittings, they're serious racers with stainless wire rigging, adjustable backstays, and four part tackles to adjust the mains'l. Their blocks and modern winches are the same found throughout the yachting world. However, these have no transoms. The quarters curve to form pointed sterns just like historic Viking boats. They are unlike any we have seen before.

While the Norse heritage is alive in the language and boats, the Norse rule ended here over five hundred years ago. In 1469 the king of Denmark gave Shetland to Scotland's King James III as his daughter's marriage dowry. The islands were largely ignored until huge shoals of herring arrived in the seventeenth century, bringing fishermen and their families in pursuit. These newcomers were not Scandinavian but were from the south. Modern Shetlanders have dark hair and light complexions, and Scottish accents echo along the narrow streets today.

These southerners also brought their architecture. Buildings overlooking Bressay Sound are dour, gray, and dignified, with none of the bright colors and bold contrasts typical of Scandinavia. Banks and public buildings stand foursquare, austere, and cold. They confront the elements with raw dignity. The main street twists and turns round blind corners. There are no sidewalks. Cars and people intermingle in a continuous, watchful minuet. Lanes, paths, and alleyways lead perpendicular to the shore, cross the main street, and then run steeply uphill. Shoppers lean into the frequent, bitter winds. Outside the town on lonely hillsides, low stone houses appear as natural as the heather, jutting from slopes like small rock outcrops.

While many Shetlanders may have Scottish blood coursing through their veins, their nearest neighbors are still Scandinavians. Bergen is less than two hundred miles away, just a day and a half by boat (unless beset with contrary winds). Torshavn, the Faroese capital, is a similar distance northwest, while Edinburgh is twice as far away and London over six hundred miles distant. The islanders foster close links with Norwegians and like to emphasize the islands' Viking past. Each edition of the *Shetland Times* dedicates a full page to Norwegian affairs. The "Shetland Bus" in World War II brought relations between the Norwegians and Shetlanders especially close.

The harbor is home to *Dim Riv*, a *Gaia* replica with colorful shields along the gunwales and a rather Disneyesque prow more reminiscent of Bambi than a fearsome dragon. Each January, "Up Helly Ah," a winter festival inspired in the nineteenth century by Viking legends, brings a thousand torch-bearing revelers to Lerwick's streets. Participants dress as Vikings (complete with apocryphal horned helmets) and drag a longship to its ceremonial conflagration. In May yachts race here from Bergen. This year thirty boats completed the course about a week ahead of *Symphony*.

Once a stopover on Viking routes to the west and south, Lerwick is still an ocean crossroads and meeting-place for sailors. Most of our neighbors in the harbor are Scandinavian. Two Swedish boats are moored by the harbor entrance. At *Symphony*'s stern an elegant sloop with a professional crew flies the swallowtail ensign of the Royal Norwegian Yacht Club. Several less ostentatious boats from Norway lie by the quay. Prominent against the wall at the root of the pier is *Dagmar Aaen*, a large German sailing ship heading to Jan Mayan and East Greenland on a filmmaking expedition. For a couple of days we're neighbors of *Sara*, a thirty-foot sloop crewed by five Norwegians of varying ages, all thrilled to have completed their first open-sea passage. Just one yacht flies the British red duster.

Soon boats are moored two or three deep against the wall. Our immediate neighbor is a thirty-foot, red-hulled sloop with *Mona Lisa* in bold white letters across her stern. She's skippered by Kjell, a retired school headmaster and frequent summer visitor to Shetland who's just made his first trip single-handed.

"That sounds pretty tiring. Were you able to sleep?" I ask.

"It was okay at first," says Kjell, "but later I just couldn't stay awake."

"I'd be worried about hitting something," I confide.

"Well, what I did," explains Kjell with a knowing smile, as though announcing a great discovery, "is put out regular calls on the radio. I made all-ship safety broadcasts warning vessels I was in the area. I asked them to look out for me. It worked just fine!"

He goes on to explain he usually makes the voyage with his paramour, who's unwell and unable to be along this year. "She's my Queen Marguerite," Kjell declares. "I call her my queen because she makes me feel like a king."

I'm too discrete to inquire how Marguerite produces such bliss.

Kjell is a good neighbor, always cheerful and responding to a "Hi!" or "How are you?" with an exaggerated "Won . . . derful" or "It is so won . . . derful to be alive." An oil lamp supplements the twilight as we enjoy a sociable evening in *Mona Lisa*'s cabin, sipping Kjell's special cocktail of whiskey and vermouth. He explains he's planning an extended visit so he can translate poetry from the Shetland dialect into Norwegian.

The following day Kjell explains that *Mona Lisa*'s cruising stores include quantities of dried fish. "It's very good, but it's not cheap," he tells us. "It's a great delicacy. It keeps for years and is a wonderful snack. You must try some."

"That's very kind," responds Les, adding, "but don't give away your supplies."

"Oh, but you must have some—it's so good," insists Kjell.

For several minutes Kjell rummages inside *Mona Lisa*'s cockpit lockers. Finally he emerges, crosses *Symphony*, and climbs the ladder to the wharf. He carries three or four large pieces of what were once fish, and a ball-peen hammer. He places the fish on the flat top of a large steel bollard and proceeds to beat the pieces vigorously with the hammer. He pauses several times, testing the consistency between his fingers and tasting small pieces. When everything is to his satisfaction, he breaks off samples and passes them to each of us. Unfortunately, despite conscientious preparation, the fish doesn't live up to Kjell's description. It's tasteless, stringy, and indigestible.

"What do you think of it?" asks Kjell expectantly.

Les and I try to be discrete, describing it as "interesting" and "different." Les's eighty-two-year-old father, who has flown from England to stay aboard with us for a few days, is more forthright when Kjell asks him directly, "Well, do you like it?"

"No, I don't!" declares Dad without hesitation.

Undeterred by our unanimous rejection, Kjell offers samples to the crew of *Sara*. Surely these true sons of Vikings will appreciate this traditional food. We feel our distaste for this "delicacy" vindicated when our neighbors all decline Kjell's offering.

A couple of days later we're chatting inconsequentially in *Mona Lisa*'s cockpit when Kjell suddenly turns the conversation to whaling. "I always carry whale meat when I sail," he tells us. "Foreigners tell us we shouldn't kill whales, but we must. It's a resource, it's there, and we must use it."

I don't really want an argument but cannot leave this view altogether unchallenged. "It's always such a thrill to watch whales at sea. We can't imagine wanting to kill them. Actually, I support Greenpeace and the ban on whaling."

"Oh, they've been up here causing trouble, but we ignore them. They just make everyone more determined," utters Kjell defiantly.

"But whaling's brought the species to the brink of extinction," I argue.

"There are plenty of whales—you see them all the time," counters Kjell.

For a moment it seems our neighborly relations are set to deteriorate, but we know neither will persuade the other and move on to other topics. However, the next morning Kjell appears wearing a T-shirt declaring "Intelligent People Need Intelligent Food," below the silhouette of a breaching whale. I ignore this childish provocation and he soon changes to a less contentious shirt. Neither of us mentions the subject again.

Our first excursion with Les's father is aboard a tourist boat visiting bird cliffs on the coast of Noss, a small island off Bressay. The motor vessel *Laerling* is about fifty feet overall with a central deckhouse accommodating the steering station and about a dozen well-packed passengers. There are seats on both fore- and afterdecks, but once underway these are cold and periodically doused with spray.

Most passengers prefer to squeeze into the cabin.

After steaming steadily for forty-five minutes round the south coast of Bressay and across a broad inlet, we approach Noss. Huge cliffs get closer . . . and closer. Long after the point where I'd heave to, *Laerling* continues boldly on. Finally, when we can almost touch the six-hundred-foot precipice, a quick burst in reverse brings her to a halt. The cliffs are an extraordinary white mass of feathers and guano. Tens of thousands of guillemots, kittiwakes, gannets, and great skuas are segregated by species along bands of horizontal sandstone. At the very top where vertical rock gives way to grassy slopes, we can just see the strange red-and-yellow bills of puffins.

A continuous clamor of birdcalls rises above the noise of the idling engine and almost drowns out the sound of waves breaking on rocks just a few feet away. The pungent smell of bird droppings is overpowering. It penetrates our lungs and combines with the swaying of the boat to make several passengers unwell. It's a memorable moment. The boat rocks just feet from the jagged rocks. Waves crash against the foot of the cliff, and pools of green water swirl around us. The noise is deafening, the smell nauseating. We feel compelled to examine every part of the precipice while at the same time tempted by the smell and noise to seek out a less hazardous and uncomfortable place.

When everyone's senses are satiated, *Laerling* continues her circuit of Bressay. I stand next to the skipper as we both stare ahead past a pair of noisy windshield wipers.

"Do you ever use the chart plotter?" I ask, indicating the small unit on the navigation table.

"Oh, yes, that thing's amazing," he responds brightly as he reaches over to switch it on. A greenish light illuminates the small screen, and the skipper begins to press buttons. When the results are not what he expects, he presses more. It's obvious he's not very familiar with the device, but he persists in pressing buttons with one hand as he steers with the other. His attention seems absorbed by the screen. I don't see him look up to check *Laerling*'s track, but he must have, as she continues on course with hardly a waver. After several minutes an outline of the surrounding islands appears and he grins in triumph.

Over the next few days we explore the islands by rental car, starting at Sumburgh Head, a huge rock bastion topped by a vacant lighthouse at the southern tip of Mainland. From a small parking area we climb a path up an airy, grassy ridge above steep cliffs. Guillemots, puffins, fulmars, and gannets crowd small ledges on the rocks. Far below, seals swim playfully in the water and bask on rock outcrops. It's sunny but hazy. From the abandoned lighthouse at the top of the cliff we scan the horizon, hoping to see Fair Isle forty miles away, but haze blankets the horizon. The island of Foula, twenty-seven miles west, is also invisible.

Just north of Sumburgh, way below the old lighthouse, we find one of Britain's preeminent historic sites next to the islands' busy airport. Jarlshof covers an extensive area of level ground a few feet above a curving shallow bay. It is covered with remains of houses going back three thousand years. These historic dwellings lay hidden beneath sand dunes for centuries until ocean storms stripped away the veil in the nineteenth century. Generations of different peoples have lived here since the first houses were built. Iron Age houses and the base of a *broch*, a stone tower used as a dwelling by ancient peoples, lie next to remains of an extensive Viking community. Most prominent and most recent is the Earl's Hall, a romantic stone ruin from the sixteenth century. It was built by Earl Stewart, the last of the Viking Earls of Orkney, and is featured in the opening chapter of Robert Louis Stevenson's novel *The Pirate*.

We mingle with visitors from a coach tour to examine the site and its ruins. A cold winds whips between the stones and we linger at those remains that provide an effective lee. Roundhouses of ancient Picts are sunk into the ground; tops once covered by turf are now open to the sky. Floors, walls, partitions, seats, and storage areas, all of rock, still stand where they were last used thirty centuries ago. Some are entered through narrow passages, and we stoop to pass beneath low ceilings. Nearby, rectangular stone patterns surrounded by well-tended grass are the foundations of the Viking houses. Artifacts in the small museum are familiar from the displays in Stavanger and Bergen: bone pins, steatite bowls and spindle whorls, line sinkers and fishhooks.

A short flight of stone steps leads to the top of the Earl's Hall and the whole site lies before us like a country park. Westward is open water. The sand looks golden in the sunshine, and the multitudes of blues and greens in the water seem more like the Caribbean than the chilly north. Braving the stiff breeze as we stare out to sea, we see the first tall black fin slice through the water. Another joins it, and another, until half a dozen cruise in company round the bay. They're unmistakable: a family of orca (killer whales).

We return to Lerwick along the island's main road overlooking the east coast. To our left, mountain slopes of heather and rough stones rise to disappear into banks of thick cloud. On the right, the land slopes away in a long downward curve to the top of the sea cliffs. Far away a round stone tower, wider at its base, stands on the small island of Mousa. It is the best preserved of all Scottish brochs. With walls thick enough to incorporate a spiral staircase, it has survived over fifteen hundred years. These towers were here long before the Vikings, who sometimes made use of them. *Egil's Saga* tells of a couple that holed up here when they were shipwrecked while eloping from Norway to Iceland. In a more curious incident, an earl besieged the broch where a fellow named Erland was holding captive his mother, Margaret. This episode was eventually resolved in a very un-Viking-like manner: all the participants were reconciled and Margaret and Erland married.

At several places round the coast, the land has been sliced away by the irresistible forces of countless tides and storms to form precipitous cliffs. Inland the ground slopes more gradually to rounded summits separated by long desolate valleys. The hillsides are treeless tracts of peat, heather, and rough grass. They're bare and lonely, rather than spectacular.

One long valley runs north from Scalloway, the former capital. It's more attractive than many, with green pasture rising halfway up the hills. Near the village of Tingwall a low peninsula projects into a lake in the valley floor. A thousand years ago this was Lawting Holm, an island approached by a series of steppingstones. Here was the Vikings' assembly or *Thing*, a combination of legislature, law court, and summer fair, where matters of common concern were resolved.

Many Shetland hillsides are marked by dark brown cuts where grass and heather have been stripped away and pits dug seven or eight feet deep. Generations of islanders have cut peat for fuel, a critical resource in a land with no trees or coal. Beside each cutting and out-side many cottages, stacks of rectangular briquettes stand drying. We pass many cars drawn up at the roadside while people chop more peat and add it to the nearby stack.

Our longest excursion takes us to the northernmost island of Unst. Away early, we motor from Lerwick to the village of Toft. This is little more than a roadside dock. A small store is closed as is a road-side café. We wait behind three other vehicles and watch a black-and-white ferry cross the sound from the neighboring island of Yell. At the dock its loading ramp clangs to the roadway, and four cars, a truck, and a small van drive off. Soon we follow in line up the ramp to the car deck. The crossing takes no more than ten minutes and we're off again along more curving, rural roadways. Soon we come to another ferry, indistinguishable from the first, which carries us over to Unst.

We head for Haroldswick, a small village at the head of a large bay of the same name. According to legend, adversaries of Harold Finehair took refuge here after their defeat at Hafrsfjord. Too arrogant or too proud to settle quietly, they used the island as a base for raids on Norway and provoked Harold to attack them and once more to demonstrate his supremacy. There's not much to see here, just a few buildings in a rather dreary landscape. Haroldswick has no conven-tional café, but the proprietor of a small grocery has set aside an area with tables, chairs, and a microwave oven where visitors can heat items bought in the store and prepare drinks of tea or coffee. We each find something to our taste and after forty minutes or so emerge rest-ed and fed.

Next to the store is a building that looks like a warehouse. However, its utilitarian exterior is misleading. It's the Unst Boat Haven, with an extensive collection of traditional boats up to thirty feet in length. All are clinker-built double-enders. We examine each boat, along with artifacts and displays recounting the history of the former fishing industry. It's sobering that men would routinely set off into the Atlantic in such small open boats. Inevitably the accounts include tales of notable disasters when the fleet, overtaken by storms, did not return and whole communities were devastated by the loss of fathers, husbands, and sons.

In a small adjacent workshop, a boat builder bends over an

inverted wooden hull. He looks up as we enter. We feel guilty at interrupting his work, but he greets us warmly and patiently answers our queries. A lean man of about fifty, Dave speaks slowly in a distinctly Scottish accent with the soft tone we associate with the islands. He has lived all his life in Haroldswick—the last apprentice in a long line of Shetland boat builders.

"Is this a traditional design?" Les inquires.

"It's a yole," explains Dave. "Once they were only round Sumburgh, but now you see a few farther north. They use them in the regattas."

"What wood is that? Can you still get the traditional woods?"

"I use larch. We get it from the mainland."

"From Scotland?"

"Yes," says Dave, and goes on to explain, "we use it with copper fastenings. Those have to be specially made."

"We've seen very few trees. What would they have used traditionally?"

"There's never been much wood here. It all came from Norway. My grandfather went there with five other men in a sixareen to fetch wood. Often boats were built in Norway, then dismantled and the pieces shipped over. When they got here, they were rebuilt. I can remember that."

"We've seen a few rowing boats, but does anyone sail these days?"

"Mostly it's the rowing boats. The regattas have gotten really popular. It's a big thing in the summertime. There was a time sailboats were common but not anymore."

"They used to sail," he continues. "My father was a fisherman, and in his day there'd be fifteen or twenty sailboats racing every Sunday night on Balta Sound."

"Are there standard designs?"

"There are no plans, if that's what you mean. We make the boats like they were in the past. The methods are traditional. Everything's lined up by eye rather than made to a fixed plan. It's always been done like that. Mind you, the builder has to know what he is doing."

A couple of miles past Haroldswick, two broad headlands, Saxa Vord and Hermaness, project into the North Atlantic, separated by a long inlet called Burra Firth. According to legend, Norwegian giants Saxa and Herman quarreled incessantly and hurled boulders at each other across the firth. Both fell in love with the same mermaid, who promised herself to the one who would follow her to the North Pole without touching land. Giants, it seems, cannot swim, so both were destined to pine forlornly on their lonely headlands. In another tale a witch turns Saxa into turf to form a hill and Herman into a wreath of mist to float over Hermaness.

Today Saxa Vord is alive with birds. A raven stands sentinel at the top of a precipice, twisting its head just enough to keep us in its watchful gaze. Fulmars circle the cliffs. A puffin screams at us in protest from the middle of a field of sea-pinks. The sun shines from a clear sky and brings blue tones to the waters of Burra Firth and browns and greens to the hills of Hermaness. We look down on the tops of skerries, white with guano, and watch lines of breakers wash over the rocks along the shore. Far below, on an isolated rock a half-mile from the cliffs, the lighthouse tower on Muckle Flugga also gleams white. It is the most northerly tip of the British Isles.

The final shoulder of Hermaness supports several tall radio masts inside a wire fence before plunging away to the rocks two thousand feet below. The summit is home to a large flock of arctic skuas (known locally as "bonxies"), large and aggressive birds that don't hide their resentment at our incursion. They swoop low over our heads, maintaining a continuous, deafening screech. We continue along the cliff top, but the attacks become more frequent and the dives more hostile. Soon the swooping birds are so low we feel the rush of air as they pass just inches above our heads. Our courage gives way to discretion and we make a rapid retreat.

We break our return to Lerwick for a brief stop at Girlsta Loch, the deepest loch in Shetland. It's not very grand, lying in a bare and rather undistinguished valley. Long ago, Ravens-Floki called here on his voyage to Iceland, anchoring his boat in a sea loch visible from our parked car. It was not a happy visit: Girlsta Loch claimed the life of his daughter in a drowning accident.

Two weeks pass very quickly. We drive Dad to the airport for his flight home and return the rental car. We get a few items at the chandlery. Local boats all fly the blue-and-white Shetland flag rather than the British Union Flag or even the Scottish Cross of St. Andrew, and we take one as a souvenir. Mostly we buy gloves. Regular ocean yachting gloves have already proved useless. Sooner or later we expect to face really cold conditions with freezing wind and spray, so we stock up here with the gloves worn by local seamen. We each buy three pairs: one of orange rubber, one of wool to go inside the orange pair, and one that combines orange rubber outside with fuzzy material inside.

We return to the customs office to clear from the U.K. The officer files the paperwork in a mechanical fashion, and we head back to the chandlery to arrange refueling. The pump at the chandlery wharf is broken, but the manager arranges for a tanker to come to the dockside. Several boats take advantage of the opportunity to fill up. We top off the freshwater tanks from a hose on pier. With everything ready there's still time for tea once more with Kjell. We slip the lines and depart on the afternoon tide.

Chapter 6

Isles of Sheep

We drift slowly north through Bressay Sound, all sails set before the lightest of winds. To port, Lerwick's houses, warehouses, oil storage tanks, and shipping facilities slip behind. We've enjoyed our stay, but we're happy to move on. It feels good to be back at sea, quietly ghosting along in calm water. We're at peace with ourselves in a moment of complete satisfaction. Our reverie is interrupted momentarily as *Symphony* drifts toward foul ground and it seems we must use the engine and destroy the tranquility. Happily the zephyrs prove just adequate to push her clear.

At last a breeze fills in and *Symphony* gathers speed. Our leisurely drift becomes a brisk downwind sail with occasional jibes to keep the sails drawing. It is a beautiful evening, the scenery is enchanting, and all is well. We're heading for Vidlin, a small village at the end of a long narrow inlet near the entrance to Sullom Voe. It's late as we approach, and the hills cast long shadows on the dark and impenetrable water. To enter the inlet we must swing all the way round to the south. We expect to motor up the bay but instead, pinching close to the wind, we ghost magically through water showing just the barest ripples. A small harbor offers the chance of a mooring, but the night is calm and we're content to set the hook. The bay is big enough to accommodate a small fleet, and we anchor in the middle and deploy a long scope. The night remains peaceful and we sleep undisturbed.

This is our last call in Shetland; from here it's straight to Torshavn, capital of the Faroes. We leave about 0530 to gain a favorable tide through Yell Sound. The pilot contains stern warnings of strong currents in the sound and of fast-moving oil carriers operating from the Sullom Voe terminal. However, this must be a slow day in the oil business, as we see no shipping. Our passage is uneventful, and we settle into one of those most pleasant days at sea when nothing happens nor needs to happen. It is enough to be, to feel the gentle motion of the boat, to sense a soft breeze on the arms and face, and to admire distant green hills and steep cliffs.

A large flock of gannets circle overhead and their brilliant white

Tjørnuvík

Gjógv

Vestmanna

ESTUROY

STREMOY

Klasvík

VÁGAR

Kvívík

MYKINES

Tørshavn

KOLTUR

NÓLSOY

HESTUR

Kirkubøur

SANDOY

**FAROES
Isles of Sheep**

SUDEROY

© 2000 Trevor Hodgson

plumage and distinctive black wing-patches show vividly against the blue sky. They fish energetically, first rising slowly on flapping wings, going high, and yet higher before pausing as they search the water for prey. Their quarry sighted, their wings form a sharp **V**, and they plummet headlong to the waves. This is no gentle dip. There's no hesitation. It's a full-blooded dive, driving through the surface and plunging to the depths. More often than not they emerge triumphant, a fish helpless in their beaks. We applaud their display. They earn their food.

Late in the afternoon we draw abeam of the Point of Fathaland, the end of the promontory forming the west side of the sound. We continue for a couple of miles to give a wide berth to isolated Ramna Stacks, and then fashion a direct course for the Faroes. We're making good time, with a fair wind and pleasant seas. The wind vane steers *Symphony* easily and we relax together in the cockpit.

A deep orange sun slides to the northwestern sea and we begin our customary watches. Les takes the first four-hour stint from 2000 till midnight, but I'm restless and cannot sleep. At 2300 I'm awake, Les is tired, and we agree to change. She takes one last look around the horizon and joins me at the foot of the companionway. We share a few moments sipping mugs of tea. Les's watch was quiet, her only sightings a couple of far-off fishing vessels. Now we have the sea to ourselves clear to the horizon. It's my turn to be lookout. My foot is already on the companionway steps to climb to the cockpit when a light flashing on a porthole has me there in a single leap. A boat like a fishing vessel is maneuvering a couple of hundred yards astern. She emits a low screeching noise. When she repeats it, I realize it's a siren. As she turns I see *GUARD SHIP* in large white letters across her black topsides. I duck back below to the radio. Almost immediately an accented voice cuts through the static:

"This is (unrecognizable) calling the yacht *Symphony*, over."

I reply immediately: "This is yacht *Symphony*, over."

"I've been trying to call you," the voice admonishes in a disapproving tone.

I ignore the implied criticism and repeat our call: "Vessel calling *Symphony*, this is yacht *Symphony*, over."

The voice continues: "We're a guard ship. Two miles ahead of you is a survey vessel. She's towing equipment extending one mile astern. You must keep clear. Over."

I repeat the message to make sure we have understood.

"Roger," says the voice.

"We'll change course to port and stay well clear," I confirm.

"Thank you."

"This is *Symphony,* standing by, channel 16."

"(Unrecognizable) . . . standing by."

Turning our attention ahead we see the navigation lights of a ship on the horizon. I adjust the wind vane to fall off at least two miles astern of the survey ship while the guard ship steams off northward and quickly disappears into the twilight. Once past the survey vessel we resume our original course to Torshavn. Les retires to rest and I continue the night-watch routine. A short spell of rain washes the deck with huge drops of fresh water. Then the wind dies.

At sunrise the sky is again a brilliant orange, but the sun soon disappears behind banks of clouds. A patch of dense cloud directly ahead is right where we expect to see the Faroese mountains. It is like a beacon guiding us to the islands. Perhaps the Vikings used these clouds to help with their navigation. But if these are waypoints, what are the clouds farther to starboard and those others on the port quarter? There are so many, how can we know which to follow? Northern waters always seem cloud-covered as low follows low in a steady eastward progression. On an Atlantic crossing a couple of years ago, clouds covered the sky every day, even in mid ocean many hundreds of miles from any islands. I often read of mariners finding their way by steering toward clouds clustered round mountain peaks. Here in the North Atlantic it doesn't seem it could be very reliable.

We watch a rare patch of blue sky. At first it expands, but behind it and getting closer, more dark clouds extend down almost to sea level. The water ruffles as a breeze wafts us with fresh air, but it doesn't last. We think of setting the sails, but before we can go forward, the breeze dies and the ripples fade away. We enjoy a few moments' sunshine, but soon the clouds return. Two small whales pass along the port side and we watch the fins of two sharks circle slowly round us before heading away eastward.

With no wind we must motor or drift. We have no autopilot, so motoring means hand steering. I favor waiting for wind, while Les prefers to use the engine. After a couple of cold, dark hours in the cockpit on watch, Les is tired and quite chilled. At the changeover she confesses to dancing and jogging in place to generate some warmth, but sharply declines my request for a demonstration. In my mind the "stay warm and wait for the wind" strategy is vindicated and I heave to until a light breeze finally fills in.

I see none of the birds that reportedly guided Viking sailors. Only the ubiquitous fulmars fly overhead, but rather than heading purposefully to land, they fly round and round in circles. Nevertheless, I enjoy watching them. In calm weather they sit rising and falling with the swell, scrutinizing our every move with their puzzled but disdainful eyes. They're at their best when a brisk wind drives the sea into steep waves with long deep valleys and whips the spray from the crests. The fulmars wheel in the air with graceful turns before plunging to the very surface of the sea, threading their way through the troughs and pivoting miraculously on extended wing feathers just inches from the water. They're very entertaining but seem to care little where land may lie. Following them would produce a very erratic course.

The pilot book declares flatly that a Faroese landfall will likely be made in poor visibility and bad weather. However, we're fortunate to arrive on a fine night with a fair, moderate wind. Les wakes me with just ten miles to go. It's late, but in the sub-arctic twilight I can make out tall cliffs of Nolsöy, an off-lying island to starboard and the dark mass of Streymoy, the main island ahead. Several faint navigation lights appear ahead and to port. Most seem stationary, but others we watch closely as they move with the erratic motion typical of fishing boats. None approach close to *Symphony*.

We've become bolder since we hove to outside Lerwick. Here there's no waiting outside for daylight—we sail straight into the harbor. A lighthouse on a nearby headland and a smaller harbor light confirm the position shown on the GPS. We pass the head of the breakwater into a large commercial port. We approach a long, empty wharf with a line of warehouses, all illuminated by a string of neon lights. It's difficult to believe such a grand mooring will remain unused for long, but no doubt if the space is needed, someone will

Buildings with rust-red walls and grass roofs crowd Tinganes, a rocky outcrop overlooking the harbor at Torshavn, Faroes

move us on. We come alongside the stone wharf and tie up to huge metal bollards. It's 0200 and still twilight, or maybe it's already getting light. A few cars cruise along the wharf, driving slowly toward the end before turning around and motoring slowly back. None stop or give us more than a brief glance.

I wake to find a man in working clothes, leaning on a bicycle and peering down from the wharf. A large freighter with *Pasadena* on her bow is already unloading astern.

"Good morning," I call, as cheerfully as possible just moments after waking up.

"Hello. You must have arrived overnight," he says.

"We arrived about 1:30."

"You have to move now. Many big boats will soon come here," he explains flatly without criticism.

"Oh . . . okay," I agree. "Where's a good place for us to go?"

"Go right to the end of the harbor. You'll find a good berth to starboard. When you're tied up, give the harbormaster a call on channel 12."

"Thank you. We're on our way."

Our visitor remounts his cycle and pedals along the wharf toward the town center.

It takes just a couple of minutes to gather our thoughts, retrieve the mooring lines, and get underway. Our directions take us toward the heart of Torshavn, past more empty wharves to starboard, and on to the head of the harbor. Just as it seems we've reached a dead end, we find a narrow entrance to an inner boat basin. Immediately to starboard the promised berth appears beside a low wooden dock. It's ideal, close to the city center, and completely protected from both the weather and the wakes of the large ships in the outer harbor. As soon as *Symphony* is secure, we call the harbormaster to report our arrival. Thirty minutes later a customs officer arrives and we sit in the cockpit to complete the usual paperwork. Surprisingly we find that the emphasis here is less on beer and wine and more on soda. It's not the contents that get official scrutiny but the containers. Cans, we learn, are illegal. It's okay to consume the soda aboard, but we're directed not to take the cans ashore.

A quick glance around shows Torshavn is quite unlike Lerwick.

There's no gray Shetland stone but an eclectic display of bright, colorful buildings. Layers of frame houses, most painted white, rise up the hill opposite. The town itself appears to be a jumble of two- or three-story buildings threaded by irregular roads. The harbor-side tourist office is a plain modern building, but the rectangular façade has been painted in bold colors with a row of gable ends. Across the mooring basin a substantial group of old buildings crowd onto a rocky peninsula called Tinganes. Here most of the walls are rust-red. The roofs are green lawns of real grass. Narrow, twisting, up-and-down streets thread between the buildings. Some tiny houses, completely black except for their grass roofs, squeeze between the larger buildings, huddled against the hillside or backed up into rocky corners. Tinganes was the meeting place for the Vikings' assembly, and today many of the buildings accommodate departments of the Faroese government. At the seaward end, the peninsula becomes a low rock slab swept twice daily by the tides.

Beyond Tinganes another boat harbor accommodates small vessels at long, floating pontoons. Most are powerboats with stern cockpits and central doghouse steering stations suitable for inshore fishing or family outings. Some have conventional square transoms, but others have curved quarters that join at a solid sternpost. Several wooden boats, all clinker-built double-enders, have long, slender oars laid along the bottom. The oars are square in section to fit against a distinctly Faroese style of oarlock where they're held by a knotted strap of leather or birch.

During the day the harbor is busy. Large freighters dock at our original berth. Quays near *Symphony* are crowded with passengers boarding ferries for the other islands. Some have "drive on, drive off" facilities for cars and trucks. A large passenger ship, with *Norrøny* displayed on her bow and "Smyril Line" prominent on her funnel, docks in front of the harbormaster's office. She's a regular visitor on her summer route connecting Esbjerg in Denmark with Bergen, Torshavn, and Seydisfjørd in eastern Iceland. The wharf directly across from *Symphony* is filled by a large sailing ship. The *STS Malcolm Miller*, part of the British Sail Training Fleet, is crewed by a mixture of professional sailors and paying guests.

Torshavn is a compact community, small enough to be explored on foot. Every fifteen minutes chimes ring out from a church near Tinganes. Various stores line the main streets but nowhere come together to form a central shopping area. Many business premises are along secondary roads, interspersed with private houses. In a bookstore full of tourist guides and local history, we buy a slim volume showing local tidal currents. It's in Faroese, but dramatic illustrations leave us in no doubt of places to avoid at full flood or ebb.

The supermarket, a quarter-mile from the harbor, displays a good selection of familiar items in the slightly claustrophobic atmosphere of a spacious basement. As expected in the Isles of Sheep, lamb is plentiful, as is beef, but we see little chicken. Labels show that most packaged goods come from Denmark. Among the usual displays of cereals and soap powder we find some items absent from our stores at home. Large baskets of dried fish remind us of Kjell and his hammer. The fish look just as dried out and tough-looking as those at Lerwick, but local shoppers inspect the wizened corpses, feel their texture between finger and thumb, and sniff their odor as though they possessed a fine bouquet. It's distressing for ardent opponents of whaling to see three or four different types of whale meat for sale, all of which appear to us unappetizing. However, most pathetic are *lundi* (puffin), packed four together on plastic trays, with tiny feet sticking straight up in the air.

Many of the other islands can be reached only by boat, but most of what we want to see is here on Streymoy, the main island, and on Eysturoy, which is accessible by bridge. We decide to explore by car, only to be taken aback by the high rental charges. The daily rate for a compact car is three times what we'd pay at home. A young man at the tourist office suggests we rent from a local garage. We select a Suzuki sedan from a typed list of available models, and with help from the staff (no one at the garage speaks English), we make a reservation for tomorrow. We're warned the garage takes no credit cards, so we get cash from an ATM in the town center.

The next morning we're off early, anxious to pack in a full day's exploring. Torshavn is going to work as we follow our directions through the central streets and up a hill on the edge of town. At the appointed address we find a small repair shop but no rental cars or office. A loud call brings the one mechanic sliding out from beneath a car, and he directs us round a corner to the rear of the garage where a small cramped building serves as the office.

Mr. E. Hansen, the middle-aged proprietor, presses hard on his ballpoint pen to register through all six copies of the rental agreement. When he's finished, I sign at the bottom, hoping I've not sold our souls (the form is all in Faroese), and we step outside to the car.

"You must fill with fuel when you return," Mr. Hansen reminds us.

"Okay. No problem."

"It must be full," he repeats, anxious that we understand his broken English.

"Yes, I understand."

"There are many tunnels. Afterward you must switch off the lights," he warns.

"Okay. Thanks."

We're assured "the car runs well," which proves a fair assessment, but it's certainly old and well used, with bodywork liberally decorated with dents and scratches. Nevertheless, it gets us round the islands and we're happy to save some money, although it still costs much more than we'd pay at home. Before returning it, we stop at a gas station to fill up. The cashier sums up well, exclaiming, "I didn't know they rented cars like that."

We soon leave the city, pass through a straggling modern housing development, and emerge onto bare hillsides. Wide empty slopes of rough grass and rocks sweep up from the tops of coastal cliffs to bare summits. The steep mountainsides rise in steps with vertical risers of gray, fractured rock separated by steep slopes of grass and scree. They are divided by long valleys with wide sweeping sides. There are no trees or bushes. In places, waterfalls cascade from upper valleys to feed streams that rush down the lower slopes before pouring over a cliff in a final drop to the fiord.

Sheep are everywhere, but we never see many together. They're usually in pairs or groups of five or six. To the Viking settlers, the Faroes were the Isles of Sheep, and even today some wool is exported. They're not the economic force they once were, as fishing and tourism are both larger sources of revenue, but there are still eighty thousand sheep on the islands, two for every person.

Many tiny *bygds*, traditional Faroese villages, stand isolated at the seaward end of valleys and are approached along twisting and undulating roads too narrow for vehicles to pass. We sense profound loneliness as we look at these remote communities separated from neighbors by long distances and rough mountain terrain. It's an atmosphere we've felt nowhere else. Tiny houses no larger than boulders appear like children's toys, insignificant against vast mountainsides. Small black buildings, low and with small windows, line fast-flowing and rock-strewn streams on their final dash to the sea. Here and there a prominent gable end is trimmed in red.

Outside the villages, cultivated terraces rise one over another, clinging to the lower slopes of the mountains. Small green potato shoots are just starting to appear. Nearby, long wire racks, five feet high, are strung from wooden posts. We learn they're to prevent hay blowing away while it dries. The villagers are prepared for gales in other ways too. From boats to trash containers everything's tied to heavy rocks or iron rings cemented to the ground.

Even in good weather, life here could be hard. Many smaller *bygds* have no church, and on the Sabbath, in the days before road transport, the faithful climbed the steep mountain paths over dividing ridges to worship in the next valley. When someone died, the deceased made the same perilous journey on the shoulders of kinfolk in order to be buried in holy ground.

Gjøgv in northwest Eysturoy has one of the most extraordinary harbors but certainly not one we'd want to visit by sea. A long, steep flight of concrete steps leads from a high cliff into a defile. A ramp runs alongside the steps all the way from water to cliff top where the end of a hauling chain still protrudes from a small concrete engine shed. Way down in the bottom is a worn concrete wharf, still with rusting mooring rings. The cliffs rise sheer from the sea and overhang on both sides, cutting off the sky but for one small patch. The air is cool and damp, heavy with the smell of seaweed. The sea rises and falls as waves roll through the entrance and water laps at the rocky sides of the gorge. The rock-strewn outlet to the sea cannot be more than twenty feet wide. A bend in the chasm cuts off the view short of the open sea, but waves break into showers of spray on a rock in the entrance. Passable by small boats in good weather, the chasm must be untenable with any wind blowing into the entrance. Our thoughts turn to the men who spent whole lives sailing in and out of this treacherous chasm. We feel a chill at the very thought.

We make the long climb to the cliff top. It's back to the car and on to the next stop, but when I turn the key, there's no revving engine, just a dull thud. Then there's nothing. We've neglected Mr. E. Hansen's sound advice and left the lights on after passing through one of many tunnels. There's no sign of life in the small black houses that line the street, but a young couple also visiting the grotto help me push the car. Fortunately we're on the top of a rise and soon have it rolling downhill. I ease it into gear and the engine roars back to life. For the rest of the day we never switch off the engine.

Kirkjubør, at the southeast corner of Streymoy, was the cultural center of the Viking Faroes for hundreds of years. We approach along a narrow road high above Hestsfjørdur with spectacular views of the dramatic islands, Hestur and Koltur. After a long steep descent we pull up at a small pier in front of a cafe and old farm. The fiord is calm. The water laps gently against rocks scattered across the bay. The pilot suggests this as a temporary harbor and we had considered bringing *Symphony,* but there's no safe refuge for anything bigger than a dinghy and we're pleased we opted to come by car.

The community was once substantial, including a large farm with fifty houses, two hundred cows, and five thousand sheep. Today there's a church, a small, never-completed cathedral, a café, and a log-built farmhouse occupied by the Pattursson family for eighteen generations. A few modern houses a little way back up the hill complete the settlement. Work on the cathedral began in the thirteenth century. It's of early Gothic style, rectangular in shape and open to the sky, and has a small two-story annex. The construction is of high standard, as befitted the bishop of the time who, according to the sagas, "more than all his predecessors, enriched the Faroese church with privileges, lands, and worldly goods."

The bishop's secular success had a downside, fostering hostility from his neighbors and insuring his constant embroilment in feuds. A suspicious fire destroyed the church and palace, and work on the cathedral stopped. The small church was rebuilt to serve as the national cathedral and is still used by the local community.

The bay here is Brandansvik, Brendan's Bay, honoring a sixth-century Irish saint who reputably sailed over much of the North Atlantic in a *curragh*, a traditional Irish boat. The story of Brendan's voyage is related in the medieval *Navigatio*, which describes fantastic lands and fanciful encounters with flying griffins and hymn-singing birds. However, it includes descriptions of icebergs and volcanoes that seem too realistic to have originated other than by a first-hand account. The first Viking explorers reported Irish clerics already settled in the Faroes and Iceland.

In the 1970s, author and adventurer Tim Severin built *Brendan*, a replica of a traditional curragh made of oxhides stitched together over a wooden frame. He then sailed this boat with five fellow adventurers from Ireland to America, calling at the Faroes and Iceland. They anchored here and visited the Pattursson family at the farm. Tondur Pattursson joined *Brendan*'s crew for the rest of the voyage and provided drawings for Severin's book. He's now a celebrated Faroese painter.

Kvivik lies a little north of Kirkjubør. The modern village straddles a shallow rocky river, and where this joins the fiord, stone foundations of two Viking buildings are protected inside a walled enclosure. A large long-house may have been a Viking hall, while a smaller building was probably a cow-byre and barn with stalls for up to twelve animals.

At the northern tip of Streymoy, Tjørnuvik lies on a dramatic, U-shaped fiord. On each side, huge mountains rise in continuous curves from shore to summit. We pause at the roadside overlooking Sundini Sound. Far below, waves crash into vertical cliffs on the northern shore and send cascades of spray high in the air. We follow a narrow, twisting road in a long, steep descent across the face of a mountain. The views are exhilarating, but oncoming vehicles force us terrifyingly close to the edge of the road and a thousand-foot drop to the water. The Viking settlement is on open ground at the head of the fiord. Excavations have shown the liberal use of wood for internal structures, a surprise in a country without a single tree other than thin juniper that is quite unsuitable for building. Such lavish use of imported timber suggests surprising prosperity so far from supplies in Scandinavia.

The Faroese National Museum is a long and strenuous walk up a hillside well north of Torshavn. We decide to take a bus and spend half a morning collecting information on routes and schedules. At a stop on the main street we climb aboard for a slow, winding tour of Torshavn's northern suburbs. No place is excluded. Stops are made in shopping areas and industrial parks. Residential streets are combed in the search for passengers. Finally we leave the houses behind and cross open hillsides of gorse and heather. The driver tells us when to alight and we step down just a few yards from the museum entrance.

Many displayed items are already familiar from museums in Norway and Shetland: stones covered with angular runic inscriptions, spindle whorls and loom-weights formed from shards of steatite, stone sinkers for fishing lines. There are cloak pins and rings, sewing needles and leather shoes, ropes and barrel hoops. Less expected are wooden items including bowls, nails, and knife handles. A gaming board is very similar to one found with *Gokstad*. Of many items illustrating domestic life, one exhibit in particular catches our attention. Labeled "butter box top" or "cheese box top," it's a circular disk about five inches in diameter with its circumference decorated in a pattern of triangles. I count thirty-two points, the same as the Greenland "sun dial." Both here and in Bergen we've found similar disks, each assigned different functions unrelated to navigation. Can the Greenland find really be something other than a sun compass? Maybe the triangular design around the circumference was not for navigation but just a popular geometric pattern.

Many modern Faroese are purebred descendants of Viking settlers. Their language is a variation of Old Norse. The islands became part of Denmark with the Norwegian-Danish union, but they avoided Shetland's fate of being given away. Maybe no one was interested in such distant, foggy, and windswept islands. In 1948 the Faroese regained control over many domestic affairs, but the Kingdom of Denmark still controls all foreign affairs as well as the military, police, and magistrates.

We must continue on our journey and we decide to call next at Vestmanna, a harbor on the southwest corner of Streymoy and a convenient departure point for Iceland. We untie the lines, and Les maneuvers *Symphony* round the long bowsprit of *Malcolm Miller* that extends well out over the channel. Once clear of the harbor the wind is variable and we continue south along the coast with the engine. Rounding Hjettsfjord the buildings at Kirkjubør appear miniscule at the foot of a rugged hillside. Gradually we work our way past Hestur and then Koltur. The diagrams in the tidal-current book have persuaded us to time passages carefully, and we enter Vestmanna Sund just after slack water for a favorable current to Vestmanna.

The fiord is wide between Streymoy to starboard and Vagar to port. The national airport is on Vagar, and passengers traveling to Torshavn go first by bus, take a ferry across Vestmanna Sund, and then catch another bus for the forty-five-minute ride to the capital. A black-and-white ferry pulls away from the Vagar shore and steams off ahead of us. We follow her into Vestmanna's large natural harbor, reputed to be one of the best in the islands. A group of seals watch our approach cautiously while a flock of eider sit complacently on the water.

The harbormaster doesn't respond to our radio call, but Les reminds me it's Sunday and we assume it's his day off. Directly ahead, in front of a group of modern industrial buildings, an empty bulkhead is long enough for several ships. We tie up at the western end. It's the first time we've moored at a fish factory. We'll find another in Iceland and they'll be common in Greenland and Labrador. We look around, getting our bearing and half expecting someone to move us on. A solitary figure strolls along the wharf, scanning the waters of the fiord and eyeing the sleek black head of a seal swimming a hundred yards away. The man is small, quite round, and about sixty. He approaches slowly as we finish tying up.

"Hello."

"Hello. Have you come far today?"

"Just from Torshavn."

"Will you stay long?"

"Just a few days. . . . Then we're heading to Iceland."

"You'd do better at the back of the fish plant. When the ferry comes in, the waves here get quite big. It comes and goes all day. Round the back there's no wash at all."

"Is there space for us?"

"Oh, yes. I have my small boat back there. I'm repairing it. It's a

Symphony at the fish factory, Wastmanna, Faroes

new boat, just seven or eight years old, but it needs much work."

"Thanks. We'll go and take a look."

We're now all on the wharf. I hold out my hand. "My name's Trevor. This is my wife, Lesley."

"I'm Chorchel," the man seems to say as he shakes my hand with a steady grip. "Chorchel Olsen." Later we discover his name is spelled "Tjorkel."

"How big's the boat?" he asks.

"Thirty-seven feet."

"Is it a family boat?"

We admit we don't understand.

"Was it passed from your father?" he asks, looking toward me.

"No, we bought her when she was three years old."

"Oh," says Tjorkel, as though this needs deep consideration.

Behind the fish plant we find a small dry-dock and a long, sheltered wharf that's empty, apart from Tjorkel's small powerboat. His advice proves sound. Ferries come and go at all times, casting their wash on the front face of the fish wharf, but no swell penetrates to our mooring at the back. Tjorkel pays a couple of visits to *Symphony*. The morning after we arrive, he's at the dock early, bringing several gifts: four frozen mackerel, several pieces of breaded white fish, a length of fishing line, sinkers, hooks, and a copy of *Almanaki*, the Faroese nautical almanac.

"Hi. Come aboard," Les calls, and Tjorkel climbs down from the dock. "Would you like a coffee or a cup of tea?"

"No, no coffee . . . but I like tea."

"We only have Earl Grey. Is that all right?" asks Les, already in the galley lighting the stove.

"Yes, thank you. I like Earl Grey."

As we sit in the cockpit drinking mugs of tea, Tjorkel apologizes for his English. We're embarrassed. True Anglo-Saxons, Les and I are both poor at foreign languages. Everyone we meet is willing to speak English, and it's so easy to let them.

"I never had lessons," he goes on. "I learnt it from British troops in the war. They were at Skansin (a fortress overlooking Torshavn harbor). They could never say my name. They called me Churchill."

"You certainly learned well," compliments Les. "We've no

Faroese or Danish at all."

"Did you ever work on the boats?" she goes on.

"I did . . . on my family's boat. I worked for years. I was also in America, in Portsmouth, on a big boat. We stayed a couple of weeks while we got the engine repaired. It was in the paper." Tjorkel unfolds a large page of newsprint and points proudly to a photograph of himself, sleeves rolled up, processing fish below decks. The accompanying notice describes the visit of a Faroese fishing vessel to New Hampshire. It's dated 1988.

The copy of *Almanaki* is full of the usual information on tides and currents and the height of navigation stars. Surprisingly it also lists members of the Faroese parliament. Much of it we can't use; it's either out of date or in undecipherable Faroese, but one table will prove very useful. Fish are important in Iceland and Greenland, and people can identify the various species. Several times we'll pull out Tjorkel's *Almanaki* to translate the local names into English.

Vestmanna is a small community surrounded by steep, grassy hills and is provincial compared with the capital. Houses are painted in bold colors, most commonly the familiar rusty red, and stand out prominently against the green mountains. Like other Faroese communities, it depended on sheep rearing until the nineteenth century when fishing became preeminent.

Having enjoyed bird watching at Lerwick, we decide on another trip, this time to Vestmannabjorgini, the cliffs and bird grottoes on Streymoy's southwestern coast. Two or three excursion boats make the run from the dock at the head of the fiord, which is also the home of the airport ferry. The road to the head of the bay follows the shore about thirty feet above the water. We pass a couple of run-down shops and several houses, and look down onto the roofs of boathouses that line the shore. Tiny potato patches are squeezed between the buildings.

The boat operators use small wooden sheds as booking offices. We select one that offers a trip this evening, but all places are taken so we book for tomorrow aboard the brand-new excursion boat *Barbara*. However, shortly after we return to *Symphony*, a car draws up on the wharf and out jumps Jackie, the wife of *Barbara*'s skipper, to ask if we want to go that evening after all. We arrange for *Barbara* to collect us directly from *Symphony* to avoid another walk to the harbor. About thirty minutes later we climb over the lifelines and join five or six other passengers in *Barbara*'s cockpit.

The current in the Vestmanna Sund is strong, and *Barbara* stays in slower-moving water almost within touching distance of rocks along the shore. Even here the engine works hard, and in places, ground is gained just foot by foot. The side of the fiord presents a changing panorama of mountains, rock faces, scree, and steep grass. Occasionally a sheep or two gaze back from apparently precarious ledges poised above tremendous drops. The skipper explains they're taken to the cliffs each spring to fatten on the luscious grass. Often they're hoisted bodily up the cliff face straight from the boats. In the fall they're lowered back down and taken off to be slaughtered. Our slow progress is unimportant as the time passes quickly. We watch the unfolding scenery, try to identify the birds that stare back from rocky perches, and carry on an intermittent conversation with a couple of other passengers.

Near the mouth of the fiord we're about to emerge into open water when *Barbara*'s engine stutters meekly and stops. We assume the skipper has paused to point out some feature of special interest and look for him to emerge from the pilothouse. However, that's not the case. He stays bent over the controls. He presses the starter. The motor whirs furiously, but there's no indication the engine might start. It sounds starved of fuel. The current now hurls us backward at a truly impressive speed. Fortunately it runs parallel to and not toward the rocks. The crew rush to set anchors, small grappling hooks with short lengths of chain and nylon lines, each about one-half of an inch in diameter. I look at them with concern, skeptical that these can hold *Barbara* against the force of the current, especially with the short rode that follows each anchor over the side. Nevertheless, after a couple of attempts, the bow swings into the stream and we appear to be set. Instinctively Les and I both note ranges of prominent rocks on shore to satisfy ourselves we're not dragging.

The crew heave open large hatches in the cockpit floor, and the skipper disappears into the dark space below with a flashlight and wrenches. I hear calls from the bilges to the pilothouse, talk of a filter bypass, and more efforts to start the engine, but all to no effect.

Soon the skipper is on the radio calling for help and we settle down to wait. An hour goes by quite pleasantly as we continue our bird watching and fragmented conversation. Nevertheless, everyone's pleased to see another boat making her way steadily toward us, following *Barbara*'s line along the foot of the cliffs. *Urðardrangur* is a traditional double-ended Faroese wooden boat, albeit powered by a diesel engine. She stands off a couple of boat-lengths while towropes are thrown and made fast. The current now becomes a distinct asset as *Urðardrangur* tows us slowly but steadily back to Vestmanna.

The skipper hands out refunds to the passengers, but we decide to try the trip again tomorrow. This time, as we climb aboard *Urðardrangur* (*Barbara* is apparently not yet repaired), there are no technical problems and we enjoy a successful expedition. The cliffs prove worth the journey, towering above us for two thousand feet. At the seaward end of rocky inlets, detached buttresses form tall, steep stacks. As we near the cliffs, the skipper issues a plastic hardhat to each passenger. Defiles, just inches wider than the boat, form grottoes, some leading to open pools where we gaze up at cliffs covered in myriad birds. One passage closes overhead to become a dark cave, and we edge slowly toward a distant patch of light. The cave is cool and damp and we're happy to return to the light and warmth of the sun. It's inspiring country. As the publicity leaflet for the cruise entreats, we "inhale the fantastic impressions we get from the 1500-feet-high vertical standing mountains surrounding us."

The following morning is clear and the forecast promises a few days of pleasant weather. We decide to leave for Iceland at the start of the afternoon ebb tide. Unfortunately Tjorkel is away from Vestmanna and we cannot say goodbye. We already told him we'd leave if the weather turned fair, and I write a brief note thanking him for his gifts and his friendship and leave it, along with a box of Earl Grey tea, in the cabin of his boat.

Chapter 7

The Edge of Hell

With our experience aboard *Barbara* fresh in our minds, we pay extra attention to the tides before leaving for Iceland. Dramatic illustrations in the tide atlas show that streams in Vestmanna Sund can get up to nine knots. We heed the warning and time our departure a little after slack water. Accordingly, just after 1330 on June 17, we leave the wharf at Vestmanna and motor slowly down the harbor. Gaining the center of Vestmanna Sund, we set the main and genoa, and *Symphony* sails smoothly ahead in a force three southerly. The barometer reads 1015 millibars. In little more than half an hour we leave the fiord with the bird cliffs to starboard and continue out into the ocean.

The Faroese west coast rises fortress-like to meet the North Atlantic in a series of forbidding rock walls. The deep grottoes we explored aboard *Urðardrangur* show as prominent dark gashes down the two-thousand-foot face. The huge scale of the precipice is emphasized by the sight of an excursion boat, just a tiny white speck at the toe of a buttress. As the coast recedes, the lush green color of the grass fades from the cliff top, rocks become gray, and gashes darker. Soon the hills and valleys merge into a uniform blue-gray silhouette.

The sky remains overcast. The wind freshens and backs southeast, giving the first indications of an approaching warm front. *Symphony* flies along on a broad reach with the knotmeter steady between six and seven knots. After an hour, conditions become boisterous and we tie a single reef in the mains'l, but *Symphony* races on with no loss of speed. At 1830 the SSB crackles a gale warning from Radio Torshavn, while the wind continues to strengthen. By our midnight watch change, it's blowing twenty-five knots and we take down the main and roll in some more of the genoa. The barometer now reads 1010 millibars. *Symphony* rolls as waves heave up on the port quarter. We continue to make fast progress toward Iceland through the rest of the night.

In early morning the sky and sea are indistinguishable shades of gray. I'm at the end of my watch, already weary from the routine. For a moment we're both in the saloon. I'm pulling off my boots as I brief Les on our position and the weather. Les is disappearing into her voluminous foul-weather jacket. Suddenly a heavy object strikes the deck with a resounding crash and has us both rushing to investigate. The mast and rigging appear intact, the sails are drawing as they should, and *Symphony* still powers forward. With my boots hastily returned to my feet and with a safety line clipped to the starboard jack line, I go forward. The problem is easy to find. The gears of the main halyard winch are lying on deck. The handle's nearby, but there's no sign of the drum. I left the handle in the winch, and it has rocked back and forth to ratchet the bolts free. I'm simultaneously relieved and mad as hell, pleased the problem's not serious—we can lead the halyard to another winch without much trouble—but angry my carelessness has lost us a winch. If I had removed the handle when I'd finished with the mains'l, it wouldn't have come off now.

It's 1330, just twenty-four hours since we left Vestmanna, and we've covered 142 nautical miles, our best day's run aboard *Symphony*. The barometer is down to 1002 millibars, and throughout the afternoon the wind continues to gain strength. At 1500 hours we roll in more sail but continue to race along with the wind behind the beam.

I stand at the top of the companionway surveying the small circle of sea that is our world. *Symphony* crashes through the waves, sending spray shooting high over the deck from the bow. We're alone on a wave-tossed disc just four miles across, hidden from the rest of the world by a shroud of thick mist. Wave after wave rolls through the curtain onto our wild, wet stage. As each one approaches *Symphony*, it gains its own distinct individuality. Some are big, some steep. Some pass easily astern, others crash into the hull forcing *Symphony* to yield before tons and tons of water. Once they're past, the waves stretch out and resume their anonymity. Over and over, the pattern repeats. Everything's in constant flow, ever changing but always the same.

We're accompanied by our regular coterie of fifty or sixty fulmars, our most familiar offshore companions and extraordinary aerial acrobats. For hours they entertain us with wheeling turns, their extended wingtips just clear of the water. They swoop low, skimming so close to the waves they seem at risk of being overwhelmed. Periodically birds interrupt their aerial ballet and one by one settle on the water, riding nonchalantly up and down as the waves sweep beneath them. They fall quickly behind *Symphony* until they're just small white smudges, alternately passing from view and re-emerging as they rise and fall on the swell. Then, all in close succession, as though directed by some silent and unseen signal, they take off and resume their acrobatics. They quickly catch us, briefly repeat their aerial exhibition, and once more settle individually on the waves. *Symphony* sails on, once more leaving the birds behind, and the whole sequence is repeated. I watch carefully to be sure it's the same individuals that return each time, but there's no mistake. The same group of fulmars stay with us for several hours and repeat their maneuver, over and over, at least thirty times. It's me who tires of the game first. When I go below, they're still there, repeating their strange routine.

When Ravens-Floki sailed here, he knew the general direction of his landfall—explorers had already sailed to Iceland and returned to Norway—but he needed to be sure of his bearings. Maybe he, too, experienced overcast and sunless weather. However, he was prepared for just this situation—he had his ravens. He released the first bird soon after leaving the Faroes, and it flew directly back to the land they'd left. A little later he released the second. It flew high into the air, completed a large circle, and returned to alight on the ship. However, when he later released the third raven, it flew straight ahead and disappeared over the horizon. Much encouraged, Floki set course in the same direction. Soon he sighted the coast of Iceland and followed it westward and round the Reykjanes Peninsula to the site of modern Reykjavik.

At noon on our second day out we record another excellent twenty-four-hour run of 129 miles. We stay well off Iceland's inhospitable and dangerous southern coast and head for Heimaey in the Westmann Islands, six miles from the mainland's southwest coast. With just eighty nautical miles to go and still enjoying fast sailing, we appear set for a very fast passage. Now the threatened gale finally materializes. The wind backs to the northeast and increases to force eight despite a recent Icelandic forecast predicting moderate conditions. I call Reykjavik Radio to clarify the forecast and, if possible, get an update. We make contact at the first attempt and provide our latitude and longitude to a courteous operator who speaks excellent English. The operator reads his latest forecast for moderate, northeast winds of force five or six, seventeen to twenty-seven knots. It's the same forecast we picked up a couple of hours ago and implies a comfortable and speedy sail to Heimaey. However, the wind howling outside speaks louder than the forecast, and three hours later, an update gives a quite different picture. It tells us what we already know: It's blowing a gale. Now we hear winds are expected to increase to forty-five knots, force nine. It's not what we wanted, but it's probably accurate as the seas get bigger and less organized, the wind continues to rise, and the first water cascades into the cockpit.

We're still speeding along with the wind behind the beam. At this rate we'll close the Icelandic coast during the early morning hours. We consider running on and heaving to nearer the coast but decide instead to stay where we are and continue tomorrow when the wind is expected to abate. When the wind veers southeast during the night, making the Icelandic coast a lee shore, we're pleased we stayed well offshore.

With all sails furled we set a parachute sea anchor to hold *Symphony*'s bow into the wind and waves. I crawl along the pitching side deck, dragging the anchor in its bag and trailing three hundred feet of three-quarter-inch nylon rode. Three fenders provide flotation for the chute. One end of the rode is already shackled to the chute and I attach the other to the main anchor chain, leaving the anchor in place. When all is ready, I cast the parachute, bag and all, over the starboard side and watch it open up and drift astern. Too late I realize my mistake. *Symphony* is still making way and the rode is wrapped round a lifeline stanchion. When the line pulls taut, it locks fast. I grab one of several pieces of line hanging from the lifelines, tie a rolling hitch on the rode with one end, and belay the other round a cleat. As *Symphony* moves with the waves, the rode alternately tightens and slackens. With each hint of slack, I take in on the temporary line until I've enough slack in the rode to slip it back over the lifelines. Once the sea anchor is deployed properly, *Symphony*'s bow comes round into the wind. Each wave heaves her bow high in the air only to release it a moment later and she crashes into the sea, showering spray in all directions. However, she no longer rolls with each passing wave and feels completely under control. I secure the anchor chain to two separate cleats with nylon stoppers, remembering the philosophy of an English rock climber who wisely counseled, "Never use just one belay when four will do."

It's good the lifelines could take the full load of *Symphony* on the sea anchor without breaking, but my haste with the chute resulted in a bent stanchion. Les and I pause in the cockpit, watching the building seas and again checking the motion until we're satisfied that everything is set properly and that *Symphony* is riding safely. With nothing more to be done on deck, we go below, where I check that all hatches and portholes are tightly fastened. We're both ready for tea and a sandwich.

Before long I'm back on the companionway steps, fascinated by the ever-changing pattern of the waves. Les is at the chart table reviewing our distance from the Icelandic coast and updating the log. Since we set the chute, the cockpit has been dry. Waves break over the bow, but by the time they reach amidships, their force is spent. Spray frequently splashes the cockpit dodger, but beneath it I'm perfectly dry. Suddenly an extra large wave rolls over the bow and cascades along the port side. It crashes into the dodger, sweeps it aside, and dumps it in a tangled heap in the cockpit. The wave rebounds from the back of my foul-weather jacket and pours down the companionway all over Les. She's not dressed for topsides and is instantly drenched with icy water through all three layers of clothing. I scramble down the ladder.

"You all right?" I ask weakly, unable to think of anything else.

"No," says Les firmly. "I'm soaked through. It's freezing." Her hair is bedraggled. Her shirt, sweater, and pants are all wet.

"Oh dear, you'd better get dry."

"It hit you first, and you're not even wet!" adds Les in exasperation.

"You get changed. I'll clear up the dodger." Luckily the dodger frame collapsed before the force of the water could tear the fabric, and I soon have it all back in place.

By eight o'clock and the start of our regular watches, Les has recovered, but I'm feeling unwell and take a couple of seasickness pills. The wind howls. Periodically a wave sweeps across the deck and water pours in through the center and forward hatches despite my

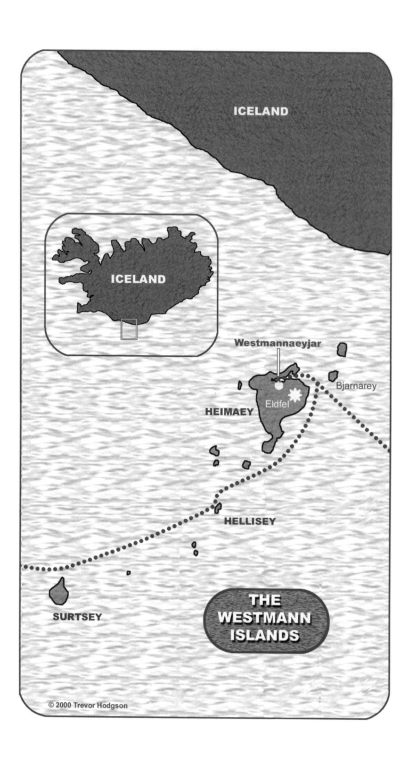

ICELAND

ICELAND

Westmannaeyjar

Bjarnarey

Eldfel

HEIMAEY

HELLISEY

SURTSEY

THE
WESTMANN
ISLANDS

© 2000 Trevor Hodgson

earlier effort to seal them. I go round each hatch once again, forcing the fastenings as tight as possible, but still, water gets inside. I monitor the radar, adjusting the gain and selecting different ranges to insure no ship can slip through to us without being spotted. Every few minutes I crouch below the companionway hatch, waiting for a lessening in the roar of approaching waves. Sensing a lull and hearing no sign of a big one coming, I slide back the hatch, scan the horizon for shipping, and slip back inside before the next wave can strike.

Eventually Les takes over and I settle in my bunk on the starboard side of the cabin, grateful for the snug embrace of the lee cloth as *Symphony* shudders from the onslaught. I drift in and out of consciousness, always aware of the storm outside, convinced I cannot sleep, while in fact time passes quickly. The wind and waves roar. *Symphony* sheers wildly as cross-waves strike the topsides. Periodically the roaring grows louder and more insistent. I brace for the coming impact. Will *Symphony* ride this as she has the others, or will she be battered onto her beam? Sometimes the roaring passes by, there's no crash, and the noise quickly subsides, but all too often there's a tremendous bang, *Symphony* lurches violently, and we wait anxiously for her to regain her balance. Semiconscious, my brain works overtime recirculating unwelcome questions: Why are we here? Why must we endure this bumping and rolling? What are we doing on this awful ocean? Can't we just sail in protected waters? There are no answers. I just want the banging and lurching to stop. From time to time I climb from my bunk and pull on foul-weather gear. It's damp and horrible. I slide back the companionway, and the raging storm threatens to invade the cabin. I reach out to clip my safety harness to a jack-line, clamber over the storm boards to the cockpit, and crawl along the deck to the bow. Satisfied the snubbers are not fraying and the anchor's still holding, I retreat back to the shelter of the saloon and the warm, dry cocoon of the bunk.

While I drift in and out of sleep, Les is restless, unable to throw off a concern that we'll drift into shoal water by the shore. We're still thirty miles from the coast and our rate of drift is less than one knot, but she cannot put aside her worries. She sits by the chart table, reading fitfully and monitoring the radar and GPS. She makes frequent visits to the companionway to check for shipping.

Eventually the noise lessens, the wind loses its intensity, and *Symphony* rides more easily. I no longer listen compulsively for the next rushing wave, and begin to relax. I dare to think the wind's abating. It soon drops to fifteen knots, but the seas remain high and become less organized. The bow still heaves violently up and down, and we delay an attempt to retrieve the anchor until the water's calmer. As the darkness and the fury of the storm fade away, Les finally manages to get some rest.

It's early afternoon before conditions moderate and we can get underway. Once more I crawl along the foredeck, as the sea still plunges the bowsprit to the water every minute or so. Hauling in the anchor chain is easy with the electric windlass. With the engine turning slowly, Les edges *Symphony* forward while I control the windlass with a foot switch. Slowly, foot by foot, the chain winds in and disappears down into the chain locker.

Recovering the last section of chain proves more difficult. Each time the rode comes taut, the anchor swings wildly back and forth ahead of the bow. The thought of winding it aboard is intimidating. There's abrasion on the nylon rode where it's been caught by the edge of the swinging anchor. By the time I have it under control, one strand is completely severed. Les motors *Symphony* forward to slacken the rode and I heave in the chain. However, with no tension on the rode, wind and waves push the bow off and we have numerous cycles of slackening, pulling, and snubbing as the final links slowly come home. After a long struggle I have the anchor secured on its roller. Les now motors forward to bring the parachute alongside *Symphony*'s port bow while I haul in the nylon rode, periodically snubbing the line to keep *Symphony*'s bow into the waves. I reach out with boat hook and haul in one of the lines to collapse the chute and heave the soggy nylon aboard. I am tired, soaked, and throwing up.

The anchor and its gear are soon stowed away. We set the main and genoa and resume our voyage to the Westmanns. Ironically, so soon after the gale, the wind diminishes and is soon just a light breeze. We can't make the speed we'd like, but it's an opportunity to dry out with the companionway and hatches open. Soon the cabin's like a laundry with clothes hung all around. Les, still exhausted after her night of little sleep, returns to the bunk. In the evening the wind dies away completely and I hand-steer and motor.

A landfall is always special. The trials of the ocean crossing are in the past, and ahead lies the comfort of a harbor berth with a stable, upright boat resting quietly by a quay. Soon we'll complete our repairs, sleep regular hours, and enjoy fresh food. We'll have a new place to explore, new people to meet, and new customs to learn. Our arrivals in Norway, Shetland, and the Faroes have all been in fog or late at night, none of them particularly dramatic. Now, Iceland compensates in full measure. The visibility is excellent. Purple bumps on the horizon gradually grow into the Westmann Isles. To the north the mainland is a range of dark mountains with shapely summits speckled with snow. The sea air is crystal clear, but gray clouds ebb and flow across the mainland mountains and the view changes constantly. Intermittently, low-angled rays of the sun illuminate tantalizing views of the upper valleys, but always the highest summit remains obscured. A long glacier follows a curving valley from the Myrdalsjökull icecap way up in the clouds as it flows steeply to the sea. Mist forms over the islands. Quite suddenly it expands and the whole island group disappears inside a gray blanket. The sun dips below the horizon, leaving a surreal twilight world before the mist drifts away as quickly as it formed and the islands re-emerge as sharp silhouettes.

Les joins me in the cockpit for the approach to Heimaey, the only town on the islands. The entrance lies between the main island to port and Bjarnarey, its close neighbor to starboard. The sea is now dark gray. In the half-light we pass steep lava cliffs that stand brooding like grotesque monolithic sculptures. The entrance is narrow. Tall vertical cliffs guard the starboard side, and irregular lava flows extend a considerable distance from the port shore. The first basin inside the harbor is crowded with fishing vessels and other small craft. Next, a large wharf, apparently a ferry terminal, has ships moored along both faces. Ahead, yet another basin accommodates several large fishing vessels moored around the walls. Some boats are rafted three deep. All have high freeboard, making it awkward for us to lie alongside. However, there's one small section of wall unoccupied. We prepare the dock lines and fenders to moor port side to the wharf. Les brings *Symphony* to a stop alongside the bulkhead, and I clamber up a metal ladder to tie off the lines.

The ladder is slippery, liberally coated with the discarded wastes of fish processing. The tide is low, and it's a long and messy climb. Nevertheless, I soon have the lines secured to large commercial cleats and *Symphony* lying quietly against the wall. With time to look around, we can see how horribly dirty the water is. Fluorescent lighting augments the twilight to cast an ethereal green glow on the scum covering much of the basin. It's not a pretty sight. We consider moving to a more salubrious berth, but we're tired and unsure where else we'll find space. We elect to stay here tonight and find a new berth in the morning.

Before turning in, I hoist the yellow Q flag to the starboard spreader and call Westmannaeyjar Radio to contact Customs. We stand by while the operator locates a customs officer. After a few minutes he's back on line to advise that we should do nothing tonight and that Customs will contact us in the morning. It's Midsummer Eve, the shortest night of the year, and a traditional party time in Iceland. The entire local population, including the customs service, is celebrating.

Reminded that it's the summer solstice, I recall the words of Dicuil, a ninth-century Irish monk who wrote of his brethren who sought solitude in the Faroes and on the rugged south shore of Iceland. He describes the light summer nights in a way his readers would no doubt appreciate: "Whatever task a man wishes to perform, even to picking the lice out of his shirt, he can manage it precisely as in broad daylight."

The gray morning does nothing to improve the harbor's appearance. At least in the half-light we were spared some details of the debris. Tall dark cliffs with steep rock faces, buttresses, and grooves overlook the basin, adding to its somber atmosphere. In several places ropes and ladders hang down in loops. We make a brief exploration of the immediate neighborhood but find only industrial buildings and shipping wharves. At one corner of the harbor a fisherman, still in foul-weather gear, is sorting his catch into large rectangular plastic bins. We approach for a close look, and he immediately offers us a large cod. Thankful and delighted, we carry our dinner back to *Symphony*. A little later two fishermen stop on the wharf.

"You're far from home. Did you sail from America?" asks the elder.

"Yes, we just arrived. We were in the Faroes."

"We're from the Faroes. That's our boat over there." He indicates a well-worn fishing trawler moored inside two other boats.

"We were at Torshavn and Vestmanna."

"We're from Klasvik."

"Ah, yes. . . . We were near there when we drove round by car."

"Have you caught many fish?"

"No. We're hopeless at fishing. Everyone catches them, but we get nothing."

"Oh, you should, they're easy to catch. They taste good too. You can catch them while you sail. Don't you have a line and hooks?"

"No. We've tried several times back home but never catch anything."

"It's a waste not to fish," says one as they take their leave to wander back along the dock in the direction of the town.

We've been watching for a customs officer, expecting him to arrive early. When he doesn't show up by eleven, I make another call to Westmannaeyjar Radio. After another long pause we're assured he's on his way. Sure enough, before much longer a young man in white shirt, clean blue jeans, jacket, and tie clambers down the slippery ladder clutching a black briefcase. His smartness appears out of place in this malodorous, greasy basin.

"Sorry I'm a little late," he says as he settles in the cockpit, his briefcase on his knee as a desk. "We had a party here last night. It was the longest day."

"We heard about that. . . . Was it a late night?"

"Very late. I was running the bar and stayed right to the end," he continues. (Aha! Good news indeed: a customs officer who moonlights as a barman!)

As we talk, the young man completes a long form with the usual questions. "The form's really for big ships," he confides, "but it is the only one."

He rips off the bottom copy and hands it to me. The rest he stuffs in his briefcase. "Tell me," he says as his case snaps close, "what's the yellow flag for?"

"Well, er . . . ," I hesitate, "it's for you. It's so you know we need to enter Iceland."

"Really? I never saw one before."

"Well, you found us anyway," consoles Les.

As he leaves, we haul down the obviously unnecessary Q flag.

Now officially in Iceland, our first task is to find a cleaner and more wholesome berth. We decide if we find nothing else, we'll lie alongside a boat in the small basin near the harbor entrance. As it turns out, we get lucky. To reach the basin we run along the back of the ferry dock and much to our surprise find it completely empty. This seems too good to be true, but a check at the harbormaster's office confirms we can use the wharf. As we finish tying the lines and tidying the deck, our two Faroese friends appear on the quay. Unable to accept that we could cruise Iceland and not catch fish, they bring yards and yards of fishing line, many large hooks with colorful plastic lures, and several heavy lead sinkers. We thank them for their kindness and promise to give the equipment a thorough test before we leave.

Heimaey is a community of about five thousand inhabitants. It is notable for its large fishing fleet—it lands ten percent of the whole Icelandic catch—and for the devastation it suffered in 1973 when a volcano overlooking the town erupted without warning. At two o'clock on a January morning, after several small earthquakes, deep rumbling wakened residents. A red glow appeared through the smoke covering the nearby mountain and then a fiery column burst upwards fifteen hundred feet into the air. A mixture of burning ash and red-hot stones rained onto the town. The people ran for shelter, but their houses and the other buildings provided little protection. From the eastern side of Helgafell a stream of lava crept toward the sea. Everyone who could, hurried to the harbor. The old and infirm were carried from their houses by firemen and driven to the airfield, where helicopters from the American base at Keflavik landed precariously through clouds of smoke and ash. About three hundred people chose to stay behind: a few shopkeepers trying to save their inventory, some public officials to guard the abandoned town, and the firemen. Most of the island's cattle and sheep were slaughtered before they starved or were buried beneath the ash. Fortunately the fishing fleet was in the harbor and available for the evacuation. If the eruption had started with the fleet at sea, the rescue would have been much more difficult.

The lava rolled over the northeastern part of the town, engulfing streets and houses. It spilled into the harbor in a flood a quarter-mile wide, threatening to close the port forever. Pumps were set up in an empty factory, and hoses laid from the harbor up the main street to the lava. Several thousand tons of water were pumped on the lava every hour. The liquid rock cooled and hardened into a wall ninety feet high running out to the middle of the harbor. When new lava flowed down, it piled up behind the wall. Most of the eastern part of the town was buried under lava 120 feet thick, but the harbor was saved. About two million tons of pumice and ash covered the area where the main fissure opened, and 112 houses were burned out or buried.

Today the waterfront is wholly industrial. We dub an area of abandoned buildings and derelict space behind our berth "the battle zone." Maybe it was the fish plant before the eruption. Now local children use it as a playground. A block or so from the harbor the town center has two hotels, a tourist office, several stores, gas stations, and convenience stores. The shops are adequate but not great. The supermarket is remarkable only for a very cold, walk-in, refrigerated room stocked with the dairy items. A movie theater runs a schedule of films showing dramatic footage of the 1973 eruption. There's a heated community swimming pool, which we discover is a feature of many Icelandic towns. Behind the downtown area are neat rows of attractive small homes.

We're surprised to find no public telephones. Calls can be made from the tourist office or the post office, but these are open only during office hours. This doesn't work too well for us, as they are open only during working hours. When they close, it's only 2 P.M. on the U.S. East Coast, and the best time for us to call is later when the family is at home. We arrange to use a phone at the reception desk of a hotel to let our children know of our safe arrival. A pleasant surprise is to find propane cylinders available at the local hardware store, and to discover that the fittings are the same as in the States. We exchange one cylinder and the storekeeper insists on delivering the new cylinder directly to *Symphony* at the dock.

We celebrate our thirty-fourth wedding anniversary with dinner at a rather dark and otherwise empty establishment at the back of the town's larger hotel. Our young waitress is from Reykjavik and the chef is a young Dane with a geekish appearance and a strange red tartan hat. Our meal includes an introduction to puffin, which is moderately good but nothing special, and an Icelandic yogurt-like dessert called *skyr*, which is an instant success.

Several tourists are evident in the streets by their casual outdoor clothing and cameras. A small but regular procession of buses leaves the town center for the one-mile journey to the foot of Eldfell, the dark mountain that has loomed over the town since it was created in the 1973 eruption. It's dormant now but still active. Most visitors fly from Reykjavik or take a daily ferry from Porkláshöfn on the mainland. They usually stay only for a night or so.

The 1973 eruption is only the most recent of many such events in the history of these islands. Each island in the group has been born in a catastrophic convulsion of fire, rocks, and lava. Just ten years before the eruption here, a whole new island, Surtsey, was formed by a mighty eruption in what until then was open sea. The volcanic nature of this region was noted by the earliest visitors. Maybe Brendan called at the Westmann Islands, as the *Navigatio* includes a vivid description of an island eruption. As Brendan and his crew rowed away from falling ash,

> The islander reappeared and hurled a great lump of slag at them. It flew two hundred yards over their heads, and where it fell, the sea boiled and smoke rose up as from a furnace. When the curragh had gone about a mile clear, more islanders rushed down to the shore, and began hurling lumps of slag at the monks. It looked as if the whole island was on fire. The sea boiled; the air was filled with howling; and even when they could no longer see the island, there was a great stench. Brendan said they had reached the edge of Hell.

The highlight of our visit is a climb to the top of Eldfell. We set off, walking through the town streets, and soon we leave behind the stores and pass between rows of small houses. Abruptly a steep wall of lava confronts us, the edge of the flow that wrought such destruction in 1973. Remnants of what used to be homes still protrude from the lava. A steep wooden ladder leads up the face of the wall to the surface of the flow and to a scene unlike anything we've seen before. A broad path of crushed lava winds between chaotic mounds. Huge, ragged lumps of rock lie in chaotic piles. Irregular hollows and deep holes make walking off the path almost impossible. The whole rock surface is covered in green lichen and moss. It's desolate, like barren moonscape. Astonishingly, patches of plants somehow survive despite the hostile conditions. Volcanic debris has weathered into a poor soil that has collected in hollows and now supports several species. Many are small and delicate and we have to get very close to distinguish plants with petals hardly bigger than the grains of soil. A few larger hollows support masses of lupins, whose blue flowers and green leaves are a vivid contrast against the black of the rock.

A short but steep little climb leads to a road that follows the boundary between the solidified lava and a slope of black cinders that rises to the mountain summit. Les points out that I'm not dressed well for exploring volcanoes. My white sneakers almost glow against the black ground and the green polyester shopping bag with the camera and binoculars is not at all rugged and manly. I ignore such conventional opinion and savor a slight feeling of eccentricity. The path curves gradually up a ridge overlooking a deep basin, once the volcanic crater. Gases vent from crevices in the hillsides, filling the air with sulfurous vapor. The climb is not long, and soon we step airily along the summit ridge before picking a spot to sit down and admire the view. Wow! The rock's still warm! Twenty-four years after the eruption and the summit rocks are still warm. It's amazing!

The summit is a world of strange minerals. The deep black of the lower slopes is offset here by rocks of rust and yellow. Fragile, sulfurous meringue spews from deep fissures. The air has the astringent smell of brimstone. Despite these signs of a violent and recent birth, the summit is quiet. The mountain has spent its anger in a brief paroxysm and at least for now is silent. There's a feeling of peace, of being apart from the world below.

Turning from the cinders at our feet, we pan slowly through 360 degrees in sheer exhilaration at the extent and variety of the view. The full magnitude of the lava flow is before us, the edge poised above Heimaey and thrust out into the harbor entrance. Other islands, formed by earlier eruptions, extend in a long, curving line to the south. Far below we see tourists exploring the crater, and beyond them a semicircle of dark cliffs overlooks the harbor and town. To the north a gray line marks the coast of mainland Iceland.

Many early Vikings sailed by here en route to Reykjavik and other western Iceland settlements. However, the first to settle on this coast was Hjorleif, who sailed from Norway with his brother Ingolf. Like so many others, they were outlaws seeking refuge from justice. Hjorleif brought with him several slaves that he captured while raiding in Ireland. Landnamabok records that the brothers parted in fog off the south coast of Iceland and each made his own way to the mainland.

Like many pagan immigrants nearing their landfall, they sought guidance from Thor on where they should build their homes. To determine the divine will, they tossed overboard the pillars from their prized high seats and followed them as they drifted ashore. Wherever the pillars landed they made their home. Ingolf, unable to find his pillars, settled about eighty miles east of the Westmanns. Hjorleif, however, continued westward and settled somewhere along the gray coastline that forms our northern horizon.

Both brothers went about establishing their new farms, but it was not long before Hjorleif's slaves conspired to lure him into a trap and killed him. Knowing full well it was only a matter of time before they'd be hunted, the slaves sought a secure place to hide. These islands to the south appeared their best chance, and they brought the women and what goods they could carry in Hjorleif's boats to seek refuge.

When Ingolf learned of his brother's fate, he guessed where his murderers had fled and followed them. The *Icelandic Book of Settlements* records the conclusion:

> They were eating a meal when Ingolf surprised them. Panic overwhelmed them, and they ran each his own way. Ingolf killed them all. . . . Many of them jumped off the cliff that has since been known by their name. The islands where these thralls were killed have been known ever since as the Vestmannaeyjar, because they were Vestmenn, Irishmen.

Which of the cliffs below our feet was the scene of the slaves' desperate suicidal leap? We can almost hear their screams floating on the still mountain air.

A French couple who've flown from the mainland for a one-day visit join us on the summit. We exercise our very limited French in a halting but congenial conversation about families and holidays. However, the afternoon is wearing on and reluctantly we start to descend. The summit ridge continues to the north as an exposed knife-edge. Unable to resist a full traverse of the mountain, a legacy of long-ago days spent climbing higher and more difficult hills than this, we cross the narrow summit and begin to descend the steep north ridge. The slope is comprised of loose cinders and is slippery where rock lies just below the surface. Most of the way we edge down cautiously step by step, but where possible, we run down, leaning back, digging our heels into the soft surface as we once did on mountain screes in Scotland. The bottom of the slope is a bank of steep black sand, and we race down the final stretch to level ground. Here the cinders have been crushed into broad roadways. As we make our way back toward the town, we are passed by a couple of tour buses. We're well pleased with our day.

Chapter 8

The Golden Circle

We spend our last morning at Heimaey relaxing and watching the world go about its business. A boat leaves for the bird cliffs with a group of tourists, followed closely along the channel by a fishing boat. Two harbor employees steadily repaint a broad yellow line along the top of the harbor wall. Eventually coffee works its morning magic and we begin preparations to leave. Filling the water tank proves more difficult than usual. The only supply is in a deep well in the deck of the wharf, and no one can locate a long metal pole needed to open the valve. Eventually I find it on a floating pontoon used by the painters. We take a short walk to the stores to mail postcards and buy fresh meat.

About midmorning *Loan Shark*, a modern racing yacht, motors into the harbor, her decks festooned with control lines and shiny winches, and a U.K. Red Duster flying at her stern. She ties up behind *Symphony*, and five male crewmen climb briskly to the top of the pier. She's returning home after racing (not very successfully) from Falmouth to Reykjavik, and has called to take on fuel. The skipper arranges for a tanker to come to the dock, and we take advantage of this to top off *Symphony*'s tanks.

We plan to leave late morning for an ETA at Reykjavik of tomorrow afternoon. The weather's warm and sunny as we motor out along the channel between a yellow buoy, marking the edge of underwater lava, and a high rock precipice. We emerge onto an ocean that's blue and still. We follow the line of ragged lava cliffs that form the south coast of Heimaey, and as the last of these falls astern, we continue toward a gently curving line of small islands.

A thick white cloud of birds circles each island, but Hellisay has an abundance unusual even here. The chart shows deep water right to the foot of the cliffs and we approach for a close-up look. We motor in until our necks ache from looking up. While *Symphony* drifts, we watch a seething mass in constant motion as birds fly off, circle round, and resettle. The noise is deafening and we must raise our voices to be heard. The smell is revolting. I photograph the multitudes above and around us while other birds sit on the water, calmly watching our every move.

The last island in the chain is Surtsey, thirteen miles southwest of Heimaey in what was open sea before 1963. Early on November 14 of that year, a Heimaey trawler was setting her nets in over four hundred feet of water when crewmembers smelled sulfur and felt a strange motion. Soon clouds of ash were flying from the sea. The volcanic eruption grew and grew. By midafternoon the column of ash and smoke was four miles high. In the next six weeks, Surtsey grew from nothing into an island topping out at more than four hundred feet above the surface of the sea.

Today the island is peaceful and looks rather ordinary with nothing to suggest its violent birth. The single summit is bare, but lower slopes are green with vegetation. Numerous birds circle the southwest cliffs. Landing is prohibited except for scientists who monitor the evolution of this unique environment. The only building is a hut used by researchers. We stop the engine to picnic in the sunshine on fresh bread, brie, and rolled lamb while drifting among our loyal following of sea birds.

Our meal over, we set a direct course south of Reykjanes, the peninsula at the southwest corner of Iceland, where we'll turn north toward Reykjavik. We expect an easy overnight voyage, although with no wind it appears we'll be using the engine. As we organize ourselves for a long session of motoring, we're startled by a huge splash on the port side. A cascade of water hits the surface of the sea, and wavelets spread out in a widening circle. What on earth was that? What could it be? We stare, unsure what to expect, excited but apprehensive. There's a long pause. Just when we begin to wonder if we imagined it, a large dark form with distinctive white under-parts, breaks the surface and rises vertically in the air. It climbs like a rocket till its waving tail clears the surface, hangs momentarily, then crashes back to the water in another mighty splash. Volumes of water shoot into the air.

As suddenly as it rose, the creature disappears, leaving only a patch of white foam and ever-widening rings of ripples. We stand spellbound, unable to speak. Before we recover, the whale explodes into the air once more and crashes back in another great cascade of water. Then it leaps again, and again . . . and again. On and on the performance is repeated. It's an astonishing experience. I run for the camera to capture at least one of these athletic leaps. I aim and shoot each time the whale leaps into the air. Shot after shot, I'm sure I have him, captured for all to see, but later, when the film is developed, I find to my great frustration I was too slow. The film is full of splashes and swirling water, but no leaping whale.

At last the whale, a minke, grows weary and leaps no more. We collapse on the cockpit seats, gibbering excitedly about this unique spectacle. Many times we've seen dolphins, whales, sharks, and seals but nothing to approach this display. The excitement leaves us drained of energy, but the show's not yet over. As the last ripples from the whale melt away, a tall black fin slices the water right alongside *Symphony*. It glides past the gunwale and is joined by another, and another—no doubt a family group, and, unmistakably, orca or killer whales. The fins of the female and young are large, but they're diminutive next to the six-foot appendage of the male. The group swims slowly, in close company, unconcerned by *Symphony,* or by us—even when we motor beside them for a better view. Eventually they swim away to the east and we break away to resume our passage to Reykjavik.

As the sun starts its afternoon descent, light zephyrs form ripples on the water. The breeze freshens and we raise sail, scudding briskly along, close-hauled. The wind is westerly and we cannot make our course directly, so we tack in toward shore and then out again as the wind slowly veers. Once twilight closes around us, small clusters of lights flicker from the shore. The night is uneventful, with occasional course changes breaking the watch-keeping routine. The morning is fair and we continue our zigzag progress to the west. The Reykjanes Lighthouse grows slowly larger. When at last it's abeam, we make our final tack and sit down to eat lunch. Then the wind dies away to three knots and we start the engine.

The lighthouse occupies a desolate perch at the end of a lava peninsula. Rocks offshore look sinister and we give them a wide berth. Six miles west, the island of Eldey, a high, flat-topped plug of basalt, is reputed to be the world's largest gannet colony, home to several thousand birds. The island has been a nature reserve since 1940 and is visited by bird-watching boats from ports on the mainland.

A hundred and fifty years ago it was the final home of the last great auks. Once counted in millions, the great auk was flightless, and used superb underwater-swimming ability to catch fish. However, its large body provided a good meal, and its feathers filled pillows and beds. Large, densely packed colonies were easily raided and the huge population gradually declined. By the 1830s the last surviving colony clung desperately to the cliffs of Eldey. Each year there were a few birds less. On June 4, 1844, a boat with fourteen men approached the island. The waves were high, but three men managed to land and found just two birds and one egg. One sailor smashed the egg, an act he later excused by claiming it was "cracked anyway," and the others each killed and skinned one adult. They sold the skins to a taxidermist in Reykjavik, and the species first named just eighty-six years earlier was extinct.

Along the Reykjanes Peninsula the lava meets the ocean in a thick, dark line. Behind the black cliffs, low-lying land stretches back to distant mountains speckled with snow. Occasional houses and industrial buildings, all in strong, bright colors, contrast strikingly with the dark lava. Small communities cluster round inlets that provide shelter for a few fishing boats. Several long, irregular promontories of lava project well out from the shore. Low-lying and difficult to see, they lie in wait for any boat following the coast too closely. Lights warn mariners of the danger, but these are at the inland end of the obstructions, leaving the seaward extremities unmarked, a practice that could well catch the unwary.

From the time we passed the Reykjanes Lighthouse, we've seen several whales and dolphins, but none have come close to *Symphony*. We've seen no boats since leaving Heimaey but several appear as we near Gardskagi at the north end of the peninsula. At first we're puzzled by their erratic courses. They spend periods dead in the water and then dart off unpredictably in brief high-speed spurts. We assume they're fishing but then realize they're whale-watchers racing to get up close for a better view.

For several hours weather faxes have shown an area of high pressure building over Greenland. Now this system begins to assert itself. Blue sky slowly drives all sign of cloud from the sky. The gray-green

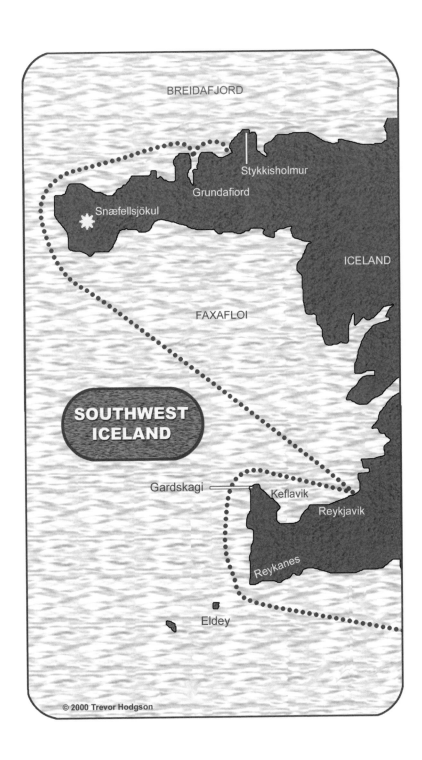

BREIDAFJORD

Stykkisholmur

Grundafiord

Snæfellsjökul

ICELAND

FAXAFLOI

SOUTHWEST ICELAND

Gardskagi

Keflavik

Reykjavik

Reykanes

Eldey

© 2000 Trevor Hodgson

sea adopts a bluish hue. Bright sunlight exposes intricate shapes in the dark surface of the lava. Patches of Sargasso weed appear bright yellow, reminders of the long reach of the Gulf Stream and its warming effect on Iceland's climate.

We give Gardskagi Lighthouse a wide berth and motor into Faxafloi, the broad bay named for the Viking Faxi who accompanied Ravens-Floki. The last cloud melts away and the inland mountains are transformed into a panorama of magnificent ridges silhouetted against the sky. To the north the veil falls from the distant ice-capped cone of Snæfellsjökul to reveal a golden jewel floating in a sea of mist. The sun warms our backs. The water sparkles. The air round *Symphony* is alive with soaring, wheeling, diving gulls, gannets, and fulmars. Fish must be plentiful. Birds rain down in continuous waves, the gannets diving hard through the surface. More often than not, they emerge with fish hanging from their bills, provoking a cacophony of calls and screeches as scavengers swoop down to steal from the hunters. Sometimes skirmishes over food escalate to major battles as neighboring birds fly down to join the fray.

Other visitors have fallen under the spell of this scene. In 1856 English Lord Dufferin sailed here aboard his schooner *Foam*, when few could afford to cruise and those who did, did it in style. He kept a diary of his experiences, and among his letters he wrote:

> The panorama of the bay of Faxa Fjord is magnificent, with a width of fifty miles from horn to horn, the one running down into a rocky ridge of pumice, the other towering to the height of five thousand feet in a pyramid of eternal snow, while round the intervening semicircle crowd the peaks of a hundred noble mountains.

Ahead, a light-gray smudge between sea and mountains slowly grows larger and eventually resolves into the buildings of distant Reykjavik. Here is Iceland's capital and home of three-quarters of its citizens. It was founded by Ingolf after the death of his brother, Hjorleif. Ingolf had cast overboard his high seat pillars as his ship approached the south coast, but they were found only after he killed the Irish slaves at Westmanneyjara. Miraculously they had drifted for miles along the south shore of Iceland, then north round Reykjanes and east through Faxafloi to come ashore at the site of the future capital. What clear evidence of the mysterious guiding hand of Thor! Accepting divine will, Ingolf established his farm and named the settlement Reykjavik, meaning "Smoky Bay," a reference to hot springs that still send clouds of vapor into the air. Today Ingolf is celebrated as Iceland's first settler. He surveys the land that was once his farm from a monument in downtown Reykjavik.

The city was slow developing. Lord Dufferin's enthusiasm for Faxafloi was countered by his disdain for what was then a remote Danish colonial outpost. He described its appearance as "a dirty greenish slope, patched with houses which themselves, both roof and walls, are of a moldy green, as if some long-since inhabited country had been fished up out of the bottom of the sea."

We follow the buoys toward the harbor entrance. Two boats some way off appear to be ferries. Like Lord Dufferin, we're disappointed by our first impression as several white oil tanks dominate the approach. I call Harbor Control on the VHF, and immediately we're directed to call again once we reach large stone pillars at the harbor entrance. We do as instructed, but the second call is anticlimactic, as we are simply advised to "anchor with the other yachts." Accordingly we head toward a cluster of masts on the east side of the harbor where we find several pontoon berths, all of which appear occupied. A head appears in the companionway of one boat. In a brief conversation shouted across the water, we're advised these are yacht-club moorings and we should find more room in the opposite corner of the harbor.

Back we go to find a long, floating pontoon that forms a basin with dockage for small boats. We tie up in an empty slip only to discover that the gates in a security fence are locked and we cannot leave to go ashore. I untie the lines so carefully set just a few moments ago and we move to the outside of the long pontoon, which we later discover is set aside for visiting yachts. Before long we're in bed. Oblivious to the sounds of the city, we sleep a full twelve hours and don't wake until 1030.

The harbor is home to a variety of boats. Nearby is the familiar form of a Viking longship, the *Gokstad* replica *Islendur*. Fitted with a diesel engine and a rather un-Viking-like central deckhouse, she carries tourists on short cruises. Most of the harbor is busy with commercial vessels. Occasionally a squat tug powers by and *Symphony* rocks in her wake. Passenger ships serving coastal communities dock behind us, while a whale-watching boat is tied up just ahead. Four mothballed whaling vessels, with crow's-nests high on their masts and deadly harpoons at their bows, lie in dry-dock waiting for a chance to return to their grizzly trade. Nearby, a busy repair yard has two large freighters on the ways. One morning *Dolphin*, a huge white cruise liner with Maltese registration, discharges passengers at a nearby wharf. The next day she's gone.

One sailing boat stands out from others despite her small size. *La India* is just twenty feet long, with sponsors' logos prominent along her tiny topsides. She's sailed by Geronimo, a gentle, charming man with long, curly black hair who left six years ago to cruise along the coast of his native Argentina. The cruise proved longer than anticipated and he continued along the South American seaboard, through the Caribbean, and along the U.S. East Coast. Last winter he stayed over in St. John's, Newfoundland. Our friendship is short, as Geronimo announces his intention to leave for Spitzbergen that evening. However, we gather for a couple of hours in *Symphony*'s saloon and I show Geronimo the videotape of the leaping minke whale. I've not yet reviewed it, so it's our first opportunity to see it too. Geronimo presses his eye to the viewfinder and starts the film. He watches quietly.

"Is it working okay?" I ask.

"Oh, yes," replies Geronimo without taking his eye from the camera. There's a pause.

"Have you found the whale yet?" I inquire anxiously.

"No, not yet," says Geronimo, still watching intently. When he reports no whale the next time I ask, I gently take the camera and peer into the viewfinder. My heart sinks! The sea spreads out before the lens; long gentle swells pass through the scene. There's a break where I stopped filming; then a huge splash fills the frame. Ripples die away and the sea is again calm. The sequence is repeated . . . and again. It's too much. Instead of several athletic leaps by a minke whale, a film to amaze the family when we get home, I've nothing but water splashing in an empty ocean. I realize I didn't allow for a slight delay between pressing the trigger and the start of filming. Each time I shot, the whale fell back to the sea while the camera got going!

As Geronimo prepares to leave, it's raining steadily, but it seems not to bother him. We feel anxious for him in his leaky foul-weather gear, a towel round his neck and his stockinged feet wrapped in plastic bags, but he shrugs off our concerns. When all is ready, he reverses *La India* from her berth and out into the harbor. She shows no lights. In no time the sails are up and La *India* disappears into the mist near the harbor entrance. We hear subsequently she succeeded in reaching Spitzbergen but only after being dismasted south of Iceland.

The next morning a large yacht from Aberdeen, Scotland, arrives at the pontoon for a week's stay and the crew decamps to a city hotel. One crewman pauses to pass the time of day as Les runs the engine in preparation for changing the oil.

"What's the clanging?" he asks.

"That's just a flapper valve in the engine exhaust," explains Les. "It's supposed to stop following seas from getting into the engine."

Our visitor is not impressed. "That shouldn't be necessary," he says dismissively.

"Maybe you're right," Les concedes, "but it's good to be sure."

"Hmm . . . I suppose so," he says and follows his shipmates along the pontoon.

Later we have a conversation with the owner.

"When are you leaving?" I ask.

"As soon as we get the engine repaired," he sighs. "Getting the right part's a real pain."

"Oh, why? What's the problem?"

"We lost the engine on the way here. We had to be towed into harbor."

"Really?"

"Yes. We had a following sea and got water in the engine exhaust."

"Wow, that can be a real problem," Les commiserates, with a straight face.

"And expensive," ruminates the skipper. As he walks away along the pontoon, we allow ourselves a feeling of vindication, even a little smugness!

After the Viking settlement, Iceland shared the suffering of her Nordic sisters as Norway slipped under the thumb of an indifferent Denmark. The climate deteriorated and life in the North Atlantic became difficult. Food was scarce and markets for trade goods declined. Along with Greenland, Iceland surrendered her independence by accepting Norwegian sovereignty in 1262. For almost seven hundred years she reverted to a European colony and only in 1944 was the independent republic restored. She's still the only sovereign Viking land in the North Atlantic. The others all remain under European rule: Shetland within the United Kingdom; Greenland and the Faroes in the Kingdom of Denmark.

When the weather deteriorated, extreme hardship was inevitable in a land with little fuel. Trees on the lower slopes that greeted the first settlers were soon consumed. Unlike Shetland, Iceland had no peat, as vegetation necessary for its formation never developed in the volcanic soil. As the climate became colder, families retreated to live in a single room, the *badstofa* (literally, the bathroom). With no heating and little food, conditions must have been harsh indeed. A vivid diorama in the Icelandic National Museum shows a family crammed into their room above the animals' stalls—we can almost feel their pain and deprivation.

Other museum exhibits include more soapstone artifacts, some of which came as ships' ballast and were formed into cooking pots here in Iceland. Most impressive are decorative wooden chests and richly carved doors. As in the Faroes, we have the oddity of a country desperately short of wood producing such lavish items. Wherever we go in the Viking lands, we're reminded of the importance of wood. We remember the church at Fantoft and the ornate *Öseberg* sled, the Bryggen, the carvings in the Faroes, and now these in Iceland. Perhaps its very scarcity here made it a symbol of wealth and power. It's clear the Vikings were able to transport large quantities of heavy lumber, and at least some had the wealth to pay the freight.

Reykjavik is modern, white, and concrete. After Bergen it's the largest city on our route and we'll see nothing comparable until Halifax, Nova Scotia, after we've been to Newfoundland. The absence of tall buildings is noticeable. Nowhere do we see structures higher than five stories. Everyone looks healthy, an impression reinforced by the bright sunshine that lasts through most of our visit. We take advantage of the facilities, catching up with newspapers and enjoying a restaurant meal. Browsing in a large midtown bookstore, I finally find an English copy of the *Eyrbyggja Saga* that I sought unsuccessfully in Hull and Bergen. This recounts stories of the early settlers in Breidafjord, our next port of call. The tourist office is an excellent source of information and we pick up all the free maps and guidebooks we need for our stay. We find no large supermarket near the harbor, but a small grocery on a busy central street is adequate for day-to-day needs. Iceland has good bread.

As at Heimaey, telephoning home is easy, provided we remember to call during office hours. There are no street phones, so we use booths at the telephone company office or tourist office. Payment is made after the call is completed, and credit cards are accepted. One Friday evening I have a moment of panic when I find I've lost a book containing all the notes I've recorded during the voyage. I remember having it in the booth at the telephone company, which is now closed. Fearful that in another working day it will be swept away and never recovered, I bang on the rear door of the office. To my great relief and surprise, my knocks are answered. A cleaning lady appears, speaks fluent English, and hands over my book. A lucky day indeed.

On weekends, crowds gather at a flea market in a large warehouse by the harbor. It's a jumble of antiques, records, magazines, collectibles, clothes, and food. Several booths have interesting-looking old books with leather bindings and gold titling. It's disappointing to find they're all in Icelandic. There are large displays of seafood. Discriminating shoppers examine piles of dried fish. Just as at Torshavn, they check the appearance, feel the texture, and hold samples to their noses to check the aroma. Kjell is clearly not alone in his reverence for this strange northern commodity, but we remain more mystified than convinced.

The most publicized outing for visitors to Reykjavik is "the Golden Circle." It's a full day's bus tour with visits to Gullfoss, a majestic waterfall; Geysir, the famous hot spring; and Thingvellir, a national park and home of the world's first national parliament. We want to visit all of these places plus a couple more: Stöng, an eleventh-century farm, and Skalholt, a picturesque church that was once the center of Icelandic religious life. We reserve a rental car and hope that we can see them all in a single day. The rental company offers to pick us up at the harbor, making it much more convenient than a long cross-town journey on public transport.

With much to see and a long way to go, we plan an early start. However, things don't look too good when the promised pick-up fails to arrive. A call to the rental office reveals a misunderstanding that's soon resolved and we're on the road about an hour later than planned. At least this car's better than the one in the Faroes, quite new and unscratched.

We soon leave the fast-food outlets, light industry, and apartment blocks of the outskirts of Reykjavik. In no time we're passing through long shallow valleys, with cows and sheep grazing on rough green pasture. Several herds of Icelandic horses graze in paddocks and we stop to allow one large group to cross the road ahead of us. Just a short distance from Reykjavik, the paved road changes to a compacted cinder track. We pass few other vehicles, and a huge cloud of dust announces each one while it is still far off. The inland valleys of both Shetland and the Faroes are barren, but this is more desolate by several degrees. There are no trees, no grass, no heather—nothing but black cinder and scattered rocks. Above are dark volcanic mountains with more black ash and dirty white snow. Thick clouds cutting off the mountain summits exacerbate the somber character of the scenery.

Though the summit is lost in the clouds, we know from our small tourist map that we're at the foot of Mount Hekla, the most celebrated of Icelandic volcanoes. It has erupted fifteen times since settlers first came to Iceland. Throughout the Middle Ages, Europeans held it in awe as a gateway of Hell itself. A major eruption in 1104 showered millions of tons of ash onto twenty or more farmsteads in the upper valley below the summit. One farm inundated by this outpouring was Stöng, perched on a hillside near the head of the valley. Ironically the volcanic dust that drove out the farmer and his family preserved the buildings from the erosive forces of wind, water, and freezing.

Stöng was built in traditional fashion with thick walls of turf laid on two foundation-courses of rough stones, and with a turf roof. It was a medium-sized farm, with a working household of about twenty people. Today a fabricated metal building protects the whole site. We enter through a door into a small vestibule that in turn leads to the main room—a typical Viking longhouse used for working and sleeping. It's just like other Viking houses we've seen, but it's a little disappointing. Its size is impressive, but it lacks the atmosphere of other sites. The metal roof is no doubt necessary to preserve the remains, but the modern scale and materials insure that it seems more like a museum than a place where people lived and worked and spent long winters round the fire.

Back outside we're temporarily dazzled as the sun breaks through gaps in the clouds. The valley casts off the dark, sunless mantle and is bathed in golden light. We emerge onto a wider road and follow it along a level valley with distant views of the dark ridges and snowfields of the central mountains. Eventually we draw up beside several cars and two buses at the Gullfoss parking lot. There's no sign of the waterfall, but a paved walkway leaves one corner of the parking area and gradually descends a hillside. Round a corner a great cloud of spray hangs over one end of a dark gash in the floor of the valley. We join other visitors on an area of rough scrub atop a small rise in the middle of the canyon.

The falls are spectacular, the thunder of crashing water tumultuous. A rainbow arches through a cloud of spray over a rocky gorge. A small, undulating path, doused continually by spray, leads along the canyon side high above the river to the top of the falls. The air is saturated with fine mist. Anyone staying more than a minute or so is wet through and we retreat quickly up a steep path that eventually leads back to the parking lot.

While Gullfoss reveals her beauty only after a short walk from the parking lot, the gush of steam and water from Geysir can be seen right across the valley. A tall gray plume of vapor rises like a beacon as we approach. Crowds at the tourist center indicate the popularity of the site. Coaches and cars fill the parking areas while visitors crowd into restaurants and gift shops. Across the road from the center, visitors stroll along pathways over slabs of light-brown rock between steaming hot springs. Water gurgles from holes, and many crevices are lined with shiny, smooth silica. Steam vents from the rock in several places. There's a sulfurous odor. Every twenty minutes Geysir shoots a spout of hot water and steam a hundred feet into the air. It starts with a violent agitation in the center of the pool where the water's at boiling point. Suddenly a dome of water rises to a height of eight or ten feet, then falls back, followed immediately by a tall column that springs upward in a succession of jerking leaps, each higher than the last. It's quickly over and the whole column splashes to the ground.

The church of Skalholt occupies a bucolic setting on a small lakeside hillock surrounded by mountains. Soon after the end of the first millennium, the national assembly declared that Christianity should replace the worship of Thor as the national religion, and Skalholt became the seat of archbishops. Today it stands in magnificent isolation, but for centuries this was the largest community on the island and the center of its Catholic Church. The current stone church is the fourth on the site. A photograph in the basement museum shows an earlier cathedral, a huge timber building, another surprising find in a land of so little wood. The museum also displays a huge stone coffin, imported with extraordinary effort to provide a special resting place for the bones of one archbishop. It says much for the power and wealth of the medieval church.

The road to Thingvellir lies along a picturesque valley with rock outcrops, mountains, streams, and deep lakes. We're excited to be approaching Iceland's national park and one of the most notable of all Viking sites. It's as picturesque as we imagined. A river winds its way through a great natural arena, a depression twenty-five miles long and ten wide surrounded by handsome mountains. A white church spire rises from a grove of small trees. A hotel is partly hidden. Thingvellir lies across the junction of the European and North American tectonic plates. The valley has subsided as the walls have moved apart. According to geologists, the valley walls are still separating by about three millimeters each year.

One June day in the year 930, representatives from all over Iceland gathered near cliffs on the northwest side of the valley for the first-ever national legislative assembly. When much of Europe was still controlled by local chieftains and struggling toward national monarchies, Vikings gathered here voluntarily to form a constitutional republic. The process was not democratic, as attendees were chieftains, each accompanied by just two advisers. The president of the legislature was the Law Speaker, elected for a three-year term, who recited the laws from the Law Rock below the line of crags. Iceland is a big country, and traveling to the Thing was a significant undertaking. The journey from east Iceland could take up to three weeks. The gatherings became much more than legal assemblies. They were great annual fairs and national conventions and became the social events of the year for farmers and farmhands, chieftains and churls, friends and enemies, boys and girls. The plain below the Law Rock became a temporary town of tents and booths. Gossip flew while news was made, stories and poems told, plots hatched, and marriages arranged. It was boisterous, vivid, animated.

We leave the car with two or three others in a small enclosure well below the line of cliffs. A bridge leads over a branch of the Oxera River and we continue up a steep path past the Law Rock where a group of tourists listen intently to an enthusiastic guide. Just below the summit we enter a chasm between two lines of rock. The higher edge forms the rim of the gorge, while the lower appears to have slipped away and down, leaving a sloping canyon wide enough for a small roadway. We follow the shady track steadily upward to emerge into sunlight at the top of the gorge. From the rock platform that forms a small summit, the view is unbroken for 360 degrees. A brass plate set into a stone plinth shows a silhouette of the whole panorama and the name of each mountain. We work our way slowly round the compass, admiring each summit and struggling with unpronounceable Icelandic names.

It's getting late. The low sun casts contrasting patterns of dark shadows and bright sunlight on the rocks. We return along the bridleway. Stone foundations of small booths used as temporary accommodation by assembly delegates still show above the rough grass. Farther down the canyon a wooden staircase descends to the plain, and a path then takes us back to the car. The evening is strikingly beautiful. The sylvan scene of the river, lake, the church, and hotel, contrasts with the starkness of the volcanic cliffs. The far side of the rift valley is already deep purple.

Our Golden Circle tour is complete. We've managed to visit all the sites without feeling unduly rushed. We freewheel down the valley toward Reykjavik and the setting sun. By prior arrangement, we leave the car in a dockside parking lot. It's been a long day and we have no energy for anything else. We enjoy a simple meal of spaghetti with sauce and a glass of red wine. Soon we're in our bunks, sound asleep.

The next day is taken by shopping for family gifts. Although everything in Reykjavik is expensive, we expect only limited opportunities for buying gifts in the more remote places we'll visit from here on. With five children and four young grandchildren to buy for, we examine everything carefully to make sure we get value for money and maintain rough equivalence among the several gifts. Anything we buy must survive several months at sea and possibly rough handling. After much deliberation we do what most tourists do and buy various items of Icelandic wool.

The next leg of our journey, another short overnight voyage, will take us north to Breidafjord, the setting of the evocative *Eyrbyggja Saga* with its tales of the early settlers, and the place where Viking adventurers first departed for Greenland.

Chapter 9

The Land of Magic

Preparations for sea always bring us twinges of excitement. We get anxious to feel *Symphony* roll with the swells and forge through the waves. We've repeated the same steps many times: checking the rigging, storing the dinghy, changing the engine oil, reviewing weather faxes, studying the latest forecast, filling the fuel tanks, and repacking everything we've used in port. As we check off items on our list, thoughts of the overnight sail to Breidafjord bring an extra shot of adrenaline. We're leaving large cities and commercial harbors for relative backwaters of rural communities and isolated anchorages. We're nearing the heart of our journey, where history and romance intertwine in a colorful tapestry. We'll visit places little changed since they were described in the *Eyrbyggja Saga* hundreds of years ago. In the "Bay of a Thousand Islands," our path first crosses that of Erik the Red, the habitual killer whose repeated brushes with the law eventually forced him from his farm and family. Already banned from the lands to the east and with nowhere else to go, he made the first crossing from Iceland to Greenland, the most challenging leg of the Viking route to America.

We make a final trip to the store for a few items of fresh food and to collect washed clothes from a nearby laundry. Soon after lunch we motor across the basin to a dockside tap to fill the water tank. As we coil the hose, *Islendur* backs from her berth and we follow her out between the stone pillars at the harbor entrance. A crewman heaves aloft her single square sail and she bears away eastward along the shore, soon disappearing into the mist. Our route lies north along the main shipping channel, where we immediately confront a tug maneuvering a tow from astern to alongside. This operation occupies much of the channel and Les gives both vessels a wide berth. Reykjavik's low, undistinguished profile and white fuel tanks soon dip astern. Only the mountains remain visible and these present a somber background shrouded in mist.

By the time we pass the fairway buoy, it's raining steadily. Our course across Faxafloi lies directly to weather. A brisk northwest wind drives the rain in our faces and raises an uncomfortable, choppy sea. We raise the mains'l (with one reef) and the stays'l, fall off to port, and sail close-hauled into the gloom. Almost immediately I begin to suffer from the erratic motion and struggle against feelings of lethargy and withdrawal. I decline Les's curry, usually a favorite meal, take a couple of pills, and lie on my bunk. As often before, I resolve that next time we set out I'll take pills before leaving port. Midnight brings the start of my watch by which time I feel a little better. By the early hours of the morning, growing hunger overcomes my remaining queasiness and I eat some of the rice and curry, which, being cold, is somehow more digestible.

Our route lies by the foot of Snæfellsjökul. After our magical but distant sight of the mountain as we arrived from Heimaey, we're eager for a closer view. At first light, things look promising. The rain stops before dawn. Broken clouds around the horizon are edged in gold. The water shimmers where sunlight finds a way through the overhead. However, the brightness is short-lived. The clouds cling tenaciously to the mountains. Soon thick shadows roll remorselessly downhill to cut off the sunlight and re-impose a dark mantle over the desolate coastline.

Our course is now northerly, but the wind veers to remain doggedly on the bow. Rather than spend time tacking, we elect to motor. Rugged hillsides of muted grays and greens rise above the sea cliffs. Patches of snow look old, grayed, and sprinkled with debris. On the shore, small and isolated orange light-towers are prominent against the dull background. From time to time the cloud ceiling rises and wisps of gray flirt tantalizingly with lower mountain ridges, but each time the summit remains obstinately obscured and the dark blanket soon descends once more.

Flocks of fulmars, kittiwakes, gulls, puffins, and razorbills follow us intermittently throughout the day. We see several dolphins some way off, but none come close—maybe we're too slow to create a decent bow wave. At any one time, five or six small fishing boats are visible, widely spread out around the horizon.

A small light at Önderverdanes marks the northwest corner of the Snæfell Peninsula, and once well past the headland, we turn to follow the south shore of Breidafjord. Deep bays penetrate to the heart of the mountains, but the summit ridge of the peninsula remains hidden by clouds. Between the bays, long ridges terminate in bold headlands. From the chart I identify Bulandshöfdi, a broad buttress flanked by steep screes. The *Eyrbyggja Saga* describes a battle fought here in typical Viking fashion with swords crushing skulls and severing limbs. After the fight a band of escaping slaves were pursued to the top of the buttress. To avoid capture, they threw themselves down the steep cliffs. As the saga prosaically records, "No living creature could survive a fall from that height."

After the battle of Hafrsfjord in Norway, critics of Harold Finehair faced a simple choice: accept Harold as lord and master or move elsewhere. Thorolf Mosturbeard chose to leave for Iceland, and after a good voyage, sailed past these headlands, following his high-seat pillars as they drifted into Hofsvag, fourteen miles ahead. We too are heading for this shallow bay, but the day is wearing on and it's clear we'll arrive rather late. Ready to rest and eat, we elect instead to anchor in Grundarfjord, the next large bay that is well protected, easy to access, and a dozen miles closer.

The entrance to Grundarfjord lies between a buoy marking a long shoal to port and a mountain of steep rock terraces rising tier over tier in a giant pseudo-gothic façade. We sail to the head of the bay where the chart shows shallow water, but as we prepare to anchor, we see the houses of a small settlement. There's a fish plant with a long, empty wharf that we explore as a possible berth. Les pulls alongside and I scramble up a metal ladder between the familiar black truck tires to secure the dock lines. On the pier opposite, several yellow-suited fishermen are hauling boxes of fish from a boat into a truck.

"Is it okay to moor here?" I call out.

A wave of the arm and a reply in Icelandic direct me to a small building at the end of the wharf. The office door is closed, but my call rouses the middle-aged harbormaster from his chair. He's thickset, with gray hair and cheerful countenance, his gaze open-eyed yet squinting. It's apparent he doesn't speak English. It occurs to me I've interrupted his afternoon sleep.

"Hello."

He grins affably and replies in Icelandic.

"Is it okay to tie up here?" I ask.

More Icelandic.

I try again. "Is okay to tie up?"

He replies, "Is okay," as though he doesn't understand. I step outside, point to the wharf, and repeat the question. The harbormaster follows to where he can see the wharf.

"Is okay," he says with a nod and a wide grin.

I return to *Symphony* and finish tying off the dock lines. A boy of about ten with a bright, shiny face and thick blond hair fishes off the front of the fish wharf. Astonishingly he hauls in seven or eight large fish one after another, loads them into a plastic crate, and rides off on his cycle, towing the crate clattering behind on a short string. Intrigued by this extraordinary performance, we cross the wharf and peer into the water. A large shoal of fish feeds hungrily round the end of a pipe discharging effluent from the fish plant.

As often after a night passage, we sleep late. When we eventually wake, the sky is completely cloud-covered. Light mist alternates with heavy rain throughout the day, and it's evening before it's pleasant enough to go ashore. Grundarfjord is an agreeable, unpretentious community, situated on the limited usable land between the mountains and the sea. Many buildings are painted white. A half-mile along the single main road, we find a small restaurant. We each have a beer. They taste good, cold and refreshing. We linger over them, savoring the taste, drinking slowly to extract every ounce of flavor. For our meal, Les chooses haddock, which she pronounces excellent, while I have a superburger and French fries. Our waitress, very obliging and very pregnant, speaks idiomatic English which, she explains, she learned in Scotland while somehow avoiding any hint of a Scottish accent.

Returning to *Symphony* we're intercepted by a group of young boys cruising the town on bicycles. We recognize the enthusiastic fisherman, who's introduced to us as Johan. He speaks little or no English. Usually polite, he suddenly appears immature, jerking his arms as though still fishing, and screaming at the top of his voice to scatter gulls. His friend, Thorgrimmur, is the son of a trawler skipper. He learned his excellent English on vacation in Africa. We learn he has hunted reindeer in east Iceland, shot ptarmigan, and netted puffin. During our stay, these boys, often with others, become our constant companions. They visit us aboard *Symphony*, relishing candy that Les hands out from a large plastic jar. They're inquisitive, showing keen interest in our voyage and in life in the U.S. Whenever we set foot ashore, our escorts materialize from side streets, apparently summoned by unseen forces. "Hee. . . ere's Thorgrimmur!" becomes our private joke. On one visit, the boys surprise us with a gift of a large vacuum-packed smoked salmon. We're caught off balance. How did these youngsters come by this fish? Is it theirs to give? Do their parents know? Did they raid someone's freezer or whisk it away from the fish plant? We decide to accept gracefully and keep our questions to ourselves. It's quite the best salmon we've tasted in a long time.

The next day is Sunday and the weather is much nicer. A freighter moors behind *Symphony*, but we see little loading or unloading and she soon leaves. The mountain ridge overlooking the town stands clear and jagged against the sky. I remember climbs and scrambles along many such ridges and imagine standing in crisp mountain air, balanced atop the world, surveying ridges and valleys, rocks and snow, the sea and islands, all with the eye of an eagle. I think of scrambling along knife-edges from peak to peak and the exhilaration of reaching a summit. However, I recall, too, the penetrating, wet coldness of the high snow-filled valleys and the miserable uphill trudges under a ton of clothes and equipment—too hot inside and too cold in the extremities. I gaze at north-facing gullies that never feel the warmth of the sun and remember the icy chill of meltwater seeping into a boot and down the sleeve of an arm reaching out for a hold. These days I'm very content to admire mountains from a distance, to be by the water, and to bask in warm sunshine.

We walk along a deserted road between rows of small houses and out beyond the village to a harbor sheltering small local boats. Where a farm road joins the highway a sign advertises holiday accommodations and horse rentals at the farm, *Kverna*. Les is a lifelong horse lover, and I know her visit will be incomplete without a ride on an Icelandic horse. Many times she has described their special gait, the *tolt*, a fast running-walk that is supposed to be amazingly comfortable for the rider. Apparently it can be experienced only in Iceland. Unfortunately I view horseback riding in the same light as bungee jumping—fine for others, even okay to watch, but on no account to

Kirkjufell towers over the fishing village of Grundafjord, western Iceland

be engaged in personally. Les taught our children to ride while I was content to watch and offer encouragement. Nevertheless, the valleys look attractive in the sunlight, and an afternoon ride into the hills might not be too bad. We walk up the road and knock at the farm door. We hear doors closing inside before a shortish middle-aged woman answers. She confirms we can ride this afternoon. We should return in a couple of hours, by which time the horses will be rounded up from nearby pasture.

We return to the village to have a light lunch and to get cash for the horse rentals. We find a bank, but it has no ATM and it seems we may have to forgo our rides. However, the manager of a convenience store—the only place open in the village—agrees to furnish the cash, with the amount charged to a credit card. Returning to *Symphony*, we're waylaid by Thorgrimmur and friends. Now pressed for time, we share a quick snack of bread and jam with the boys and return to *Kverna* at a brisk pace.

Gudfinna, the proprietor and trailmaster, understands my appre-hension at climbing onto a horse and gives me what she calls a "kind" animal. She tells me the horse's name, which sounds like "Dunna." It takes a little time to saddle five horses for Les, Gudfinna, her twin six-year-old sons, and myself, but eventually we all mount up. Les and Gudfinna keep a tight hold on Dunna's head while I make an undignified lunge onto her back. Everyone else leaps up with appar-ent ease. With final adjustments to girths and stirrups, the horses walk slowly in line up rising ground behind the farm. I'm content to follow a little behind Les. Dunna has spasmodic bursts of enthusiasm, strid-ing out and threatening to thrust her nose into the nether regions of the animal ahead. Then she falls behind, her energy apparently spent. Several times she stops, looks back longingly, and takes a step or two toward the farm before I can pull her round with the reins.

We climb steadily beside a stream that flows through a deep val-ley in a series of rapids and deep pools. The horses' plodding steps appear awkward and they seem about to trip over their own horse-shoes. Where the track approaches the edge of the valley, I look straight down past Dunna's flanks to rocks and surging water far below. I feel acutely out of control, my life dependent on a horse of uncertain sense and clumsy feet. I'm glad when these spots are safely behind. On the relatively level floor of a high valley, we stop to rest the mounts. The terrain is rough, with no vegetation to obscure the views, and the landscape is big and empty. Far, far below, the buildings of Grundarfjord nestle below the cliffs of Kirkjufell. *Symphony* is just visible as a tiny white spot by the harbor wall.

Gradually my apprehension diminishes. The level going is more comfortable and I begin to feel at ease. In places we ride side by side and Gudfinna describes extended summer treks across mountain ridges to the Snæfellsjökul icecap. I can appreciate the appeal of such expeditions, of carrying along everything needed, of visiting remote places and camping out beneath the stars. Not so long ago this was the only way to travel across this vast island. When Lord Dufferin made the thirty-five-mile excursion from Reykjavik to Thingvellir, his party and their equipment were borne by twenty-six horses under the care of three guides. Baggage traveled separately from the lord and his companions. Servants set up the camps while the lord played chess! Now, that sounds like a fine sort of camping!

Our return lies across a low ridge and down a neighboring valley. The descent begins steeply and we dismount and walk the horses. We pause to admire Grundarfoss, a high and picturesque waterfall cascading down a rock cliff, before continuing downhill toward the farm. When we reach level ground, the horses break into the *tolt*. The other riders shoot ahead, and it takes only a gentle toe tap to send Dunna flying after them. I quickly discover that Les's promise of extraordinary comfort is less than completely accurate. The legs of the animals beat the ground at an astonishing rate. Certainly their backs remain remarkably level, but they vibrate rapidly up and down, resonating with every step. Shock waves pulse through my posterior and spread through every part of my torso. I cannot imagine such discomfort for an extended period. It's an experience appreciated fully only after the pain has stopped. The rest of the party must be blessed with different anatomy, as they're fulsome in praise of this excruciating mode of travel. I recover somewhat when the pace slackens to a walk and we all arrive back at the farm, well satisfied with our afternoon ride.

Once the horses are unsaddled, we tour the stables, and then we're invited into the farmhouse. We enjoy tea served from a thermos—as we've seen in Icelandic cafés—accompanied by chocolate cake. Trophies for soccer and riding, won by the family's eldest son, line the living room wall. Ragnar, Gudfinna's husband, joins us. He turns out to be Thorgrimmur's uncle!

Grundarfjord has been a rewarding stop—the better for being unplanned—but we've already stayed longer than intended. The sail to Hofsvag is short and we leave late in the afternoon to take advantage of a favorable tide. Thorgrimmur and his friends line the wharf, waving farewell as we pull from the dock. We promise to exchange e-mail when we return home. As *Symphony* gathers way down the fiord, the waving figures become smaller and their plaintive shouts of "We'll miss you" grow fainter.

We sail close-hauled on starboard tack through a narrow passage between the rocky shore and an area of foul ground. Once well clear of the north slope of Eyrarfall (which forms the east side of the bay), we go about onto port tack to follow the coast eastward. *Symphony* glides along gracefully on a beam-reach, heeling gently in complete harmony with the sea and wind. Multitudes of small islands lie to port and a range of rugged mountains to starboard. It's a beautiful evening, perfect for sailing, in an extraordinarily beautiful setting.

To enter Hofsvag we must pass through a narrow gap between two islands, then immediately turn to port to avoid charted but unseen rocks. We roll a deep reef in the headsail to slow *Symphony* for better control while maneuvering, and rehearse each step so we both know what to expect. As often happens, an awkward passage, well-studied in advance, turns out less trying than expected. Soon we sail serenely into the anchorage where we hand the mains'l, roll in the rest of the genoa, and start the engine. Our small-scale chart has no depth markings, and we explore cautiously down the bay until the water shallows alarmingly and rocks and weed threaten to entangle the keel. Retreating, we find a spot in the southwest corner of the bay near Purkey Island and anchor on the edge of deeper water. On the first attempt, the anchor drags through the soft bottom. It holds on the second try and I let out a long length of chain. As the bottom may be foul, I set a trip line using a fender as a marker buoy. Finally I fix a nylon snubber to the chain with a rolling hitch.

The next day, breezy, wet weather returns. We busy ourselves on board. Les bakes bread. I catch up on my notes, send e-mail to each

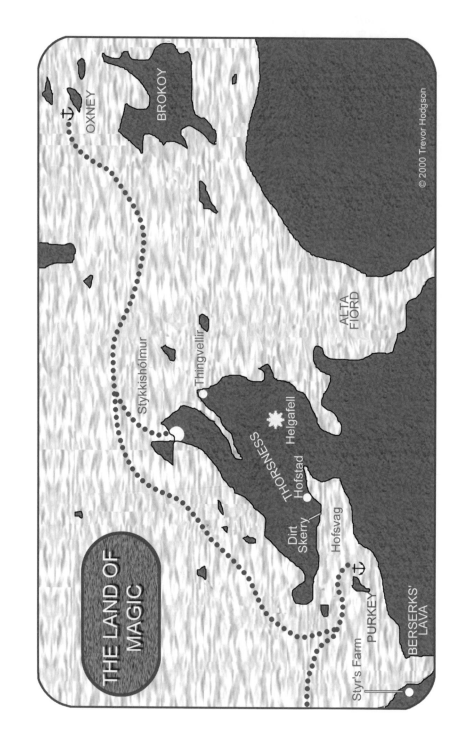

THE LAND OF MAGIC

OXNEY

BROKOY

Stykkishólmur

Thingvellir

ALTA FIORD

THORSNESS

Helgafell

Hofstad

Dirt Skerry

Hofsvag

Styr's Farm

PURKEY

BERSERKS' LAVA

© 2000 Trevor Hodgson

of our five children via SSB, and keep a check on the anchor. We have no tide tables for Hofsvag, so I produce our own, noting the depth sounder at regular intervals. It is very approximate as *Symphony* swings with the tide, but the readings produce quite a smooth graph and serve well enough to estimate the tidal range and give approximate times for high and low water.

Our two-horsepower outboard lives on a board mounted on the stern rail. A couple of days ago I found the engine steering-arm lying in the cockpit next to the bolt, now sheared off, that had attached it to the engine. How it broke is a mystery. Anxious to avoid a long row to shore, I set about making repairs. I try drilling the broken bolt in the steering-arm but make no impression on the tough steel. After several tries I give up and settle for strapping the handle to the engine with duct tape. The engine itself starts well with just two pulls of the rope—not bad, as we've not used it since we left Hull.

In the afternoon the weather is visibly improved, and by evening we're ready for a walk. As we head ashore, the outboard cuts out several times. Each time, a pull on the starting line gets it going; then it stops again and I resign myself to a long row back after all. Landing on a beach of coarse, black sand, we scramble onto a rocky headland. The beauty is captivating. Craggy mountains present a jagged line across the sky. Islands and rocks lie scattered across Breidafjord. The air is still, the water of the bay unruffled. Only the plaintive calls of redshank break the silence. We sit and let the magic of the place waft over us. The shadows lengthen and the mountains grow dark. It's time to head back. Our return takes us through a miniature valley where a stream makes its final descent to the sea over a picturesque waterfall. Back in the dinghy I row slowly, unwilling to break the spell by disturbing the water with anything but the slightest ripple. Aboard, it's difficult to turn in. It's so light, so perfectly peaceful.

We're at the heart of the land of *Eyrbyggja*, the romantic tale set in the violent days following the original settlement. It has colorful characters that stride boldly across a magical landscape. Happily many features described in the saga can still be recognized. After Thorolf's high-seat pillars drifted into this bay, he made his home where we can now see a modern farm. He named the bay Hofsvag (Temple Bight), and his farm Hofstad (Temple Farm), both of which still appear on current maps. Nearby, he raised a temple to Thor with wood brought specially from Norway. Helgafell, the pagan holy mountain, is clearly visible to the east, and the Berserks' Lava, where Swedish berserks built a path for the love of a woman, sweeps down the mountains to the west in a wide, rumpled, gray-green band.

Berserks were noted for furious fighting. When not in their excited state, they were good servants, willing and strong, but if crossed, they went into frenzied rage. A Viking named Vermund brought two berserk brothers, Halli and Leiknir, to Breidafjord, to help him in a dispute with his own brother, Styr. However, the berserks proved so troublesome he thought it better to give them, and the problem, to Styr. Before long, Halli fell in love with Styr's daughter, demanding her hand in marriage, and when Styr refused, the Swedes became threatening, breaking open his bed closet by forcing apart the joints with their fingers.

Now Styr, too, was anxious to be rid of the berserks. He turned for help to Snorri the Priest, who lived at the farm at Helgafell. Snorri was brilliant, conniving and ruthless, a man of great foresight, with a long memory and a taste for vengeance. He was destined to become the most influential person in the region. He advised Styr how to be rid of the mighty troublemakers. Styr promised his daughter to Halli provided he earned the marriage by work. The Swedes must clear a pathway over the lava field, build a boundary wall between the farms of Styr and his brother, and construct a sheep enclosure on the lava. The two men, summoning all their strength, completed the work in a single day, tossing aside great lumps of lava. Meanwhile, Styr had a bath dug into the ground with a trap door overhead.

When the berserks returned, tired and weak, their frenetic strength exhausted, Styr thanked them for their work and invited them to use the bath. When they were inside, Styr closed the entrance and piled rocks on the trap door. Before the entrance he laid a fresh oxhide. Then he poured hot water through an opening. The scalded Swedes ran for the door and broke it open. Halli slipped on the raw oxhide, and Styr promptly killed him. When Leiknir tried to escape by the trap door, Styr impaled him on a spear and he, too, fell back dead. Styr gave them a good pagan burial, laying their bodies in a hollow in the lava, "so deep that one can see nought therefrom but the heavens above it, and that is beside that self-same road." He threw rocks over the graves to be sure the berserks could not rise up to haunt the neighborhood. Subsequently it was Snorri himself who married Styr's daughter. The *Eyrbyggja Saga* concludes that "both men might be deemed to have gained from these events, and this alliance. For Snorri was the better counseled and the wiser man, but Styr the more adventurous and pushing."

The lava is clearly visible from *Symphony*, inviting us to visit the scene of the berserks' labor. First I clean the outboard fuel system and check that the engine runs smoothly. We hesitate to leave *Symphony* in the brisk wind, but the anchor seems secure and she's riding comfortably. Finally we decide to go. Again the dinghy is lowered over the side, the seat fixed in place, the engine and oars passed down from the cockpit, and a fender pressed between the inflated sides to provide a second seat. The camera and binoculars follow in a yellow, waterproof, plastic bag. With one final check of the anchor, we're on our way, drifting easily downwind to the shore. It's still four hours to low tide, but we haul the dinghy well back from the water.

Black pebbles and black sand make for difficult and tiring walking. Many stones have curious holes, as though attacked by toredo. We head away from the shore up a steep grass bank, stepping carefully over a flimsy wire fence to gain the small valley we descended last night. Already we're too warm, and we strip off our plastic rain gear and stow it in the yellow bag. A climb by the waterfall and a short walk across a barren area where stone has been extracted brings us to an unfinished road.

We follow this road westward at a brisk walk, with many stops to admire the scenery and look at birds. It seems a long way and our legs are feeling the distance before we near the lava. There's no sign of a path. A middle-aged man answers our knock at the door of a farmhouse. When we inquire in English, he indicates we should wait and disappears back inside. A woman, presumably his wife, arrives to tell us that we're close to the berserks' footpath, that it's near a bend in the road and marked by a small sign.

A short distance from the farm, the road turns inland. This appears a likely place for a path to strike off through the lava, but still we see nothing. We're about to continue along the road when Les spots a small board, low down and way off to the right. Little more than a post, the white-painted sign is about six inches by twelve. There are no letters or markings, but once we cross an area of rough grass, there is indeed a footpath, just wide enough for one person, leading off through tumbled blocks of lava. The ground to either side is chaotic and impossible for walking. Boulders are piled on boulders, all covered in green lichen. Deep gaps between them wait to trap the legs of scramblers. However, our path continues purposefully through the chaos, winding between the disordered piles of volcanic rock.

After ten minutes we round a corner to find a depression with another small white board. Can this be where Styr laid the bodies of the slain berserks? I descend carefully into the hollow and lie on my back on the uneven bottom. As I look up, the lava obscures the surroundings—I see only blue sky. When the hollow was excavated, archeologists found two male skeletons. Apparently they were not especially tall but appeared unusually strong.

The path emerges on a cliff overlooking a bay of blue water speckled with whitecaps. Brown seaweed lines the shore and covers the shallow areas. Innumerable islands lie scattered across the bay. Breidafjord's north coast, thirty miles away, is a fuzzy, dark line along the horizon. The path leaves the lava here and continues over broken ground to a farm, built on the site where Styr once lived. We sit on the rock, enjoying the view and sunshine. We each have a Milky Way bar. The return, first along the path, then following the dirt road, is tiring. It seems a long way, slightly uphill and into the wind, which has freshened. As we trudge along, we have time to be concerned for *Symphony*, and it's a relief when we climb a gentle hill to see her riding safely among a sea of white horses.

It's obvious the dinghy ride will be exciting. Two-foot waves sweep past *Symphony* directly onto the beach, where they burst on the rocks into clouds of spray. We don our rain gear and seal the binoculars and camera in the yellow bag. The waves batter the dinghy, making boarding and maneuvering from the shore awkward. Already we're wet through. The engine starts immediately—just as well, as I doubt I could row directly into the twenty-five knot wind. The dinghy plows doggedly into the short waves, sending showers of spray over us. Slowly, so slowly, the tiny outboard gains against the elements.

Relieved, we finally grab *Symphony*'s gunwale and clamber aboard. Once dried and warm, we celebrate a great expedition with beer, smoked salmon, fresh baked bread, cake, and tinned pears!

On a small rise overlooking the bay, Thorolf's thingmen held Iceland's first assembly fifty years before the national gathering at Thingvellir. Thorolf venerated the meeting-place and declared it should not be defiled by bloodshed or human excrement. Dritsker (Dirt Skerry), a small island just off the peninsula, was designated the local toilet. Unfortunately not all were willing to observe Thorolf's rules, and a bitter fight occurred when some later settlers refused to observe the sanctity of the meeting-place. They declared they would "ease themselves on the grass as anywhere else . . . and would not wear out their shoes going to the skerry for their needs." Thorolf's supporters fought a bloody battle with the newcomers, with men killed and wounded on both sides. No place defiled by such bloodshed could be used for assemblies, and subsequent meetings were moved to a new site farther east.

The next day is perfect for a visit to Helgafell with a look at Dritsker on the return. The morning is calm. Early clouds clear away to leave just a few wisps of cirrus gently caressing a blue sky. Helgafell is only a little over two hundred feet high, a molehill compared with the mountains along the rugged southern horizon. However, it stands alone, dominating the farms on the coastal plain, and has been a special place from the moment the Vikings arrived. Thorolf insisted "no man might look at it without first having washed. Nothing was to be killed on this mountain, neither cattle nor human beings." He believed here would be the final resting place of himself and his relatives.

We motor slowly toward the head of the bay, peering into the water as rocks and weeds get steadily closer. Two large jellyfish float past, each a foot across and trailing long orange tentacles. When rocks clip the bottom of the boat, we head for a muddy beach and haul the dinghy well back from the water line. A scramble up a grassy bank takes us along the side of a very shallow inlet. Rocks protrude from water, intermingled with bright green vegetation. We follow a farm track, cross a surfaced highway, climb over a fence, and ascend a low, rocky hill. Descending into a wide valley, we find an extensive

Lesley on an evening stroll by Hofsvag, western Iceland

system of drainage ditches blocking our path. We have to search to find a place to cross and eventually step across with water just lapping the top of our sea boots. Large black-backed gulls wheel and scream overhead. In a side channel, Les discovers a family of red-necked phalaropes that make her bird-watching day.

Back on dry ground, a wide farm track leads round a small hill and through a farm gate to a simple, white church nestled at the foot of the mountain. We rest by the gate while members of a coach party examine the church before filing up Helgafell in a long, slow line. The church interior is simple and painted white, with unusual, curved, wooden pews. Nineteenth-century plaques on the west wall commemorate prominent local citizens. At the foot of the Helgafell path is a grave. An inscription reveals that it is the resting place of Gudrun, a powerful matriarch at the time of settlement and an important character in *Eyrbyggja*.

It's legendary that anyone climbing to the summit of Helgafell for the first time, without speaking and without looking behind, will have a wish granted. We follow the winding path in silence, eyes focused just a few steps ahead. At the top we're quiet while we each make our wishes, and then exclaim in celebration at the extraordinary view. A small stone shelter stands on the highest point, where Snorri the Priest spent long periods in deep contemplation. Maybe it was here he conceived the plan to eliminate the mighty Swedes. He could not have found a more magical place. To the north, tiny white houses cluster together at the village of Stykkisholmur. Beyond are the island of Flatey and the dark outline of the northwest fiords. Eastward, Breidafjord narrows and is packed with myriad islands that merge in the haze and fade into the distant mountains. To the southeast, Altafjord penetrates deep into the mountains of the Snæfell ridge where the sun catches jagged peaks and highlights ridges and buttresses. The Berserks' Lava tumbles down a valley like a long green glacier. As we scan the panorama, reluctant to leave, a pair of ravens circle just below the summit. Round and round they go, their long primaries extended in ragged curves. To Thorolf these were Thor's messengers, and their presence at such a holy place highly significant. It's easy to understand the power of such thoughts on this lofty pedestal surrounded by such awesome scenery. The ravens utter several haunting calls before completing a final circuit and flying off to the west.

A path leads along the summit ridge and down to a road. Harvesting is underway at a farm in the valley, with three tractors working together to cut, bale, and plastic-wrap a field of hay. Three great northern divers, two parents with one young chick, swim on a lake while a golden plover searches for pickings by the side of the road. Where we reach the surfaced highway, yellow signs warn of water bubbling to the surface at 80 degrees centigrade. The idea strikes us as amusing.

Back at Hofsvag, the tide has receded, leaving an inlet of rocks surrounded by shining mud. The dinghy is stranded at least a quarter-mile from any water deep enough to float it. We half-carry, half-drag it along the beach, returning in relays for the fuel can, engine, life jackets, and yellow bag. We struggle to keep the vulnerable rubber away from the rocks and stones, but long before we reach the water, our arms tire and the dinghy slips and scrapes on the beach. One chamber buckles with a hiss of escaping air and our spirits collapse with it. Suddenly we feel vulnerable. *Symphony* is a quarter-mile from shore, and the dinghy our only way of reaching her. The tender has just two inflation chambers, and one is now holed. We carry a repair kit and pump, but they're both aboard *Symphony*. Will one float be adequate for us to reach *Symphony*? If not, what then?

The dinghy's a sorry sight. One tube inflated as normal, the other limp and useless in the water. Our salvation is the fender we use as a dinghy seat. I lash this to the deflated tube. The result's a sad-looking raft of rubber and plastic, but at least it floats reasonably level. I clamber aboard the sound chamber. It's a precarious perch, but to our relief the fender has enough buoyancy to keep the dinghy more or less level and prevent the whole thing from sinking.

Before embarking on our perilous ride back to *Symphony*, I pay a brief visit to the site of Thorolf's assembly. Les prefers to explore the shore for shells and small creatures. The headland is covered with rough grass. As I climb a short rock step near the high point on the promontory, a bird takes off from right under my foot. Instinctively I leap backwards, then regain my balance to discover a nest with three large eider eggs. I take a couple of photographs and head back to the shore.

Thorolf's Dritsker is directly ahead, linked to the promontory by a strip of wet rocks, sand, and seaweed. As I pick my way cautiously toward it, I'm suddenly the target of aerial bombardment. Instinctively I duck as red-white-and-black projectiles scream low overhead. These oystercatchers defend their territory as resolutely as any fierce Viking. I move off a little way and the birds perch on near-by rocks, still screaming their protests. I'm ready to retreat. We climb aboard the dinghy and slowly paddle toward *Symphony*. With considerable relief we finally clamber aboard.

It's time once more to work on the dinghy. Luckily the repair kit still contains both patches and adhesive. It's a simple task to clean off the surface, spread the glue, and when it's dried, place a patch over the small slit. Nevertheless, I'm relieved when we inflate the chamber and there is no sign of escaping air.

Our final expedition at Hofsvag is to the site adopted for the regional assembly after the Dirt Skerry battle. Here, for the first time, we meet up with Erik the Red. Erik came to Iceland with his father when they were banished from Norway for murder. First, they settled in the wild northwest fiords, as all the best land was already taken. Nevertheless, Erik made a good marriage to a lass called Thjodhild, and together they farmed at Haukadale a few miles east of Helgafell and started a family. However, Erik's old habits proved too hard to forgo and he was hauled before the assembly to account for more violent killings.

No doubt the assembly was a rowdy affair with arguments shouted back and forth and scuffles between rival factions. The practice of avenging any wrong, real or imagined, on the perpetrator and his household provided copious material for claim and counterclaim. It was submitted that Erik's slaves "accidentally" started a landslide that destroyed a neighbor's home. He also feuded over bench boards with Torgest, his wealthy neighbor. Erik took the boards by force and in the process killed several men, including two of the farmer's sons. The case came to trial here in the spring of 982. When judgment was declared, Erik was banished from Iceland for three years.

The present farm here is still called Thingvellir and approached along a long, unfinished road. On the right (south) of the road, tractors are cutting and baling hay. An elderly woman answers our knock at the door and directs us to her son who's driving one of the tractors.

We feel guilty taking Kristjan from his work, but he readily jumps down from his cab and walks with us toward the promontory where the assembly was held. He's home on vacation from his work in Kansas.

A large area of cut grass extends along the top of steep but short cliffs. One section is unmowed, and Kristjan explains this is where booths stood that provided accommodation at the assemblies. He remembers when outlines of former buildings were visible in the grass, but these have disappeared. Remarkably the site has never been excavated, but a preservation order prohibits mowing this area. He points out the Blood Rock where the convicted suffered painful deaths and the Hanging Stone where miscreants were tied and left to be drowned by the rising tide.

Erik's three-year banishment posed a dilemma. He was already outlawed in his native Norway and there was no safety for him in the lands to the east. Now unable to stay in Iceland, his only hope of freedom lay to the west. Sailors had already sighted land over the western horizon, describing it as a wild and unattractive place with nowhere suitable for settlement. However, without real alternatives, Erik decided to explore. While he prepared for his expedition, he hid on the island of Oxney five miles east in the inner part of Breidafjord.

We set out for Oxney on a foggy but calm morning. Visibility is about a mile and we navigate cautiously between rocks and islands, monitoring the GPS and radar. To starboard the entrance to Stykkisholmur harbor looks rock-strewn and intimidating, while to port tall granite cliffs on the island of Thorisholmi loom overhead. Here, navigation becomes more challenging, as there's no large-scale chart for the inner part of Breidafjord and the sheet we have has few depth contours. We take a mid-channel course and try to stay well clear of any obstacles.

Eventually we approach a foggy, wet, miserable-looking Oxney surrounded by deep water and circled by strong currents. Even close in, the depth sounder shows 150 feet, then 120, and then 80. We're now very close to shore. Finally we drop the anchor in 40 feet, just two boat-lengths from weed-covered rocks. The tripping line and its fender are still attached to the anchor and I leave them on—it will be helpful to see how *Symphony* moves with the current. Les reverses the engine and we both look for marks ashore to check the set of the anchor. Suddenly there's an unmistakable clunk and the engine stops abruptly. I feel sick. I know immediately what has happened: The tripping line has drifted to the stern and is now wrapped firmly round the propeller shaft. We have to move fast. The anchor seems to be holding, but we never finished setting it. The current's pushing us off the rocks, but it will soon reverse.

I inflate the dinghy at top speed, glad I completed the repair. With a second anchor and rode piled up in the stern, I row well astern and toss it over the side. We take up the slack in the rode, and both anchors appear to hold, with *Symphony* between them. Les now repeats the exercise to set another hook from the bow to prevent any drift toward the rocks.

With *Symphony* as secure as possible, we turn our attention to the rope round the propeller. We have scuba equipment with us, carried for just such an emergency. However, I always imagined that if I had to go over the side, it would be in warm, blue, tropical water. Plunging into this cold, fast-flowing, opaque-brown liquid was never part of the plan. It's foggy, wet, and cold; the water temperature is 45 degrees. I'm intimidated. My confidence is further depressed when I discover we have no diving gloves or hood on board. I must dive bareheaded and barehanded. It's going to be really cold!

Even in ideal conditions, squeezing into a wet suit is difficult and frustrating. By the time I've donned a buoyancy jacket, tanks, boots, weights, and mask, I feel so awkward I just want to roll over and lie in the cockpit. Spurred by lack of alternatives and the urgent need to fix the problem, I eventually position the dinghy by the stern and slide into the water while Les hangs onto a safety line tied around my waist. The initial cold shock is less severe than I expect.

As I thought, several layers of tripping line are tightly coiled round the shaft, and the fender is wedged between the propeller and the hull. Working is difficult. The current pulls my legs up level with my head and I cling desperately to a blade of the propeller. Hanging on with one hand and legs spread astern, I try to cut away the rope. My knife makes little impression on the tangled line, but after what seems an age of cutting and chopping, the fender shoots to the surface and drifts away. I hack at the line vigorously, but it's no good.

I'm tired and cold and have to get out of the water. I bob to the surface and swim stiffly to the ladder. My hands cannot grip. Only by
hooking my wrists round the sides of the ladder and with a helping
pull from Les can I haul myself and the heavy diving gear from the
water.

Sitting in the saloon swathed in towels, my body slowly regains
some feeling. The more comfortable I get, the more difficult it
becomes to get back in the water for another attack on the tangled
line. However, after several hesitations, it's back on with the cold, wet
diving gear, into the dinghy, and over the side. The current now flows
even faster. This time, a kitchen knife with a serrated edge proves
more effective than my boat knife. Very slowly I cut away all the line
except for three turns wedged rigidly between the shaft zinc and the
stern tube. I try and try but cannot make them yield. Again I emerge
shivering.

"It's no good, I can't get the last bit," I admit, flopping onto a
cockpit seat.

"How much is left?"

"Just three strands, but they're packed tight between the prop and
the stern tube."

"Maybe it'll start now."

"Maybe. Take it easy, though."

Les turns the ignition key. The starter whirs round, then the
engine splutters with one of the sweetest mechanical sounds ever
heard. Then it stops.

"Hey, try that again."

When the engine starts and keeps running, it is one of the happi-
est moments of the voyage. It's a long time before I'm dry and warm,
but I'm at peace. Things are back in control. It's such a feeling of
relief. Our crisis has occupied most of the afternoon and into the
evening. *Symphony* is still riding well to the three anchors and we see
no reason not to continue our visit to Oxney. We've worked too hard
to leave now without stepping ashore. Just a few pulls on the oars
bring us to a small cove where we tie up to a rock. In foul-weather
suits and inflatable life jackets, we climb to a cairn on the top of a
small hill. Oxney presents a dull and wet panorama, with areas of
rough ground separated by patches of bog. It's not pleasant walking.

Satisfied we've trodden on Erik's island, we return to *Symphony*.

One by one we recover the anchors and stow the yards of line. At last the main anchor is secure on the bow roller and we motor very slowly to Stykkisholmur. There's still no wind for sailing. Fearful the rope has damaged the propeller shaft or engine, we stay on very low power and avoid reverse altogether. At first we hardly dare hope it will keep going, but it does, and soon after midnight we edge slowly between the sentinel rock buttresses and enter Stykkisholmur harbor. Visibility is good from the combination of harbor lights and arctic twilight. *Baldur*, a large, very modern, slab-sided ferry, is berthed to the port side of the entrance. Fishing boats occupy all the dock space while ahead, small boats crowd around floating pontoons. There appears to be little room, but a man aboard *Baldur* leans over the rail and motions us to tie alongside a fishing boat at his stern. Rarely have we moored with greater relief. We're so very pleased to have arrived, to have an engine that works and a boat safely in harbor. We've made it! We've extricated ourselves from a tricky situation without help. We feel good. It's time for mince with mash and peas, a beer, and bed.

The next morning under an overcast sky, we meet Oscar, our neighbor, a young fishing skipper who's painting his boat while his partners take a vacation. Formerly harvesting sea urchins, he now fishes for sea snails that are processed locally for shipment to Japan. He strips thick chips of paint from a mast, sending bits flying in all directions, including liberal quantities over *Symphony*'s deck.

Symphony appears undamaged by her tangle with the tripping line, but we want to check the shaft and propeller before continuing our voyage. Across the harbor a projecting wharf has a gently sloping sandy bottom off each face. It's just what's needed for drying out. Oscar directs us to the harbor office to make the necessary arrangements. This proves easy to find, but the harbormaster is not, as his posted hours are apparently only a general guide. Finally, in the evening, we find him in his office in animated conversation with another man. Konrad (the harbormaster) speaks no English, but his visitor translates. A long discussion goes back and forth but finally he concurs with our plan to dry out against the wall and we agree to be there tomorrow at 1:00 P.M.

The following morning the sun appears for the first time since our walk up Helgafell and the barometer rises slightly. We have a regular breakfast of tea, followed by coffee, then porridge. At 1215 Konrad arrives. It's Oscar's turn to translate as we arrange for docking alongside the wharf. We motor *Symphony* slowly across the harbor to the waiting men, who help to secure her starboard side to the wharf with her bow facing out to deep water. Konrad is obviously concerned. It cannot be often that a keelboat dries out here, and he's fearful she'll topple. With no common language, we work through hand signals to set the lines. Doubled dock lines run from the port side, across the deck to large cleats on the wharf. The main halyard is tied off to another cleat on the far side of the dock. Konrad takes a separate line from the mast and attaches it to a crane used to unload fishing vessels.

The water is slow to recede, but eventually *Symphony* settles on the hard sand. Once she's safely grounded, Konrad relaxes and leaves in his van to return in a couple of hours. As the water falls away from the propeller, we see that the rope has already disappeared. A closer inspection from the dinghy confirms that *Symphony* has suffered no damage from her visit to Oxney. We take the opportunity to replace the shaft zinc and clean some light fouling from the rudder.

It's a sunny Sunday afternoon. The fine weather brings many townspeople to the harbor, and our activities attract a lot of attention. Whole families set off in small motor cruisers while others return, often carrying several large cod. Konrad offers us a snack of dried fish. We accept, but it does nothing to improve our opinion of this "delicacy." Konrad exchanges greetings with everyone in sight. He stops one boat party returning with several large fish. After a brief exchange in Icelandic, the skipper hands us a fine specimen of cod. When the tide returns and *Symphony* is afloat once more, we collect the various lines. Soon she's once more tied alongside Oscar's boat.

Chapter 10

First Ice

In midafternoon we cast our lines from Oscar's boat and motor slowly out between the rock buttresses at the harbor entrance. There's no wind. Overcast, hazy sky allows just occasional glimpses of the sun. Water swirls round the rocks on each side demanding our full attention and we line up range marks on the cliff astern to ensure we stay midchannel. Past a rock outcrop we turn west on a course marked by well-spaced buoys between small islands and isolated rocks. Höskuldsey, a low, rocky island surrounded by extensive reefs, lies off the port bow. Helgafell is prominent to the south, and widely separated farms show as white dots against a dull background of rough vegetation. The Berserks' Lava stands out clearly against snow-sprinkled mountains. A few small fishing boats, dotted round the horizon, rock in the light swell, each with a retinue of gulls.

Fishermen have cast lines in these waters since Viking times. Thorstein, son of Thorolf, earned the epithet Codbiter through his success at bringing home a good catch. One evening while Thorstein and his crew were fishing here by Höskuldsey, a shepherd gathering sheep watched the basalt columns on the north side of Helgafell swing open. Great fires burned inside, horns blared, and a celebration was in progress. He saw Thorstein welcomed to the feast and invited to occupy the high seat opposite his father. The shepherd's description of his vision distressed Thorstein's wife, as she rightly saw it as foreboding "something very sinister." The following morning her worst fears were confirmed when men brought news that Thorstein had drowned.

Despite Thorstein's unhappy fate, Les suggests we try our own luck with hook and line. Thanks to Tjorkel and our friends at Heimaey, we have plenty of gear and we did promise the Faroese we'd try our luck in Iceland. This may well be our last opportunity.

We stop the engine, and the world pauses to appreciate the profound silence. *Symphony* no longer forces aside the water but floats gently with a long, languid rhythm. It takes a little time to get ready. We retrieve the fishing gear from a bucket in the head. Grotesquely large hooks with colorful plastic sleeves are each attached to a leader, which is tied in turn to a monofilament line. The line tangles round the hooks, one end persistently re-twisting as we attend to the other. After forty minutes of occasionally testy work, we have ninety feet of line neatly rolled round a piece of wood, with nine vicious hooks and one heavy lead sinker laid out on the cockpit seat. Carefully Les dangles the weight and hooks over the side and pays out the line. The water is sixty feet deep. The sinker barely touches the bottom before the line tugs at her hand. Les jigs it up and down. Clearly no fish can have succumbed so quickly; the line must be caught on some rock or debris. Hand over hand she hauls the line back up. Amazingly, when the hooks break the surface, a good-sized cod twists this way and that on the end! She hauls it aboard, removes the hook, and dispatches the fish with a slash across its throat worthy of a seasoned angler. Immediately she sets about cleaning it. Gulls congregate alongside, and by the time she's finished, the sea is awash with white plumage as hundreds of birds squabble for advantage in the coming scramble for food. When we toss them the scraps, the whole mass heaves into a ball of screeching bird-life tearing at the scattered remains. At least nothing is wasted.

With dinner safely in the icebox, we continue west along the south coast of Breidafjord. The dark, jagged silhouette of the Snæfell Peninsula is clear against the sky. At last we have our closeup of Fuji-like Snæfellsjökul. As the sun sinks toward the horizon, its final rays illuminate the summit. The glistening ice-cone adopts a soft pinkish tone as its lower slopes slip deeper into darkness. The cliffs and gullies fade away, leaving the illuminated summit suspended in blackness, a gigantic jewel resting on a velvet cushion—a mystical farewell to the Land of Magic.

The scenery can be little changed since Erik the Red departed on his historic Greenland voyage. He left clandestinely, fearful of capture by his enemies and accompanied only by his closest followers. He crossed Denmark Strait to the east coast of Greenland, sailed south round Cape Farewell and then up the west coast. He spent the first winter on an island later named Eiriksöy in his honor. For the three years of his banishment, he explored the Greenland coast before returning to Breidafjord, full of praise for the land he discovered and named Greenland because "if it has a good name, people are more likely to go there."

Erik was persuasive and soon a flotilla of no less than twenty-five ships set sail for Greenland. This time it was no clandestine affair but a major event for the entire region. The departure of so many people must have left many gaps in the halls of Breidafjord. What a magnificent spectacle the boats must have presented as they followed the coastline westward. The emigrants no doubt had mixed feelings as Snæfellsjökul sank to the horizon and they thought of the homes and friends they were leaving behind.

Erik's route remained the standard way to Greenland for three hundred years. However, when the climate deteriorated in the thirteenth century and more ice swept along the East Greenland coast, it was no longer feasible. Ships then traveled farther south, as described by sailing directions in the *King's Mirror*:

> When one sails from Iceland one must take one's course from Snæfellsnes… and then sail due west one day and one night, then steer southwest…. And then one day and one night due northwest, and so one comes under the aforesaid elevation, Hvarf in Greenland.

Once Snæfellsjökul is astern, we turn south, as we intend to call at Keflavik to pick up mail, stock up with food, fuel, and water, and wait for a suitable weather window for the crossing to Cape Farewell. Winds are light, first westerly, then veering northwest. *Symphony* glides along through a night of crystal clarity. Multitudes of stars glisten in the sky. We sit in the cockpit bundled in warm clothes and wonder at the magnitude and splendor of the heavens. Eventually tiredness drives us back to our three-hour watches, and by dawn, high clouds cover the sky of a gray and uninspiring morning. Crossing Faxafloi, we encounter once again the swirling, swooping, diving congregation of sea birds. By the time we're off Keflavik, dark clouds in the southwest confirm the approach of deteriorating weather. In the harbor three or four fishing boats take up most of the space along the wharves. The harbormaster meets us at the dock and directs us to a berth at the inner end of the harbor. We are, he says, the first yacht to tie up there this year.

Keflavik was once a small trading post and fishing port, but a U.S. air base and the construction of Iceland's Leif Eriksson International Airport have swelled the population and improved the local facilities. The high street has a couple of hotels for airport passengers and several stores and eating-places. It has a significant fish-processing industry, while tourism is increasingly important. Two large shipyards have several ships stored ashore, many chocked on sloping ways. We're surprised at the number of wooden boats.

The next day the clouds are lower. The wind gains strength and blows straight through the entrance, driving waves into the harbor and noticeably raising the water level. *Symphony* works up and down against her fenders and we adjust the lines several times to keep her from the dock. When the wind reaches force seven, we become concerned. The motion is uncomfortable and waves threaten to damage *Symphony* against the wharf. A sheltered space behind a large fishing vessel, just long enough for her, offers some protection across the corner of the dock. We decide to move. Fearful of being blown against the fishing boat or dock if we try to maneuver at slow speed, we stretch long lines across the intervening water and winch *Symphony* over to her new berth. Our move is timely. The wind now blows right into the harbor. The water rises and we watch our former berth disappear completely beneath the rising tide.

Returning from shopping, we collect an entourage of young Icelanders and arrive back at *Symphony* accompanied by four or five boys and girls. They're sociable kids and speak excellent English. We learn who is related, what their parents do, where they go for vacations. They're excited to be invited aboard and explore the interior with much curiosity. Les gives each of them a few pieces of fruit candy, which again proves a huge success. Cruising the harbor is popular with local adults as well as adolescents. Cars motor in a steady procession along the line of boats. At the end of the quay they execute slow three-point turns and make their way back, perhaps pausing by a trawler to talk to the crew. Several stop beside *Symphony* to inquire where we've been and where we're headed. We hear many accounts of long-ago visits to the United States, all recalled with obvious pleasure. Four or five visitors ask how much we paid for

Symphony, a fascination for cost that seems peculiarly Icelandic.

In the evening, after a tasty chicken and rice dinner, we're reading below when a call from the dock brings us both to the cockpit. "Hi, *Symphony*. Anyone aboard?" A slim, fortyish man is perched on the edge of the wharf.

"Hello, how are you?" Les calls back. "I'm Lesley, this is Trevor."

"I'm Woody. I was just wandering around and saw the flag. Where are you guys from?"

"We live in New Jersey."

"How on earth did you get here?"

Les very briefly describes our route.

"But that's marvelous. I dream of one day taking off in a boat and here you are doing it."

"Would you like to come on down?" I ask.

"Well . . . er, sure," replies Woody, as though surprised to be asked. "I'll just have to lock the car."

He climbs easily down the ladder to join us. We all go below.

Woody is a medical administrator with the American military, in Keflavik for an international conference. His description makes it sound very important and we don't question him too closely. He once lived on a boat in a marina and has ambitions to move aboard again some day and perhaps head for the warm sun and palm trees of a tropical island.

"So what's stopping you?" asks Les.

"I'm still looking for the right female so I can enjoy cruising properly," responds Woody.

We talk well into the evening, sipping glasses of beer before Woody climbs into his rental car to head back to the U.S. base.

As we finish our coffee the next morning, we're surprised to hear again the familiar call from the dock. "Hello, *Symphony*."

Woody's back, this time bringing a copy of *USA Today* and a welcome bag of oranges and lemons.

"Say, why don't you guys come up to the base? You can get showers," he offers. This opportunity is too good to pass up, so we lock the companionway hatch and pile into Woody's car. We feel very important as a security guard waves us through a checkpoint, and soon bask in lots and lots of fresh hot water.

As we leave the base, the sun is shining—the day is fine. The wind is moderate. Our weather window is here! However, it's Sunday. We need more water, but there's no one on duty in the harbor and all the taps and hoses are locked away. We fill two three-gallon water jugs from a faucet at a convenience store, then make another round trip with the same two jugs. We're ready to leave. We say farewell and thanks to Woody, who drives off with two colleagues to explore Reykjavik.

Early afternoon we motor once more into Faxafloi and again meet great flocks of birds. The wind is southerly and the course downwind as we follow the shore toward the Gardskagi lights. Once past the shoals extending from the point, we turn west onto a close reach on port tack and behind a ketch with a red-and-white hull. For a while it seems she might accompany us to Cape Farewell, but her course is unsteady. One moment she sails close-hauled heading south toward Reykjanes, the next she falls off to parallel our course for Greenland. Finally she hardens her sheets and draws away to the south. A freighter leaves Faxafloi in a long turn to port. It's evident she could pass close to *Symphony*, but her final course is unclear. Will she go ahead or fall behind? I call her on the VHF.

"Vessel in approximate position six zero degrees zero six north, twenty-two degrees four five west, this is yacht *Symphony*, over."

There is a short pause before a heavily accented voice responds, "Yacht *Symphony*, this is (indistinguishable), over."

"We're on your port bow. Do you wish to pass our bow or our stern, over."

We are surprised to hear "I will hold my course," as the freighter appears set to pass very close.

"Thank you. Will that take you ahead of us, over."

The skipper of the freighter is uncompromising: "I will hold my course."

"Thank you. This is *Symphony*, standing by, channel 16."

I still don't know whether the freighter intends to pass ahead or behind. She cannot hold her course, as she's still visibly turning. The skipper's unhelpful response is very different from our usual experience in calling ships. After momentarily heading directly toward us, the freighter continues her turn to port and passes close behind.

The Reykjanes Peninsula slips slowly toward the horizon. Eventually only the two Gardskagi light towers remain in view. First one disappears, then the other, and once more we're alone at sea. We feel liberated physically and psychologically. The flurry of departure with the need to get things done—to buy provisions, fill tanks, and phone relatives—is all over. We've traded the convenience of life in port for the seductively simple issues of a high-seas passage: the safety of ourselves and *Symphony* and our progress to our destination. Our routine adapts quickly. Watch follows watch. The wind is variable and sail change follows sail change. Les cooks dinner and I wash the dishes during my midnight watch. I note the schedule of weather and ice broadcasts and monitor each in turn. We suffer the deep tiredness that always accompanies our first two or three days at sea.

Light winds on the port quarter continue through the first night, but by 0700 they die away, leaving *Symphony* drifting aimlessly. We resign ourselves to lack of progress and exercise what patience we can while going nowhere. Already, hopes of a fast passage are gone. We spend the whole day rising and falling on the swell, catching handholds and bracing ourselves when *Symphony* lurches unpredictably. The uncomfortable calm continues through the night, and toward morning, fog settles around us. Finally, early morning on the second full day of our passage, a light breeze sets in from west of north and *Symphony* glides along with renewed freedom. By evening, the wind freshens and we're sailing close-hauled on the starboard tack as *Symphony* forges into moderate seas. Two fishing vessels pass close by heading toward Iceland and a little later a third appears dead ahead with no way on. She's ablaze with deck lights. We change course to give her sea room and as we pass she greets us with a blast on the horn and a wave from the pilothouse.

For four days we make good progress in typical North Atlantic weather with brisk winds, overcast skies, and no sign of the sun. *Symphony* romps ahead, now on port tack. We pass north of a low and the wind backs slowly to the east. We don't touch the wind vane, but *Symphony* turns with the backing wind and we're whisked magically along a curving course toward Cape Farewell.

Six days out from Keflavik, radio conditions are unusually clear. The ham bands crackle with news of a storm far to the south packing

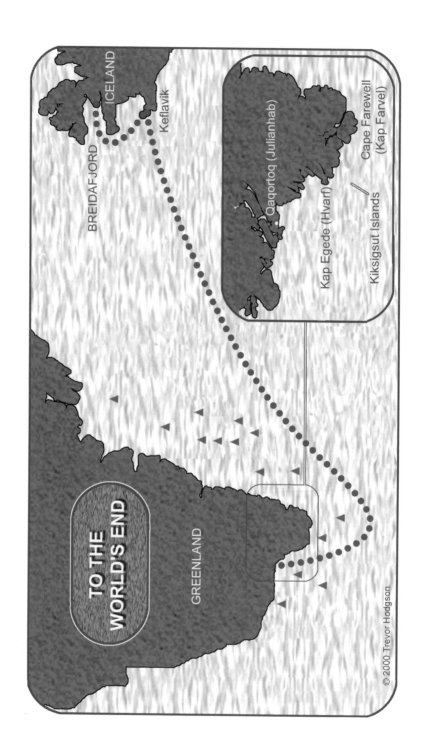

TO THE WORLD'S END

ICELAND

BREIDAFJORD

Keflavik

GREENLAND

Qaqortoq (Julianhab)

Kap Egede (Hvarf)

Kiksigsut Islands

Cape Farewell
(Kap Farvel)

© 2000 Trevor Hodgson

winds of fifty knots. It's unlikely to threaten us as it's heading west in the Atlantic off Georgia and the Carolinas. However, the weather fax shows a low approaching from Newfoundland. It looks menacing, with dark isobars packed in tight curves. I estimate its likely path from an upper air chart. It appears we're in for some heavy weather. Sure enough, the next morning a rising wind and gathering clouds confirm the approach of the low. Les bakes raisin scones. Later we set the stays'l and reef the main. We debate whether to set one reef or two, and it's soon obvious we should have gone for the second. The sailing is rough but we make rapid progress. The sun makes a brief appearance—the first since Keflavik. The wind rises and the sea begins to develop distinct patterns. Waves form and quickly get bigger. As water begins to break into the cockpit, we drop the stays'l and lash it to the lifelines. Soon we heave to with just the double-reefed main. I lash the clew with extra lines to relieve the reef line. *Symphony* no longer fights the seas but rocks slowly up and down as the waves sweep by beneath her.

The water contorts into large swirls of white and green. Long white streaks run downwind from the crests of the waves. Water sluices along the side decks, and spray repeatedly cascades into the cockpit. One wave, running across the others, heaves up amidships and crashes over the deck. Water pours into the saloon despite the tightly dogged hatch. After a couple of hours the cabin is quite wet, but it seems the seas are moderating. Certainly the gusts are less severe. However, we've been caught before by apparent lulls when we've relaxed our guard, only for a storm to return with full vigor. This is the case now. The wind rises again to 27 knots, then 28, 31, 33, 38 knots. The motion is erratic and uncomfortable. Seas break around us, and spray again rises in sheets from the bow.

We feel safe and well protected aboard *Symphony*, but the turmoil outside is enough to stir our adrenaline. If necessary, we can close up the companionway and wait it out below where it may be uncomfortable, but at least it's relatively warm and dry. How different for Erik and his companions, protected only by leaky tarpaulins. Life had to be very wet, cold, and miserable. The steersman would struggle to keep the ship's stern to the waves, as she's thrust first one way, then another, in a furious sleigh ride. The crew would bale frantically and try to calm the frightened animals, while the women comforted children huddled in the bottom of the boat. Uncertain of their position, the sailors would scan anxiously ahead, fearful for the sound of breakers. For them it was a battle for survival. Of the twenty-five boats that left Breidafjord with such high hopes, only fourteen arrived to set up new homes in Greenland.

As waves roll after waves, cross swells force irregular pillars of water high above the others, forming grotesque figures before tumbling back into aqueous oblivion. Viking sailors returned to port describing an ocean inhabited by strange creatures. The *King's Mirror* describes many monsters sighted in Greenland waters, including the merman, a tall figure with a human form but no hands and a body that narrowed below the shoulders. He wore a peaked helmet. For a companion he had the mermaid, with a woman's body and a fish's tail complete with scales and fins. However, she's not the seductive siren of popular imagination, as she is described as "having a large and terrifying face, a sloping forehead and wide brows, a large mouth and wrinkled cheeks."

Secure in *Symphony*'s cockpit, I scan the angry seas for signs of fantastic creatures. Can these contorted waves be malevolent beings rising in anger? Are these descendants of mermen and mermaids? I see no monsters, but my eyes are skeptical and I've been taught to seek rational explanations for natural phenomena. I see the forms Vikings saw, but my modern mind cannot endow them with spirit and character. Maybe the Vikings' world was more frightening than ours, but it had a richness we try to visualize but can never feel.

Toward evening the seas begin to subside. We're three hundred miles farther south than Keflavik and the nights are longer and darker. The temperature is noticeably colder. We're nearing Cape Farewell, where icebergs swept south by the East Greenland current turn northwest toward Julianhåb. I've been monitoring ice faxes , and they show mostly open water around the Cape. A couple of black triangles indicate bergs east of the Cape with more in Julianhåb Bight. They appear widely spaced, but we're unsure how many bergs are represented by a single triangle. By the time the wind and seas have dropped, it is getting dark so we decide to remain hove to until morning. We now do this each night for the five hours of darkness.

This next morning is as calm as yesterday was furious. There are no bergs in sight, but I place a call to Ice Central through Julianhåb radio on 2182. There's no reply. A few minutes later I try again and this time hear "*Symphony, Symphony*, Radio Julianhåb, over." Our thrill at our first Greenland contact subsides when we're told our signal is weak and breaking up. However, it seems we can be understood, as we're patched though to Ice Central. I request an ice report and give our position. Through the static I hear good news: "Julianhåb is open all the way from Cape Farewell. There are no concentrations . . . just scattered bergs." I ask if that means we can just head straight for Julianhåb. The ice man repeats his message, adding encouragingly, "You should have no problems." I thank Ice Central and we press on, keeping a good lookout for "scattered bergs."

On July 29, eight days out from Keflavik, Les wakes me just as it gets light. It's calm. There's no wind, no waves, no ripples. Visibility is only about two miles, and overhead the sky is blanketed with cloud. More clouds are banked around the horizon. We motor steadily north, well west of the Kitsigsut Islands. One gray, fleecy cloud gradually creeps closer than the rest and seems to thicken as we approach. Finally it materializes into a shining lump of frozen water and we're face to face with our first berg. Many times we've imagined our first encounter with ice, wondering if it would be threatening, in bad weather, or at night. Now here it is, calm, peaceful, and benign. It drifts on the smooth sea like an abandoned sailing ship, a silent and icy *Marie Celeste*. We motor as close as we dare, mindful of its immense underwater volume.

This berg is but the first of many. One moment we're motoring across an empty ocean, the next we're in a world of floating ice mountains. We motor close in to take pictures—lots of pictures—quickly exhausting a roll of film. It's soon clear our first berg was not at all extraordinary, not really large, nor particularly attractive, nor colored especially well. In all respects it's far surpassed by the splendid ice sculptures that now float past on both sides. The whole panorama is decorated with floating white ornaments. There are far too many to count. Our apprehension gives way to fascination with the variety of shapes and sizes, and the extraordinary shades of white, blue, and green. Several bergs provide roosts for birds. Some bergs lie at the head of long streams of growlers. These apparently small lumps of ice have most of their mass below the surface, waiting to snag the hull of a careless boat. We fear these most and give them all a wide berth.

Les takes over the helm and I retire to the chart table to check for e-mail and to get the latest weather faxes. Suddenly there's an anxious call from the cockpit: "Trev, there are two bergs ahead. Is it okay to go between them?"

I check the radar. "There's just one . . . dead ahead," I call, adjusting the range and filter settings to insure I'm not missing something.

"Well, there's two out here," Les replies. "I can see them."

Still a novice at tracking bergs, I make more adjustments but still see only one berg. However, by now this is really close. Just as keen to miss a single iceberg as a pair, I race for the cockpit.

Through the fog I do indeed see two bergs, one on each side of the bow. Both have steep ice faces that rise from the sea and disappear into low overcast. Les slows *Symphony* to bare steerage and edges closer. Suddenly we see a faint shadow behind the walls of ice, and the pieces all fit. We're heading into a huge ice horseshoe. A chilly lagoon beckons us into its icy arms. The buttresses at each end were visible through the mist but not the more distant, curving ridge that connects the two. We turn sharply starboard to go round the side of the white monster.

In the afternoon the sky brightens and visibility improves, first extending to the natural horizon, and then the ceiling rises to reveal the coast of Greenland. Eventually mountain summits stand clear against the sky, a panorama of fantastic sharp ridges, vertical rock faces, snow-sprinkled slopes, and steep ice patches. One bold headland dominates the view at the seaward termination of a mighty ridge. It's Kap Egede, towering precipitously eighteen hundred feet from sea to sky. To Vikings it was Hvarf, the classic landmark for ships arriving in south Greenland. It stands sentinel at the southeastern extremity of Julianhåb Bight where the mountains fall back from the coast and the terrain becomes less rugged. Gaps in the hills provide entries to long fiords that once sheltered the farms of Eystribyggd, the Greenland Vikings' eastern settlement.

Ahead, a long promontory stretches along the horizon and terminates in Cape Desolation. Above the sawtooth ridges, the sky takes on a lurid yellow glow. We must be getting close to Julianhåb, the largest town and major port of southwest Greenland, as it lies this side of the promontory, near the mouth of the fiords. We'll call there to take on fresh food and water, and to introduce ourselves to Greenland before proceeding up the fiords to the sites of the Viking farms.

The weather now begins to deteriorate. We've been granted a window to enjoy our first magical view of Greenland's mountains. Now the curtains close to obliterate first the mountaintops, then the lower slopes. Soon it's misting, and then it turns to rain. Only the nearest part of the rocky coast is visible. The chart shows a light marking the entrance to Julianhåb Fiord, but it's obscured by densely packed bergs. The main channel is clear and we turn up the fiord. To starboard the rocky island of Akia has scrubby low vegetation. The rock is red and reminds us of the islands that shelter the Norwegian coast. The rain casts a dull pall over the scene.

Les steers *Symphony* across the fiord to Julianhåb harbor. Before entering we heave to and radio the harbormaster. It's late evening. Julianhåb Radio patches the call to the harbormaster's home. After a long wait, a woman's voice answers. I explain we're a sailing vessel looking for a berth. There's another pause, then the reply is a shock: "You cannot enter, we have no room." In disbelief, we try to explain that we're at the end of a long voyage, that we must report to Customs, that we're a small vessel and won't occupy much space. It's a frustrating and unsatisfactory negotiation. The harbormaster speaks no English and his wife is translating. Nevertheless, the message is clear: a large freighter is due in the morning and no space is available.

The call over, Les and I have a conference. We're tired and disappointed. We were both looking forward to a good night's sleep securely berthed in port. Nowhere else have we been turned away, not by large ports like Bergen or Reykjavik, nor villages like Stykkisholmur. Anchoring outside the harbor is unattractive. A large berg floats close by the harbor entrance. The water is deep, the bottom rocky, and no doubt anchoring is difficult. The pilot indicates an anchorage off Akia across the fiord, but this is inconvenient for Julianhåb. After some hesitation, Les calls back on the VHF. First she goes over much of the same discussion until as a last resort she asks if we might raft alongside a fishing vessel. There's another pause followed by a very different response: We can enter the harbor and tie up at the main wharf. The harbormaster will come to the dock and direct us to a suitable berth. As we motor slowly through the entrance, a small powerboat passes. A diminutive figure, dark-haired and dark-visaged, is at the helm. A rifle is propped against his seat and a dead seal is lashed across the small foredeck.

The harbormaster arrives with his wife and son. They explain they first expected a ship much bigger than *Symphony* and direct us to an unoccupied section of wharf where we tie up to large metal cleats. The dock is modern, with steel bulkheads, and there's not a truck tire in sight. It's been a long day. We have spaghetti and meat sauce with wine for dinner and fall into a long, deep sleep.

Chapter 11

The World's End

It's already late when diffused light filters through the portholes and works its way into my consciousness. For the first time in nine days *Symphony* is still and there's no call from Les to take over the watch. I roll over and settle in to sleep longer. Distant sounds, faint echoes of people working, grow steadily more audible. I ignore them at first, but they grow more insistent and I become curious. A cup of coffee seems more and more desirable. Finally the need to visit the head forces me out of the bunk.

I push back the companionway hatch and a flood of gray daylight invades the saloon. Everything seems in order. *Symphony* rests quietly against the red hull of *Aleqaittuk*, a coastal passenger boat. A freighter, also red, is moored just a few yards astern. Shipping containers swing beneath tall cranes from the freighter to the wharf where trucks and forklifts scurry back and forth to prevent the pile from getting too high. My half-awake mind struggles to assimilate these new images. Suddenly I realize things aren't what they were! There was no red boat when we turned in last night. We had tied up directly against the steel bulkhead.

Les is now wide awake. We both dress quickly and climb up onto *Aleqaittuk*. A crewman by the cabin entrance speaks no English, but he calls a colleague who emerges to explain how we became neighbors. *Aleqaittuk* arrived late to find all dock space occupied. The crew shouted and banged on *Symphony*'s hull, but when this failed to arouse us, they assumed we were not on board. They untied our lines, tied *Symphony* alongside *Aleqaittuk*, and reset the lines—all while we slept! Several sailors join us at the cabin doorway. Our neighbors aboard the ferry show their amusement at our confusion with wide, toothy grins. We chat for a while in halting English, learning that *Aleqaittuk* operates between here and Narsarsuaq, calling at small communities on the way. It seems we've taken her regular berth. Everyone is extremely good-humored. Later, to avoid our having to move each time *Aleqaittuk* arrives or leaves, the harbormaster finds us a new berth on the opposite side of the wharf.

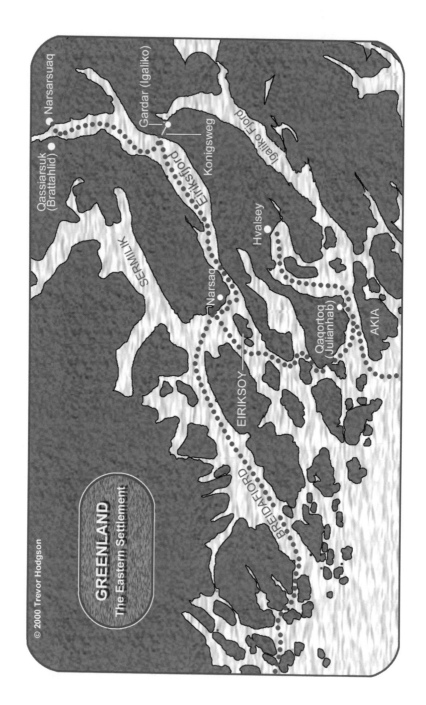

© 2000 Trevor Hodgson

GREENLAND
The Eastern Settlement

Narsarsuaq

Qassiarsuk
(Brattahlid)

Gardar (Igaliko)

Konigsweg

Igaliko Fjord

SERMILIK

Eiriksfjord

Hvalsey

Narsaq

Qaqortoq
(Julianhab)

AKIA

EIRIKSOY

BREIDAFJORD

Julianhåb spreads over seven small hills between the fiord and the inland mountains. A few small historic buildings, remnants of an eighteenth-century Danish trading post, cluster round the only fountain in Greenland. A shallow river flows down from surrounding hills to thread its way between the houses. A road bridge is a favorite fishing spot for young boys. Modern buildings surrounding the center are frame-built and relatively small, while a little farther out, blocks of apartments appear to be community housing. Occasional cars and trucks drive along the mile or so of surfaced road. Most side roads and pathways that weave between the buildings have rocks protruding through compacted mud. The town is busy and people walk briskly about their business. Several greet us with shy smiles as we pass on the street. Men of various ages sit in an uneven line along the front of one old building. In the afternoon many clasp bottles of beer—sold only between noon and 3:00 P.M.—and by midafternoon their smiles are very genial. One small, elderly woman with wrinkled features, dressed completely in black, stops to engage us in animated Greenlandic. She seems distressed. We cannot understand her and stand bemused until she turns away, muttering incomprehensibly as she goes.

The huge rust-red storage buildings of the Royal Arctic Company dominate the harbor. Pallets and shipping containers occupy much of the wharf. A stack of deteriorated animal pelts lies neglected by the road. The dock is the busiest place in town. Apart from a few people who take the helicopter from Narsarsuaq Airport, everything and everyone coming to Julianhåb must come to this wharf. It's now the height of the short tourist season and Greenlanders from other coastal towns are visiting relatives and friends. A small crowd gathers on the quay to bid farewell to each departing ship. The bright red coveralls of employees stand out among a few Danish, German, and Norwegian tourists who gather on the wharf in hiking pants, parkas, and boots.

Finding particular stores here is not easy. Most are difficult to identify, as they show only simple Greenlandic signs and their warehouse-like exteriors have no windows or product displays. We interrupt a dockworker long enough to get directions to the local food store.

Locating it proves easy as it's "the blue building on the hill" and clearly visible from the harbor. The supermarket stocks a wider range than we expect. We wander along shelves of generally familiar items, with most packaged goods coming from Denmark. We buy a few things not available on passage: fresh meat and fish, fruit, bread, cheese, tomatoes, and rolled lamb.

Although the supermarket is in general like those elsewhere, the town market offers shopping unlike any we've seen before. It's a concrete structure, rather like a large run-down bus shelter, overlooking the harbor from a small level area by the main road. Three or four men dressed in thick dark trousers and heavy jackets stand in the open doorway. Earflaps on their black caps hang loose. The men appear bored and resigned to a long day with little excitement.

The interior of the market is dim. Other than the doorway, only two small windows, high on one wall, admit any light. The merchandise is displayed on folding tables. To the right, piles of cod, salmon, and arctic char all look very fresh, while on the left are assorted chunks of dark red meat, still on the bone and very bloody. This can only be seal meat and it's not at all appetizing. Two men stand by the tables. One calls out and smiles broadly as he brandishes a piece of seal meat. Outside the market, women tend displays of dried fish and cuts of reindeer. However, most shoppers hover round a low bench against the wall of the market piled with fresh fish. Les watches local women make their selections and in turn points to a large, dark-spotted, silver fish. The fifty-or-so-year-old Greenlandic stallholder speaks no English, but a woman in line translates the cost.

The lack of a bag for our purchase produces a minor crisis. After much consultation among the vendors and some searching behind tables, a plastic bag is found somewhere inside the market and provided for an extra charge. Later we learn we've bought ocean catfish.

Greenland is very different from other places we've been. Somewhere between here and Keflavik we've crossed a distinct ethnic, cultural, and climatic boundary. To the east, complexions are fair and eyes are blue, the people direct descendants of Scandinavian settlers. Very similar languages, all derived from Old Norse, are spoken throughout Norway, the Faroes, and Iceland. Street names commonly end with some variation of the Norse word for street, *gata*. Øvregaten runs right behind the Bryggen in Bergen, and Havnargøtn runs by the harbor at Torshavn, as does Geirsgata in Reykjavik. Here in Kalaallit Nunaat (Greenland) the people are small and their faces noticeably darker. English is less common. There are few street signs and the map is a profusion of unpronounceable q's and k's quite unlike anything European.

It seems odd that we're actually four hundred miles farther south than Reykjavik. We left Icelandic evenings of extended twilight and arrived here to find real nights with five hours of darkness. Despite its name (reputedly bestowed by Ravens-Floki) Iceland has a mild climate, warmed by the North Atlantic Drift. Here in Greenland, icebergs float past the harbor entrance emphasizing the significantly lower temperature. Cold itself is not a problem, but we now begin a protracted battle with condensation inside the boat. Every part of the boat, and everything in it, is damp. Try as we might, we cannot get rid of it. By the time we reach Newfoundland, we're resigned to stripping out everything as the only means of getting dry.

While ships have long been important in all the Nordic lands, in Greenland they're still essential for everyday life. No roads connect coastal communities, and inland travel through the mountains and over the icecap is impossible. Vehicles operate within villages, but trucks serve only local needs and cars are an expensive luxury. All goods and people move by ship. Those living outside the town use small powerboats to get to stores and schools, and to obtain medicine and other supplies and services.

Shortly after we return to *Symphony*, two customs officers climb down to the deck from the wharf. One seems nervous, apparently in training or under supervision. It has started to rain and the paperwork in his hand is wet. He sits at the saloon table puzzling over the form as though it's unfamiliar. His companion looks on but makes no effort to help. Fortunately the text is in English as well as Greenlandic and Danish, and I speed the process by offering answers to the questions over the officer's shoulder while pointing to the appropriate box.

We declare the familiar items: a few personal details, information about *Symphony*, and a record of the alcohol on board. Eventually the form is completed to everyone's satisfaction and our visitors leave, directing us to report with passports to the police. We do, but find the police post closed. A woman leaving the building confirms that policing is over for the day and will resume at nine o'clock tomorrow morning. We return conscientiously and a young Danish officer, apparently surprised we bothered to call, glances quickly through the pages of our passports. Having completed the right motions, he hands them back and wishes us an enjoyable visit.

At the post office we have difficulty understanding how to make international phone calls. A short Danish man with a large, round, bald head overhears our conversation and explains the workings of the system and times of operation. His advice is good and we get through without further trouble. Our daughter is relieved to hear we've arrived safely and in turn reassures us that all's well at home. Julianhåb is a small place and we run into our Danish friend again at the local garage, which it seems he operates. He explains that the Inuit name Qaqortoq is replacing the Danish Julianhåb and tutors us in the correct pronunciation. "Q," we learn, is pronounced "ch" as in the Scottish "loch" and requires blowing while partially closing the back of the throat. We practice hard and feel accomplished when local people appear to understand us and when radio operators respond to our calls.

One historic building now serves as the local museum, with a small but interesting collection. A room dedicated to artifacts of the ancient Inuit is filled with kayaks, skin clothing, and primitive tools. Another displays items from the Viking period including a replica of a bishop's miter, wood carved with runic inscriptions, and a soapstone spindle weight.

From *Symphony*'s berth we can see the skeletal antennae of Radio Julianhåb on a hill overlooking the harbor. A visit to the station is a chance to meet the operators and offers a little (much needed) exercise as well as a bird's-eye view of the village. An irregular route leads uphill past a large school and between several houses. There's no sign to identify the radio station building. Through heavy double doors, up a flight of stairs, and along a long empty corridor, we find two casually dressed men surrounded by several control panels with numerous knobs and colored lights. They welcome us and proudly show off the station equipment and maps of their broadcast area. They issue forecasts in English, but names of areas and places are all in Greenlandic, which the Government encourages in place of the

Danish names shown on charts. We've been unable to locate any of these places, rendering the forecasts of little use. Other mariners have obviously had the same problem, as we're handed a chartlet with a numerical code for each area included in the broadcasts.

On the walk downhill the village and harbor spread out before us. Qaqortoq (as we now call it) lies in a bowl surrounded on three sides by rocky, brown hills. A river flows from an inland lake through town. White, brown, and yellow houses are spread over the lower slopes. However, our eyes are irresistibly drawn to the bright red ships and the rusty-red Royal Arctic warehouses. Trails of light mist hang over the harbor and settlement. The water itself is dark gray, while several crisp white bergs float by the harbor entrance.

Our brief tour of Qaqortoq ends back at *Symphony* with both of us ready to sit and relax. While lighting the stove to heat water for tea, I glance aft, through the cockpit to the stern. Something isn't right. I look again and realize the ensign is missing. Someone has climbed aboard during our absence to unclip the flag from the staff. I feel a rush of anger. Our home has been violated. I scan the wharf in a futile hope of spotting the perpetrator among the stacks of shipping containers. I well know there's nothing to be done. A quick look round shows nothing else amiss. By the time I've finished a cup of tea, my anger has subsided and I'm ready to see the theft as a high-spirited prank. Now I imagine the flag on the wall of a small home and a Greenlander with a cheeky grin pointing to it proudly as a trophy snatched from "the American yacht."

"Qaqortoq" means "the White Place," from field ice and ice floes that collect in the fiord. The largest community in southwest Greenland, the town stands near the seaward end of a complex of fiords that extend inland for sixty miles. For over four hundred years this was Eystribyggd, the Vikings' eastern settlement, a community of four thousand people living in farms along the shores of the fiords. Another system of fiords near modern Nuuk (formerly Godthåb) was called Vestribyggd, the western settlement. Before heading to Nuuk and on across Davis Strait to Labrador, we want to explore these southwestern fiords. At the top of our list is the best preserved of all Greenland's Viking remains, the church at Hvalsey.

The morning is not promising. The sky is overcast and light drizzle ensures that everything drips with water. There's no wind. As we breakfast beneath the dodger, a small powerboat pulls up to a nearby slipway. A family of five, apparently from an outlying community, climbs ashore and heads for the stores with shopping bags. They leave the boat just as we'd park a car at home. About 1030 I untie the lines and Les backs *Symphony* from her berth and motors into the fiord, detouring round a large berg grounded just outside the harbor entrance. The town soon disappears behind a steep rocky bluff and we turn north into Qaqortoq Fiord. It's wide and dotted with bergs. On the starboard bow, three or four modern buildings perch on a small strip of land at the southern tip of Arpatsivik Island while abeam the view extends across a wide stretch of open water to a backdrop of mountains.

Where the fiord curves round north of Arpatsivik, we maneuver carefully to avoid an unseen mid-channel rock, the only obstacle on the chart. Qaqortoq Mountain rises in rough, rocky steps to over three thousand feet and towers above a wide coastal slope of rough grass. The sun breaks through the overcast to add sparkle to waterfalls cascading down rocky channels. We search the shore for the church. There are several rock piles, but all lack the regular form of a building. We move closer. Finally we distinguish a small stone building low down below a rocky cliff. It looks minute, emphasizing the massive scale of the mountain behind.

The fiord is deep, only shallowing close to the shore, and we approach slowly with our eyes fixed on the depth sounder. Two hundred yards from the rocks the anchor clatters to the bottom in thirty feet and sets first time. We're keen to explore, but when the engine stops, we're captivated by the profound stillness. The clouds have rolled away to reveal a beautiful, spring-like day. There's no one around. There are no other boats. All we can see is ours. We pause to inhale the mountain air and absorb the majesty of the scene. It's too nice to hurry, so we spoil ourselves with a leisurely picnic of rolled mutton, ham, brie, pâté, and crusty, fresh bread with glasses of cold white wine.

Such a lunch deserves a siesta, but after no more than a brief rest, we force ourselves to get going. I heave the dinghy from the lazarette where we stored it in Iceland and inflate it on the foredeck. A short row takes us to a rock platform. We tie the painter to a rock, scramble up a six-foot bank, and continue up a grassy slope.

The long sides of the stone church lie parallel to the shore. Window openings in the four-foot-thick south wall frame exquisite views of the fiord. The rough walls, the rectangular plan, and patterns of light on the rough stone remind us of Kirkjubør's unfinished cathedral and of Viking churches we've seen in the Orkneys. The main doorway in the gabled western wall overlooks extensive stone piles that were once walls of a farmhouse, great hall, and byres. The sunshine casts sharp shadows. The air is still. Calls of distant seabirds provide a musical background. Yellow flowers carpet the hillside. We sit on a low rock wall watching a pair of snow buntings fly industriously to and from their nest in the church wall. Before each sortie, the male perches momentarily on a prominent rock. He surveys his domain, then swoops low over the rough grass in the search for food.

In 1406 an Icelandic ship arrived here and stayed four years before returning with a hold full of hides and walrus tusks. It was an eventful and historic visit. Kollgrim, a local man, seduced Steinum, an Icelander traveling with her husband, by "enticing her with the black arts." The consequences were severe, as Kollgrim was burned here "in accordance with the law." I look up and down the shore. Just where in this idyllic place did flames rise up to consume the hapless Greenlander? It's difficult to imagine such an event. Steinum suffered too. After the death of her lover, she was "never in her right mind" and soon died.

Much happier was the wedding in September 1408 of Sigrid, a local girl, to Torstein, one of the Icelanders. The banns were called on three Sundays, and the bride's family, her friends, and the crew of the Icelandic ship packed the church for the marriage. After the ceremony, the wedding party filed out to a reception in the great hall. It was a time for celebration, of looking forward to a new family and a happy future. Maybe the sun shone as it does today and celebrants spilled out onto the terrace to enjoy the magnificent setting.

Sigrid's departure for her new life in Iceland must have been tearful. Travel between Iceland and Greenland was infrequent and unreliable and it was unlikely she'd see her family again. In this moment of personal sadness no one could foresee or comprehend the catas-

The ruined farm and church at Hvalsey. A wedding here was the last recorded event at the Norse colony in Greenland

trophe that would soon engulf the whole community. As the Greenlanders watched the ship's square sail grow smaller, they couldn't know it was their last goodbye to the outside world. For many years the world heard nothing of Greenland. When the next European ship eventually called, there was no sign of the community, not here at Hvalsey, not at Gardar, not at Brattahlid, not anywhere. The entire Viking settlement had disappeared without a trace. The colony founded by Erik over four hundred years before was gone.

What could have caused such a calamity? Many explanations have been offered, but the full story is still unclear. From the thirteenth century the climate deteriorated, adversely affecting livestock and crops. Ice extended from the north, obstructing traditional sailing routes. The Inuit, better adapted to the harsher climate, gradually claimed more of the northern territory, and conflict was inevitable in the competition for food and living space. The Viking colony always needed overseas trade exporting furs, ivory, and falcons and other exotic wildlife in return for manufactured goods and critical supplies of timber. Without timber to build ships, descendants of Viking sailors became dependent on others to carry their goods.

In 1262 the Greenlanders became subject to the king of Norway for the promise of at least one trade ship each year. The promise wasn't kept and this lonely European outpost was simply ignored. It's a tribute to the settlers' resourcefulness that they survived so long.

To reach our next anchorage near the village of Narsaq, we first retrace our morning's route. Our anchor comes up enveloped in a forest of thick yellow weed that takes several minutes of prodding and pulling with the boat hook to remove. We return along Qaqortoq Fiord, sipping mugs of tea as *Symphony* motors through smooth water. Slowly the sky darkens and a light wind fills in on the bow.

Near Qaqortoq a humpback gives a magnificent display of arched flukes as he slides below the water. A few moments later a solitary seal watches us inquisitively, heedless of nearby hunters who covet his fur and meat. We urge him to flee for safety. A coastal freighter overtakes us and turns into Mato Løb, a narrow passage leading between the mountains to the next fiord. This is our route too and we follow as she steams unhesitatingly through a particularly thin section between steep rock walls. Through a landlocked bay, we turn left and

An iceberg near Narsaq in southwest Greenland

then right to join Eiriksfiord.

The fiord is divided by the island of Eiriksöy (now Igdlutalik), where Erik the Red reputably spent his first winter after sailing from Iceland. It's a rather ordinary, featureless mountain and we search unsuccessfully for any site that might have been that historic camp. Leaving Eiriksöy to starboard we work first one way then the other to find a clear passage between packed icebergs. Some are immense, towering overhead and dwarfing *Symphony*'s mast. Many glisten as the light catches them, but one is extremely dirty as though dragged through a huge cauldron of mud. A powerboat passes at high speed in the opposite direction, its young crew perhaps heading for a night out in Qaqortoq. We continue to thread our way between closely packed bergs all across Narsaq Fiord and enter a large bay marked on the chart as Narsaq Ilua. To reach the anchorage we must pass through a formidable line of monstrous icebergs grounded along the sixty-foot depth contour. We edge slowly through, but we're barely clear when a sudden crash has us looking anxiously astern. Water swirls and froths and ice bobs to the surface where a large chunk of berg has split away and collapsed into the water. We head for shallow water at the head of the bay and find good holding at the first try in seventeen feet.

Tonight dinner is special. As we boarded the dinghy to leave Hvalsey, we found an extensive colony of mussels. We gathered enough for a meal in a plastic bag and placed them in a bucket of seawater, to clean them as we sailed. They make a fine starter and are followed by tender chicken, rice, and tomatoes. Dessert is canned pears and the meal is accompanied with red wine. We feel very satisfied with a fine meal to end a memorable day.

The next morning is calm and sunny. The air is still. The few sparse sounds have the clarity of fragile crystal. Cries of birds circling the cliffs have unusual intimacy. Distant shouts of three people walking on the beach are unnaturally audible. The sun illuminates the smallest details of the rocks and imparts subtle colors to bare mountains cleft by snow-filled gullies. The bergs glisten. Occasionally a loud crash shatters the stillness as large lumps of ice break from the bergs. They tumble into turquoise water so clear that patches of sand and clumps of bottom weed are clearly visible. Places like this are hard to leave and such moments live long in the memory. We sit together on deck quietly absorbing the scenery, the sounds, and the atmosphere, anxious that our senses capture every aspect, every nuance, of the moment.

Our route continues up Eiriksfjord (Tunugdliarfik on today's charts) toward Erik the Red's farm at Brattahlid. We expect to see several boats conveying people to and from the airport at Narsarsuaq, but apart from a distant view of *Aleqaittuk* we see only two small powerboats. A few bergs add exquisite decoration to the mountain scenery but pose no obstacle to our progress. Before pressing on to Brattahlid, we plan to visit Gardar Cathedral, once the center of the Church in Greenland. These remains overlook a neighboring fiord and are reached by the Königsweg (King's Way), a rough bridle path across an isthmus two miles wide. We intend to leave *Symphony* in a small bay while we walk to the cathedral. The bay is open to the west, and we edge close to the southern shore to gain what shelter we can and drop the hook in thirty-five feet. A small motor cruiser is moored close to the beach, where there's an upturned, open boat and an inflatable. Thick clouds roll over the mountains and it starts to rain. We sit under the dodger and watch a camping party paddle up in three kayaks. They huddle beneath plastic sheets until the shower blows over and then set up three tents on a small rise.

We hesitate to set out for Gardar, as dark clouds threaten more rain and cast doubt on our getting there and back without a good soaking. We always worry about leaving *Symphony* unattended in remote places. Our greatest concern is that the wind will increase, the anchor drag, and *Symphony* will run ashore. However carefully we secure her, we're always relieved when she's safe at anchor on our return. The sky brightens a little and after several hesitations we decide the weather should be okay for a couple of hours. We stuff rain gear and cameras in the waterproof bag, launch the dinghy, and row to the small sandy beach. A single-track dirt roadway leads to a low ridge with dramatic views both ways along Eiriksfjord. Then it descends to another bay and joins the Königsweg that leads gradually uphill away from the fiord.

Once, this bridleway connected the colony's political center at Brattahlid with the bishop's seat at Gardar. Its natural line across the flank of the mountain was no doubt taken by the most powerful in the land. The surface is pebbled and the grass at the side provides easier walking. A long slope on our left leads down to an extensive farm where harvesting is in full swing. Three tractors follow each other round a large field, leaving behind cylindrical, plastic-wrapped bales of hay. From a small plateau we can look down into Igaliko Fiord and the scattered houses of the village.

The roadway descends in a long, well-graded curve. Guided by a small map from the Qaqortoq tourist office, we search for cathedral remains in an area of rough, open ground east of the village. There's no sign of ruins, and the landscape doesn't match the map. We stride out to intercept a solitary hiker, a rather austere European woman with anorak, hiking boots, and small backpack, who directs us to the center of the modern settlement. It turns out our map is a simple plan of the ruins and neglects to show its location right among the modern houses.

Remains of the cathedral walls are not evident until we're quite close. Local residents using stones for more recent construction have exacerbated the erosion of six hundred harsh winters. Tall grass obscures sections of wall, and some exploring is needed to appreciate the full extent of the ruin. A couple of lintels mark former doorways. A faded tourist sign identifies the site and provides a little background information. Modern buildings nearby with painted sides and metal roofs are not at all picturesque, and the rather overgrown site looks ignored, like a neglected garden. This was once the most westerly of all Christian cathedrals. Sounds of medieval Latin wafted across the fiord as the church tended the souls of four thousand of Christendom's most isolated adherents. In 1492, as Columbus set out on his historic expedition, Pope Alexander VI wrote: "The church at Gardar is situated at the World's End."

Little remains to suggest this former importance. Gone are the ceremonies, the colorful robes, the bell calling the faithful to worship. The only sounds now are the desultory chopping of wood and the plaintive cries of gulls circling overhead. However, if the site is neglected, the setting is splendid. Vikings certainly had sharp eyes for beautiful scenery. A wide plain leads down to the fiord that is ringed by high mountains. I take several photos.

The return to the top of Königsweg is steep enough to get us in

Ice blocks the way to Brattahlid

low gear, but quite short. At the summit the rain, which has been long threatening, at last begins. Fortunately it proves to be just a short shower. We cover the long downhill walk to *Symphony* at a brisk pace. In thirty minutes we're relaxing on board, well satisfied with our excursion and pleased to find everything shipshape. We haul the dinghy onto the foredeck and lash it to the lifeline stanchions. It's time for dinner.

As we clean the last spaghetti from our plates, we feel a gentle but distinct bang on the hull. We both leap up and rush to the cockpit. A growler, a small berg no more than three feet high, has been carried into the bay by the incoming tide and now drifts slowly alongside. It has dealt *Symphony* only a light blow and caused no damage. However, through the twilight we see a much larger piece of ice drifting down on us. It's time to move. Once the anchor's up and stripped of its long strands of fibrous hair, we motor to the northern corner of the bay and reset it. Here we're in shallow water and well away from any visible bergs. It's more open to the west, but the wind is light and easterly. Even when the wind builds later, we're well protected in the lee of the land and enjoy a comfortable night.

The next morning *Symphony* is shrouded in mist. The air feels damp. We're slow to rise—Brattahlid is just a dozen miles up the fiord and from there it's only another two miles to our overnight berth at Narsarsuaq. We have a leisurely breakfast. As we stow the final items in preparation for leaving, we feel a strange presence. Overhead a dark shadow moves slowly through the fog. Suddenly a huge bird flies overhead with wings maintaining a slow rhythmic beat. It completes a leisurely circle and settles on a ledge halfway up a vertical cliff. It sits imperiously, surveying the bay and keeping us under its watchful gaze. There's a scramble for binoculars, then great excitement. Distinctive brown plumage and lighter chest feathers identify our first closeup view of a white-tailed eagle.

There are no bergs in the anchorage, but as we turn from the cliff we see that the fiord, yesterday all open water, is now full of ice. The easterly wind has carried hundreds of bergs from a glacier at the head of a nearby tributary fiord, packing them together to form an imposing barrier across our route. Suddenly we have serious doubts of reaching Brattahlid. The ice is too thick for a direct passage, so we set

Symphony anchored at Brattahlid, the home of Erik the Red

off across the fiord—along the edge of the pack—in the hope of finding open water. A visible thinning of the ice toward the far shore encourages us, but there's no open passage so eventually we turn up the fiord to seek a route through. Les steers while I stand at the bow, boat hook in hand, to fend off ice that gets too close. I scan ahead and call to Les on the best way through. We weave between growlers and I push away small pieces. With several long detours to avoid the larger bergs, we eventually break out into open water after a passage that proves easier than we expect.

The chain again rattles through the bow roller and we anchor a few yards off the village and sheep-rearing station of Qagssiarssuk. Once, this was Brattahlid, home of Erik the Red and the center of Viking social and political life. We land at a sandy inlet and walk just a few yards inland past a small house to find the remains of Erik's farm in classic Viking position on sloping ground.

Like Gardar, the grass between the walls could do with a trim. A modern green sculpture overlooks the stone foundations from a small rock outcrop, and another commemorative plaque is set into the ground. No doubt these were commissioned with appropriate ceremony and fine words. Now they seem abandoned like confetti left by departed wedding guests. Nevertheless, of all the sites we visit, Brattahlid is special. Here's the home of the complex man who pioneered the most challenging leg of the first known crossing of the Atlantic Ocean. He made this place the acknowledged center of the most distant outpost of European culture. It was a remarkable achievement. Following his banishment from Iceland, he survived three years in Greenland with no help from the outside, explored hundreds of miles of coastline, navigated miles and miles through treacherous waters, and then found his way back to Breidafjord. It was a great feat of self-reliance, exploration, and navigation. He then returned with his fleet of émigrés and established a flourishing community in this beautiful but harsh landscape. The homicidal son of a homicidal father, Erik was also a farmer, sailor, explorer, settler, community leader, and chieftain. Violent, brave, and proud, he exemplifies many aspects of the complex Viking character.

It was here at Brattahlid that an aging Erik passed the torch of exploration to a new generation of Vikings. His own eldest son, Leif,

realized the family destiny to complete the first European voyage to
America. Leif is known to history as Leif the Lucky, the bringer of
Christianity to Greenland and the discoverer of America. Apparently
he had none of his father's antisocial tendencies, so while Erik is seen
as a scurrilous brigand whose courage and initiative evoke admira-
tion, Leif has become a pure romantic hero.

Prominent among others who gathered at Erik's fireside on long
winter nights was Thorfinn Karlsevni, a prosperous Icelandic mer-
chant who led perhaps the best organized expedition to Vinland, the
newly discovered land to the southwest. His wife, Gudrid, was by his
side to hear the plans for settlement. She accompanied her husband
on his expedition and gave birth to Snorri, the first American child
born of European parents.

A small white-painted church stands behind the farm in an enclosure of rough-cut grass. Large, round hay bales lie along the perimeter. A few feet from the church door is the raised sod base of a tiny
rectangular chapel. Reputedly, Erik's wife, Thjodhild, prayed here
when she converted to Christianity shortly after coming to Greenland.
Erik venerated Thor throughout his life, and religious differences
became an emotional issue between Erik and Thjodhild. Both were
willing to sacrifice for their beliefs. Thjodhild refused to share Erik's
bed as long as he remained a pagan, while Erik refused to relinquish
his commitment to "Red Beard."

> Erik was reluctant to abandon his old religion; but his
> wife, Thjodhild, was converted at once, and she had a church
> built not too close to the farmstead. This building was called
> Thjodhild's Church, and there she and the many others who
> had accepted Christianity would offer up their prayers.
> Thjodhild refused to live with Erik after she was converted,
> and this annoyed him greatly.
>
> *The Saga of Erik the Red*

Brattahlid occupies an attractive setting. Like those at Hvalsey
and Gardar, the ancient stones set against a background of icebergs,
fiord, and towering peaks form a striking composition. Our eyes roam
the surrounding mountains. Below bare summits lie steep slopes,

green with vegetation. In naming the land "Greenland," Erik may have stretched the truth in an effort to lure visitors. For several months each year the land is bare and inhospitable, hidden beneath layers of thick snow and ice. However, few who come here and see it on a day like this can feel disappointed or mislead.

We sail directly across the fiord toward a gap in the encircling ring of mountains. For many years Narsarsuaq ("the Big Plain") was a U.S. Air Force base, one of a chain of stations linking North America and Europe. When the Americans left in the late 1950s, it became the region's major airport. A little west of the airport is a small harbor that is our own overnight berth. A large gray bulk obscures the wharf. As we get closer, it becomes a fisheries protection ship occupying the whole outer face of the dock. Fortunately, local fishing boats on the inside face of the wharf have left just enough room for us to tie up. Once *Symphony* is secure, we climb up to the wharf where a small elderly Dane greets us eagerly, announcing, "The Queen is coming . . . here . . . tomorrow afternoon." It seems Margrethe, Queen of Denmark, is celebrating twenty-five years on the throne, with her first visit to her Greenlandic realm since 1979. She's scheduled to arrive by private jet and board the Danish royal yacht, *Danabrög*, for a tour of coastal settlements. The naval vessel at the dock is part of the royal escort.

The morning of the royal visit is sunny. A Danish "inspection ship" (frigate) arrives, bristling with antennae and carrying a helicopter on her aft deck. She ties up for a couple of hours to take on stores (forcing the fisheries vessel onto a precarious berth at the very end of the wharf) and then moves off to anchor in the fiord. Shortly after lunch an excited call turns all eyes down the fiord where *Danabrög* steams toward us, framed by icebergs and mountains. She's a classic steam yacht and reminds me of photographs of the early-twentieth-century ships of the New York Yacht Club. Her varnished woodwork is smooth and shiny, and polished brass fittings glint in the sun. Her approach brings to the wharf several officials with well-braided caps. *Danabrög* draws parallel to the quay, and monkey fists arch through the air and bounce on the dock. The crew of the fisheries ship scurries to retrieve them and haul in the heavy dock lines. White-suited sailors quickly secure the lines on board. A boarding ladder swings down to the wharf. A marine guard marches stiffly down the steps, stops when his feet reach the quay, and snaps to attention, drawn sword at the ready.

Immediately several crates are carried aboard from a waiting truck. While the navy restocks, we walk to the settlement. A pickup is parked by the roadside. One section of roadway is screened off by a combination of small orange cones and water-filled plastic bottles. A gray-haired Dane is supervising a young Greenlander filling potholes with concrete. Obviously everything must look its best for the royal visitors!

Buildings straggle along the airport perimeter. We pass a small generating plant, workshops, and apartments. A large bus stands outside a modern hotel waiting to shuttle passengers two hundred yards to the airport buildings. A museum, probably once part of the U.S. base, has two rooms devoted to displays of local Viking artifacts including: an oar blade, a wooden model of the stern of a ship, wooden toggles, the plank of a ship, and a shroud pin found at Brattahlid. There are also good displays of Inuit history, lots of artifacts and photographs from the former U.S. base "Bluie West One," and a collection of photographs of life in modern Greenland.

The headquarters of Ice Central are in the main airport building. There are few people in the small departure area as we approach a security guard by a metal detector, who directs us to a small doorway. We walk into the office and begin to introduce ourselves:

"We're traveling by sailboat. . . ."

"Ah! You must be *Symphony!*" calls out a middle-aged Dane with a smile. We're taken aback. It never occurred to us we'd be remembered for one brief radio call several days ago. Ice Central is operated by the Danish Meteorological Institute, and Søren and Gert are on assignment from the Danish navy. They spend six months here on duty and then get a period at home. It's much better, they tell us, than being at sea. They give us a booklet outlining the history of Ice Central and show us their huge operational map that dominates the center of their office. The Americans left it behind over forty years ago.

Despite everyone's excitement and the preparations of the navy, the royal visit does not go as planned. First the royals are delayed by storms in the north of Greenland. Then the queen injures her knee and must fly home to Denmark, leaving her husband, son, and daughter-in-law to continue a rescheduled tour on her behalf. The navy is given a new rendezvous with the royal party farther along the coast, and both ships steam off in the middle of the night.

The next morning is wet and we stay below. By half past one the sky is clear and we decide to hike to the edge of the inland icecap. A young Danish woman at the small tourist office describes it as a three-hour walk each way, but later we discover that the start of the trail is itself about an hour from the harbor. We hesitate to leave so late, but there's plenty of daylight remaining and we hope to make up a little time along the way. The start's very promising. We've walked just a short way when a pickup stops and the young driver offers us a ride to the beginning of the trail. We accept readily.

The trailhead is at the end of Hospital Valley, once a significant U.S. medical facility, now eroded to a solitary, tall chimney projecting above low vegetation. A broad path leads off through beautiful and well-named Blomsterdalen, "Flower Valley." Les makes several stops, crouching in the undergrowth to photograph plants with the camera just inches from her subjects. We pass two groups of walkers already returning; the members of one party in particular look very tired. The path continues through a wide, cultivated valley. We step carefully on large steppingstones across a fast-flowing river and arrive at the foot of a very daunting, steep cliff.

Four or five serious-looking hikers are resting. Their companions, who are still descending, cling to thick blue ropes fixed at intervals to the rock. We wait and watch. The hikers move clumsily and make the climb seem difficult. They appear thankful to reach the bottom and we set off with some trepidation. The cliff is certainly steep. Several rock steps are covered with wet, slippery earth and we're pleased to have the ropes to hang onto. It's strenuous but fortunately not difficult. Soon we're at the top where the trail leads off downhill into a shallow valley. The grade is moderate, but it's discouraging to lose much of our hard-won altitude. Worse, we know we must climb it again when we return. At least the walking is easy here along a path winding between smooth, glaciated rock outcrops.

The ice proves worth the effort. The glacier terminates in a steep edge twenty feet thick. The surface is inundated with grit where it has scraped the valley sides, and the top is a confused jumble of sharp ridges separated by irregular chasms. Some areas have been washed by running water and display dazzling blues, greens, and whites, like the bergs in the fiord. Elsewhere the surface is dull and opaque.

We stay just long enough to eat a chocolate bar, as the air near the ice is chilly and it is starting to drizzle. We make good time on the return leg but cannot outpace the weather. As we near the high cliff the rain becomes heavy. The steep descent proves not too difficult but needs care. The sloping rock ledges are slippery. In places we push between thick, wet bushes growing in pockets of soil. The fixed ropes are reassuring. Soon we stride purposefully along past irrigation pipes and on through Flower Valley. All the time, rain pours down. Our thin plastic rainsuits are quite inadequate and soon our clothes are soaked. The sight of the hospital chimney makes us feel nearly home, but there's no pickup to carry us the last three or four miles. By the time we reach *Symphony*, we're more than ready for dry clothes, food, and sleep.

For our sail back to Narsaq along Eiriksfjord, we're joined by Robert, an air traffic controller from Melbourne, Australia, who's exploring Greenland in his hiking boots and with a large backpack. We've run into him several times since we docked at Narsarsuaq: on the wharf, at the top of the steep cliff on our way to the icecap, and again in the small grocery as we bought fresh food. Robert intended to travel aboard *Aleqaittuk*, but she's apparently disabled and not expected to resume service for several days. He prefers to hitchhike rather than wait.

The ice that filled the fiord two days ago has disappeared, leaving only a few bergs and we enjoy a beautiful, peaceful motor cruise under a sunny sky. The mountains are stunning. The sun penetrates cracks and gullies to reveal extraordinary detail. I try to assess rock faces and fissures as climbing routes. Once, the easier lines would have made appealing expeditions. Now, I'm content to defy gravity vicariously and to admire the beauty of the cliffs from the comfort of the cockpit.

It's evening when we arrive at Narsaq. As we motor to the harbor, we're surprised to see a sailboat—the first yacht we've seen since leaving Reykjavik. Mark and Marina from *Jonathan* help with our lines as we tie up in the fisherman's harbor.

"I've met you before," declares Mark, to our astonishment.

"Oh . . . I don't remember," I confess. "Where was that?"

"I don't know, but I recognize *you*," he says, indicating Les, "and I remember your boat."

"I know," he exclaims after a pause, "it was last year in Kirkwall (Orkney Islands); you gave me a weather fax."

Les and I now recall the brief conversation and *Jonathan*'s bright-red hull by the harbor wall. "Of course," we reply in unison. "It's a small ocean, isn't it?"

Mark and Marina had sailed directly from Holland and joined the Greenland coast farther north. Their route south through inland channels is the reverse of the one we will follow to the western settlement. Mark recommends some anchorages, and before leaving Narsaq I photocopy sections of his charts at the local post office. We enjoy a convivial evening, first squatting on the dock and later gathering in *Jonathan*'s cockpit.

Narsaq is the most attractive village we visit in southwest Greenland. It rests on a sloping plain nestled at the base of two-thousand-foot Qaqqaqsuaq Mountain and looks across the fiord toward Eiriksöy. The higher elevations are rocky and barren, but lower down, steep slopes are covered in vegetation. From the harbor we see groups of blueberry pickers, tiny dots among the low bushes almost halfway up. Several historic sites, both churches and houses, surround the village. The modern settlement was established as a trading post in 1830, and now the population is engaged mainly in fishing, sheep rearing, or working at a fur workshop.

The day after our arrival is special for the two thousand or so residents. *Danabrög* arrives this afternoon with the royal party on their reorganized tour. The five or six boats in the fishing harbor all dress ship for the visit. We pull our signal flags from beside the chart table and string them along the headstay and backstay. In midmorning the navy arrives and we exchange waves with the crew of the fisheries vessel as she again ties up by our stern. They seem like old friends. A red police boat takes up a berth on the outside wall of the harbor while the inspection ship anchors in the bay between several bergs. By midmorning the dock is populated with navy men, civilians trav-

A young Greenlander with her grandmother after welcoming royal visitors to Narsaq

eling with the royal party, and local inhabitants here to see what's going on. The most colorful character is an artist commissioned to produce a set of eighteen paintings illustrating the royal tour. He wears a deep-red jacket and Sherlock Holmes hat. He puffs continually at a curved pipe, completing an effective caricature. I spend several minutes watching him sketch the assembled boats from a vantage point above the harbor.

Shortly after lunch the immaculate *Danabrög* ties up at the Royal Arctic dock, cheered by a large welcoming crowd. As her lines come ashore, her flags too break out aloft. For a time we join the crowd watching the royal comings and goings. The scene is splendidly colonial. The visitors return the crowd's cheers with the practiced waves of those accustomed to applause. There's one charming moment when a small girl in national dress, encouraged by her elderly grandmother, presents a bouquet to the princess. The brief ceremony ends with the visitors driving into town in a long procession of assorted cars and sports utility vehicles.

When the crowd disperses, Mark and Marina leave to continue their cruise southward. Robert goes with them. We wave farewell to *Jonathan* as she leaves the wharf with flags still fluttering from her stays. We're almost ready to leave ourselves, but first we walk the half-mile to the village to find a laundry. The last time we washed clothes was in Reykjavik and we're now running out of clean items. Two young Greenlandic girls, cruising on bicycles, pull alongside us. We describe our voyage, and they talk about life in southwest Greenland; more importantly, they explain the workings of the community laundry.

First we must buy a smart card from the nearby Spar grocery. Once we have this, we find the laundry a little farther along the unfinished road in the bottom of one of many tall apartment buildings. Identified unflatteringly as "Block E," it's well equipped with several large machines, spin dryers, and electric tumbler dryers. Most are unused, but a child watches from a stroller as her mother stuffs clothes into a front loader and an older man sits reading while his washing spins back and forth. While our own clothes are washing, we finish our shopping at the store, buying fish for dinner and a selection of rolled lamb, salami, fresh bread, and cookies for lunches. This store is more limited than many we've seen; it's a surprise to see a display of escargot shells on the bottom of one shelf.

By evening the royal festivities are over. First the inspection ship raises anchor, maneuvers carefully round the bergs, and steams slowly away. Then *Danabrög* casts off her lines and follows, while at the stern the royals wave decorously to the crowds. The fisheries ship backs from her berth and follows the other vessels. Finally the police boat takes up her station at the rear of the line and the whole flotilla disappears down the fiord.

Chapter 12

Snorri

It's time to head to Nuuk, but we take one more walk to the village. For the first time we find the small museum open, where a helpful curator describes some archeology underway at local Viking sites. Les is fascinated and I must keep her moving or she'd stay the rest of the summer! At the grocery we buy chicken and vegetables. The local market is in full swing in a nearby open space. Like the one at Qaqortoq it has displays of fish and seal meat, but there's also a table piled with sheep carcasses still complete with their fleeces. We buy fresh arctic char.

We leave the harbor a few minutes after 1300. A few days ago the fiord was full of ice; now it's almost clear.

"So where's all the bergs?" I ask Les rhetorically.

"I don't know . . . but I'm not complaining," she responds, happy to see clear water and have the prospect of a fine sail.

"It moves so fast—mostly driven by the wind."

"Hmm. Just as long as it doesn't blow back before we get out of here . . . ," she says, anxious to get on with the next leg of the voyage.

We leave Narsaq Fiord and turn along Breidafjord toward the ocean. It's long and straight, leading between red granite hills backed by steep slopes rising to a rocky skyline. A large black mountain dominates the view astern. At the head of one tributary fiord a huge glacier towers over the water.

"Wow! Let's get a closer look," cries Les enthusiastically.

I'm the party pooper. "Are you sure?" I ask. "We've no charts for there. It'll take at least a couple of hours."

"But look, it's so impressive."

"I know, but I'd rather anchor in daylight."

"Oh, I suppose so," she concedes reluctantly.

"Maybe we'll see others."

"Maybe," Les sighs. We continue down the fiord.

This morning in Narsaq we enjoyed bright sunshine but now the weather slowly deteriorates. Mist gathers round the hillsides and spreads out across the water. Soon light drizzle wets the sails and envelops us with the smell of damp earth. Inugsugtot Light on the port side marks the mouth of Breidafjord and the exit to Julianhåb Bight. The coast runs west before turning north at Cape Desolation, but our route cuts inside the cape along a series of inland passages that wind between innumerable islands. On the north side of the fiord a metal pole on a tiny rock outcrop marks the entrance to the first waterway. A cross on the chart showing a rock in the center of one particularly narrow section makes the passage seem problematic. In practice it proves easy and we find adequate water to pass mid-channel. More metal poles mark the route along Nordlige Mågeløb, across a stretch of open water, followed by the entrance to another narrow passage.

We plan to anchor at Skipshaven, an abandoned fishing station in a tiny inlet on an island called Ivnarssuangup Nuna. Two large bergs partly blocking the entrance appear grounded. One is surrounded by open water and easily passed, but the second lies very close to the rock cliff, leaving just enough width for us to squeeze through. We eye the berg towering overhead. Is it stable, or will huge blocks crash down as they did at Narsaq Ilua? Any falling ice will drop perilously close to *Symphony*. We're wary, too, of ice projecting into the channel, unseen in the impenetrable, dark green water. We press on, one eye on the ice in the sky, the other probing the water for obstructions. The air chills in the shadow of the rock buttress. We edge very carefully and uneventfully past into a small landlocked basin with rock slabs reaching to the edge of the water. Two buildings along one side are extensive but derelict. The roof of the larger one sags badly, and planks of siding have sprung from their supports. The smaller structure at the root of a short, dilapidated jetty appears intact but badly run-down.

The basin is too small for *Symphony* to swing at anchor. However, ringbolts have been set into the rock sides and we moor in the center of the basin with shore lines from both bows and both quarters. I attach the last line, from the port quarter, to a large cleat on the disintegrating pier. The whole wharf is rather shaky, but the inlet is completely landlocked and there's no strong wind in the forecast. I reckon it'll last until we're long gone. We enjoy a perfectly quiet, completely restful night.

The old building by the pier was apparently an office and abandoned rather carelessly. Pieces of furniture and fishing gear are spread about. Business documents, mostly invoices on thin, dull yellow paper, litter the floor. I examine a couple, but they're neither recent nor particularly interesting. The larger building is full of rotting animal skins, rusting anchors, more papers, and miscellaneous junk of all kinds. A cursory check reveals nothing worth scavenging, but heading back to the pier I discover a large coil of thick blue polypropylene line. *Symphony*'s dock lines are adequate for tying to floating pontoons but are really too short for fixed wharves and large tidal ranges. Securing her in the basin required all our lines with two of them joined together. Here's just what we need! I heave the whole piece into the dinghy and return to *Symphony* with my trophy. It's soon cut into four extra long dock lines and the ends sealed with a hot knife.

The next morning, between breakfast and getting underway, the tranquility of the inlet is shattered by the sound of a large outboard engine. I glance up to see four youngsters roar past the end of the inlet in an open boat. Their heads swing round as they catch sight of *Symphony* and they turn in a swirl of spray and head toward us. The boat comes smartly alongside and several hands grasp the gunwale and hold her away from *Symphony*'s topsides.

Four grinning twelve-year-old faces look up from the boat. At first, conversation is awkward as we have no Greenlandic and the boys have very little English. However, we exchange friendly gestures, and when we invite them aboard they have no problem understanding or hesitation accepting. One boy ties their short painter to a lifeline stanchion and one by one they clamber aboard. Les and I each write our name in a notebook, and Kaaleeraq, David-Nuka, Alibak, and Augustinus slowly and carefully add theirs below. They appear fascinated by *Symphony* and explore the main cabin and forepeak. The head evokes special approval! The electronic instruments bring cries of amazement. Les distributes boiled candy from her plastic jar to a moving mass of outstretched hands. The boys explore the deck with the same enthusiasm displayed below, checking the anchors, and examining the winches and the various lines. Eventually they climb back aboard their own boat. Byes and farewells fly between the boats and the boys roar off into another U-turn to return the way they came. We return to our preparations for leaving.

Les cleans the fish we bought in the market. I tidy up and begin to retrieve mooring lines. The tide is rising with current flowing into basin so I can remove the forward lines and leave *Symphony* swinging on the two at the stern. We're about to power up and retrieve these when the sound of an engine announces our visitors' return. This time two boats sweep back into the inlet. The second, with a middle-aged man and another boy aboard, comes alongside while the others cruise in circles near the entrance. The man is Kristjan Larsen, small in stature and with a grayish countenance. He climbs aboard quickly when invited, but his son of about ten takes off in the boat in a cloud of spray. I stay in the cockpit to watch over *Symphony* and Les conducts Kristjan on a below-decks tour while keeping up a halting conversation. Kristjan sees the fish in the galley.

"*Lax,*" he says, pointing and nodding. "*Lax.*"

Les is not at all convinced that the fish is salmon, so she pulls out Tjorkel's *Almanaki* and pours over the multi-language table of fish names.

"*Lax?*" she says doubtfully.

"Yes," nods Kristjan.

"Or is it *eqaluq* (arctic char)?"

"*Eqaluq*, yes . . . *eqaluq*," agrees Kristjan enthusiastically.

Kristjan satisfies his curiosity and is ready to leave, but his son is still hot-dogging round the harbor and it takes several shouts to entice him back. Finally the bow of the boat turns toward us. Now I'm worried. He's coming much too fast. Closer and closer, the boat surges on with no hint of slowing down. I watch helplessly, in despair, certain he'll crash straight into *Symphony*'s topsides. When it seems nothing can prevent a collision, the boy pushes the gears into reverse. The engine roars in protest. Just a few feet in front of us the boat slows to bare steerage in a shower of white water, and the ten-year-old calmly walks forward to grasp *Symphony*'s gunwale. Wow! Such boat handling in one so young is amazing.

At last we say good-bye to our new friends. Three boys climb onto the pier and release the last mooring line. As we all smile and wave, both boats slowly leave the anchorage. Underway, we have an escort for the first quarter-mile. Then the boys tire of our slow speed and with more waves turn back to their homes.

We follow the waterway through a succession of open bays and rock-lined waterways. For the most part it's broad and easy to follow. However, in one spot the bottom shallows, leaving only a narrow channel. It seems inevitable that a large berg is grounded on the shoal, reducing the clearance to little more than the width of the boat. We approach apprehensively, knowing we're again getting close up and friendly with a berg. We can almost touch it as we pass. Cold air wafts over us, but before we can worry too much we're through into open water.

It turns into a beautiful day with blue sky and puffy white cumulus clouds floating from horizon to horizon. We're surrounded by mountains, but those to the southwest are especially dramatic. Serrated knife-edge ridges link shapely peaks that tower over deep valleys. It's another range to excite the eye of a mountaineer. Late in the afternoon we arrive at Bjorn's Haven, just five miles before the waterway reaches the ocean. A turn to port takes us into a well-protected, elongated bay, and we anchor just inside the entrance near the western shore. The anchor sets fair at the first attempt in thirty-five feet.

The wind rises through the evening and Les keeps an anchor watch until 0230. With unusually good timing, the wind dies away just as I'm about to take over. However, by morning it's again blowing briskly and the weather's threatening. Low clouds scud overhead, cutting off the mountains at half height. Qaqortoq Radio forecasts winds of force nine. It's an easy decision to stay where we are until the gale blows over and we settle down for a day at anchor. By mid-afternoon the sky is brighter and the wind begins to relent. Les decides to try her luck once more at fishing. When she gets a noticeable tug almost before the lure reaches the bottom, it seems she indeed has the golden touch. Up comes the line. Alas, the catch is no culinary delight but a sculpin, an ugly and inedible creature with huge spiny fins! He goes right back in the water. However, Les still has her magic. On the second try she takes just three minutes to haul in a good-sized cod.

The next morning, immediately outside the anchorage we're confronted by the Knecket, the narrowest part of the passage. The

A mountain north of Cape Desolation, Greenland

constriction is approached along a straight channel with low rocky islands on each hand. To our relief there's no ice. As we've found several times before, sections described with special relish in the pilot can be passed without too much difficulty by staying midstream.

A profusion of scattered islands and rock outcrops screens the coast where the waterway emerges into Davis Strait. We turn north along an irregular channel through rocks and islands rather sparsely marked with metal poles. A wide bay, Alanngorsuaq (Copper Mine Bay), affords us extensive views of inland mountains. Immediately north, the mountains extend right to the coast and project westward to form the north side of the bay. Here they rise majestically, direct from the water's edge. Long rock slabs steepen into huge buttresses that in turn sweep skyward into lofty pinnacles. Not one scrap of vegetation softens the harsh angles of rock. They're bold and brash, with every detail exposed.

After cutting through a group of islands we set a course outside all the offshore rocks. The wind now fills in from the east, broad on the starboard beam. We roll out the genoa and stop the engine. However, no sooner is the sail set and windvane steering than the breeze becomes playful. Each time we adjust the lines it changes direction, strength, or both. Periods of light breeze are interrupted with fluky gusts to thirty knots. We begin with the full genoa, then step by step roll it in until it's little bigger than a handkerchief. Soon a gusty force six on the starboard quarter produces wild and uncomfortable rolls, but it's exhilarating sailing.

It's getting late before we near our overnight anchorage. In the twilight we see a line of islands ahead stretching out from the land. Surrounding the islands are many rocks, some visible while others lurk below the surface, forming an effective screen across the harbor entrance. It's clear getting in will be a challenge. I select a rather indirect approach so we can use prominent natural features as range lines. While still well offshore we turn toward the harbor through a channel of dark green water with whirlpools and white water on both hands. First, water swirls around a submerged shoal on the port side, and then to starboard, waves beat against small rock outcrops. We feel anxious, not from any immediate threat, but in reaction to the tumult around us, the crashing of the seas, the howling of the wind, and our awareness that the tricky sections are still ahead. We run in very close to white water pounding the rocky shore of an island before we turn to starboard and favor the port side of a constricted pass to avoid mid-channel rocks. The harbor opens up ahead, but the navigable channel is narrow and close alongside a rocky promontory to port. We leave the lee of the islands, and the wind screams through the rig. Waves roll in unimpeded from the open bay and sweep past us to break against rocks just feet away. As each wave strikes *Symphony*'s hull, she rolls wildly and Les struggles with the wheel while I check our bearings and cast anxious glances toward the rock wall just a few feet downwind.

Finally we reach water, sheltered by the south side of the bay. The tension eases. Our terse comments, which have all related to piloting or the proximity of one hazard after another, give way to expressions of delight at the calm water, the lack of noise, and the attractive land-scape. We babble on, releasing the tension we were too preoccupied to recognize. We maneuver past one more underwater rock, but with no waves battering us, this is straightforward. We anchor in the center of a landlocked basin at the head of the inlet. By the time the anchor is secure the surrounding hills are dark.

Morning dawns calm and sunny, but by 0830 the wind is again on the rise. *Symphony* seems secure in her sheltered basin and we dinghy ashore and walk up a hill to the north. The slopes are covered in coarse, tufted grass, but sheltered hollows harbor a surprising variety of flowering plants and large mushrooms. We certainly didn't expect large mushrooms, but here they are! I like mushrooms and these look appetizing, but Les delivers a spirited lecture on the hazards of eating unknown fungi and reminds me we're far from any medical help.

From the top of the hill we look down into the next fiord and beyond that to an arm of the sea filled with countless bergs and growlers. Rocks protrude through the grass on the summit ridge and we choose two as seats while we enjoy the panorama. Birds are noticeably absent, but any disappointment is dispelled when we spot two gyrfalcons on the hunt for prey. They circle the crags, working in spirals, first westward and then to the east before taking off and dis-appearing over the crest of a ridge. This is another compelling place, a vast panorama of mountains and fiords, of steep slopes and rock faces, of sheltered inlets and open water, of islands and ice. An entire summer could be spent here walking and exploring. It's tempting to forget Nuuk today and indulge ourselves for a few hours. However, new horizons beckon and we retrace our steps to *Symphony*.

We carefully reverse our course of last night, but it's no longer the same world. The wind has settled to a fresh breeze. The threatening waves have become long, lazy swells. Wavelets now lap gently on the islands, and the sun has rid the rocks of sinister hues. Soon we clear the off-lying hazards and resume our way north. We head for one more inland passage, intending to call at Parmiut before sailing offshore to Nuuk. However, the southeast wind has wedged several bergs between the rocky islands in the channel entrance. Maybe with time and persistence we could find a way through, but instead we sail four miles west to open water and set a course directly to Nuuk. A beam wind carries us swiftly along with only the genoa set and we both have uneventful watches.

In the evening we're surrounded by a large pod of perhaps twenty whales, all with small fins. Some lie motionless on the surface, possibly asleep. Most are very active. Plumes of gray vapor shoot into the air as they surface. Moments later they arch their backs and dive. Some breach, showing off their tail fins. One whale surfaces, almost touching the port gunwale. He seems as surprised by us as we are by him, gives a loud grunt, and immediately submerges. A few minutes later he reappears well astern and blows off a great cloud of vapor.

The rugged mountains that so impressed us near Cape Desolation have given way to lower and rounder summits altogether less grand. Deep valleys allow glimpses of the central ice. As evening approaches, the mountains fade slowly to indigo tinged with pinkish haze, then back to blue. The moon, well into its third quarter, rises before sunset. At first it's diaphanous but later solidifies and brightens before following the sun behind a bank of clouds. The sky turns golden, then red. A broad orange band around the horizon turns powder blue. In the twilight the ever-present icebergs stand out as white islands in a sea of indigo. They turn golden with the sun's last rays, and as the light fades they become dark silhouettes against a gray background. Jupiter shines behind us, bright and solitary in a dark continuum of sea and sky. In the short hours of darkness, the sky is a dazzling display of stars. Gray streamers dance across the northern sky like muslin drapes wafting in the wind. We watch entranced. They're unlike anything we've seen before—our first display of Northern Lights.

This is our first overnight sail since reaching Greenland and our first in the company of icebergs. By now we're used to seeing them and at least in good weather we feel comfortable navigating round them. They show up on radar at a range of about five miles, giving plenty of warning even at night. The growlers are a different matter. Some stay close to parent bergs, but others drift off on their own. They're too small to appear on radar, but their low profile can mask a considerable mass of ice below the surface. Once it's too dark to see them, we heave to and drift until dawn. We continue our watches, monitoring the radar for ships and bergs and periodically climbing to the cockpit to check for anything the radar may have missed. Tonight we stop in the middle of a triangle of large bergs. We track them closely through the night but appear to drift along maintaining roughly the same positions. It's watchful but uneventful.

Just north of the small community of Friedrikshavn the coastal mountains fade away and the central icecap sweeps to the very edge of the sea. The ice extends north and south as far as we can see, and inland rises steeply to the horizon. Debris colors the surface dirty-brown except where thin films of meltwater reflect the light. North of the glacier the mountains rise again. Dark and mysterious near the coast, they are higher inland and more rugged, with snow slopes and glaciers. A family of seals floats by on a bergy bit, taking their ease stretched out in the sunshine. They return our stares unconcerned. Multitudes of fulmars wheel and turn overhead.

Ahead, a thick layer of fog forms a dense white blanket, while around *Symphony,* visibility remains good. For a while the fog seems to retreat before us, but in the end chilly, damp mist closes round us. Periodically we break out into clear patches and see mountaintops rising over the mist. We continue for a couple of hours with eyes and ears straining for signs of ships or ice. Finally we heave to early and begin our regular night watches.

The next morning I get underway while Les sleeps. The wind is from the northwest at ten knots with visibility no more than 150 yards. I unfurl the genoa and set the windvane for a northerly course. It's cold and wet in the cockpit. I peer forward into the gloom, conscious there'll be little time to react should a growler materialize ahead. My glasses mist up every twenty seconds, forcing me to wipe them continually. Every five minutes I make a dash to the chart table to check the radar. Periodically the fog lifts enough to raise hopes of it clearing, but each time it returns. After a couple of hours the sun briefly penetrates a hole in the mist, but it, too, soon vanishes. Midmorning a silvery light shines through fog and it seems a little warmer. A few solitary puffins, fulmars, and shearwaters appear out of the mist and show a passing interest in *Symphony* before being swallowed by the gray blanket.

Puffins always bring smiles to our faces. We find several just bobbing on the surface. As we approach they paddle away from *Symphony*, turning their huge bills one way, then the other to look back at the strange intruder. Just as we pull ahead of them and it seems they'll resume their rest, they take off. Their takeoffs are not elegant. They flail the air and water with stubby wings, and their legs whir furiously as they raise reluctant bodies slowly from the surface. When it seems they'll never leave the sea, they lumber ungainly into the air. They're not good at landing either. They descend with feet outstretched and crash into the surface. When slowed by the water they paddle away, still glancing back anxiously over their shoulders.

Les wakes and after coffee and breakfast declares herself ready to take over. I still feel quite awake, excited to be nearing Nuuk, and we continue sailing together. I make a small course adjustment to keep us well clear of a line of rocks along the shore. Suddenly we have several radar targets. One is stationary, three quarters of a mile to starboard, and I assume it's a berg. Another passes half a mile astern— probably a boat heading for a small harbor. Yet another boat overtakes us, passing unseen and proceeding toward Nuuk. Only after we enter a passage between the mainland and the island of Simiutat do we see another vessel, when a boat going the other way passes close alongside.

The fog finally parts to reveal an entrancing picture of rugged mountains, of sunlit brown rock floating above a sea of delicate mist. I think of the stylized delicacy of oriental art. We continue through a series of channels protected by coastal islands. Suddenly gunfire crackles ahead. In the distance three small boats move quickly but erratically. Drawing closer, we see darkly clad figures balancing upright on foredecks and leaning back on a line from the bow. Rifles are slung across their shoulders or carried in a free hand. On sighting their quarry these Inuit hunters race off in pursuit. Close to the seals, gunfire rings out from the bow rider and other hunters. We hear many shots, but as far as we can see there are no kills.

Navigation here needs care. Isolated rocks, charted with only an innocuous "+", appear close to the natural course line. A small red freighter passes as we approach a section where the waterway narrows and makes two sharp turns. This is the main approach to Nuuk from the south, and three separate ranges mark the center of the channel. The freighter proves a good pathfinder and we follow her until the town of Nuuk comes slowly into focus.

Oil tanks and loading facilities line the port side of the entrance channel while the starboard side is low, rocky, and undeveloped. At the end of the oil jetty a port turn brings us face to face with prominent red buildings that are a trademark of the Royal Arctic Company. We continue into a sheltered basin. Along one side is a big blue fish plant. The other side is bounded by a steep rock cliff skirted by a long wooden wharf. A substantial wooden stairway leads from the harbor to a row of buildings at the cliff top. Boats are moored along both sides of the harbor. Most rafts are two or three deep, but some lines stretch five boats wide and almost close the central channel. As we look for a friendly boat to tie to, we notice a small gap on the very end of the fish plant wharf. It's only about half as long as *Symphony* so she projects beyond the end of the quay, but we manage to secure her with adequate lines and we have direct access to the dock.

Extensive development here in the last thirty years has produced a modern community of fourteen thousand inhabitants. It is the largest town in Greenland and the seat of the Home Rule government that manages domestic affairs. It's about a mile from the harbor to the center of Nuuk. A good climb up the wooden stairway brings us to the cliff overlooking the harbor. From here it's a fairly level walk to town. On the cliff top, small concrete business premises are interspersed with wooden frame buildings, while a little nearer town several barrack-like apartment buildings have every appearance of community housing. Downtown is a mixture of modern hotels, Nordic-style government buildings, and lines of small shops and cafes. Unfortunately the post office and other downtown open spaces are conspicuous gathering places for some residents with alcohol problems. We spend a few moments browsing in a rather nice bookstore. Nuuk occupies a peninsula, and the original landing place is the opposite side of town to the modern harbor. It's overlooked by a varied collection of old buildings. Most prominent are an excellent museum and the "official" Santa's Workshop complete with cutout wooden Christmas tree.

Like other Greenland towns, Nuuk has an outdoor market. A low and dark building houses seal meat, while open-air stalls covered with cardboard sheets offer large pieces of caribou, and both fresh and dried fish. One whole table is covered in kittiwake, complete with bedraggled plumage. Another is piled with large cuts of caribou legs, thighs, and torsos. There are no standard cuts. A stallholder stands ready with his saw and hatchet to slice off any piece a customer will buy. Les draws lines across a thigh with her hand, and soon a large piece is sawn off and wrapped in a plastic bag.

Next Les examines the fresh fish.

"*Lax,*" offers the woman stallholder.

After her conversation with Kristjan, Les is not to be fooled. "*Eqaluq?*" she inquires.

"Yes." The confirmation is instantaneous.

It may not be salmon, but arctic char has replaced Spekekjøtt as the gastronomic discovery of the voyage. We buy a large fresh fish and some smoked char that, with bread, onion, and tomato, has become a favorite lunch.

Greenland's national museum is quite small, but its collection is extremely well displayed. There are more of the artifacts left wherever Norsemen settled: soapstone loom weights, spindle whorls, lamps (complete with a moss wick, and blubber for fuel) and bowls. There are also textiles, spade blades, whalebone, metal rivets, iron keys, combs, and game pieces. Inuit tools and clothing are in a separate room and include dramatic, five-hundred-year-old mummies of six women and two children. These were dug from ice at Qilakitsoq, near Disco Bay three hundred miles north.

In a large shed next to the main building are several kayaks. These extraordinarily delicate boats look very unstable and difficult to manage. They're not vessels in the ordinary sense but rather an extension of the hunter himself, with low freeboard and a small screen on the foredeck to confuse the prey. They're specialized and refined, totally customized for hunting seals. Anything not essential has been eliminated. I don't fancy them. In unskilled hands they're just a quick way to an icy bath. I'd have to ride in the much larger and more conventional *umiak*—the "women's boat"—capable of carrying a whole family on long expeditions through the fiords.

Between the departure of the Vikings and the arrival of Danes, Nuuk was witness to an amusing encounter between English explorer John Davis and native Inuit. While sailing in search of the Northwest Passage, Davis entered Godthåb Fiord and named it Gilbert Sound after his patron. As he reports in his papers, the Englishmen landed on a rocky island, and the Inuit greeted them with a "lamentable noyse . . . with great outcryes and skreechings" like "the howling of wolves." The English party included a four-piece orchestra that accompanied dancing sailors. Ten kayaks approached, and when their paddlers landed, the English "allured them by friendly embracings and signes of curtesie." A sailor alternately struck his breast and pointed at the sun in gestures intended to break the social ice. After depositing caps, stockings, and gloves on the ground as gifts, the Englishmen performed country dances before marching off to their boats with the band still playing. This bizarre approach seems to have worked. Trade between the communities was brisk, with the English buying sealskin garments and boots—just like today's tourists.

Greenlanders are generally more reticent than people we have met elsewhere. English is much less common here, a distant third after Greenlandic and Danish. However, two hunters do pause briefly to talk. One sits on the dock by *Symphony* in a worn, red, foul-weather suit. We strike up a halting conversation. He lives at Parmiut and traveled two days by small boat to reach Amerilik Fiord, a huge indentation in the coast a little south of Nuuk. He has shot four deer, which he says is not bad, but not outstanding. Another hunter, with long, dark hair and dressed in blue overalls, has also just returned from Amerilik. We sit on a bollard while he describes his hunting. He tells me he can live quite well on the proceeds and is never short of food or other essentials. A pleasant man, he explains his dream of visiting the U.S. "For this to be possible," he says with a smile, he "must shoot many deer."

The Seamen's Home is a modern, multi-story building at the landward end of the fish factory wharf. It stands apart from adjacent warehouses and storage sheds, with yards full of buoys, anchors, chain, and other miscellaneous fishing equipment. It's a family hotel and the most convenient place to make phone calls home. It accepts payment by credit card. We take advantage of its showers with lots of hot water, and on two nights we eat in the large cafeteria that provides good, inexpensive food.

The next morning is sunny but cold and we begin serious preparations for departure. Les changes the engine oil and transmission fluid while I tighten the shaft stuffing box. We pull everything from the lazarette and re-stow it—two weeks of packing and unpacking has left it all in complete disorder. Before any passage I like to organize the navigation items to refocus my mind on the voyage ahead and on the challenges of route finding and communications. I stow the Greenland charts and pull out those for northern Labrador, update the sail plan, and list relevant radio frequencies and broadcast schedules. I store key waypoints for our next landfall in the GPS.

While our supply is not critically short, we want to fill a propane tank before we leave. At the Royal Arctic office we're directed to a small filling station across the harbor. We motor over in the dinghy with the empty cylinder. The small floating fuel dock is deserted, but in a small sales office at the top of a steep ramp we find a helpful (English-speaking) young man. There are no filling facilities in Greenland—all cylinders are shipped empty to Denmark to be refilled. Naturally they all have Danish fittings, which are not compatible with our American-made hoses. Nevertheless, he takes us to an outhouse to examine his small stock. Amazingly, among assorted cylinders is just one with American fittings. Why it's here is a mystery. It must be an error, as no one in Greenland could use it. Feeling lucky, we buy it.

Today is the day to leave. Les, as usual, is up first and makes morning coffee. Suddenly she exclaims: "Guess what's arrived in the harbor!"

I'm dozing, not yet ready to take on the day. "I've no idea—what now?" I respond, mildly irritated by an impossible question.

"Get up," she calls, "*Snorri*'s here!"

Snorri is a replica Viking knarr, a trading ship, which is re-creating Leif Eriksson's voyage of a thousand years ago. She's the star of the "Viking 1000 Expedition," retracing Leif's route from Brattahlid to Vinland powered only by sail and oars. We heard she had left for Labrador a couple of weeks before we arrived in Greenland. I climb from the bunk and look out of the companionway. There, looking rather small beside a fishing boat, is indeed a knarr. Several crewmembers are gathered in the stern in what appears an ardent conversation.

Later, on the wharf, we meet Dean, one of *Snorri*'s crew. "Hi. We're from the sailboat on the end of the wharf."

"Hello."

"What are you guys doing here? Shouldn't you be in Labrador?"

"We came in overnight. We were towed here by an icebreaker."

"Oh, no, what happened?"

"We got to the middle of Davis Strait, and the steering oar broke."

"Can it be repaired?"

"We're talking about that now. We just had a conference. There's no time to set out again now. I think we'll have to come back and try again next year."

We commiserate with Dean, and through him invite his shipmates aboard for morning coffee. Soon half a dozen modern Vikings are sipping coffee and swapping stories in *Symphony*'s cockpit. Their spirits seem good given their disappointment and the effect of sleepless nights. *Snorri*'s voyage is a major undertaking and they've all made significant commitments to be part of the expedition. The abrupt termination of the voyage must be terribly disappointing.

We leap at the invitation to go aboard *Snorri*. Skipper Terry Moore and expedition leader Hodding Carter answer our questions about the boat's construction and operation. She was built from plans used for *Saga Sigla*, which were based on a wreck found in a Danish fiord. She's an open, beamy boat. Only tarpaulins provide protection from the sea. Terry and Hodding praise her sailing in words echoing those of Magnus Anderson about *Viking*. She's surprisingly fast, and the hull flexes as she snakes through the waves. Our most surprising discovery relates to the oars. These pass through holes in the hull, positioned for rowing from a standing position. There are only six oars. *Snorri* is heavy, and in good conditions the rowers can reach only about a knot—not a lot to stem a foul tide or pull off a lee shore. With unfavorable winds a voyage to Newfoundland would take a long time. Maybe this is why sagas never report any expedition to America returning the same season. We already know that winds can be light in the Greenland summer, and ships can wait a long time for a favorable breeze.

The crew invite us to a barbecue behind the Seaman's Home. We feast on caribou and musk ox with green salad and baked potato. Our usual contribution to social occasions—a flagon of wine—proves popular. Each crewman on *Snorri* affirms his intention to return next year to complete the voyage. Naturally the steering oar is a topic of hot debate. The relative advantages of flexible and rigid couplings are debated back and forth. We wonder how Vikings managed with only the natural materials at their disposal. The cooking fire dies to red embers and we gather round with hands outstretched for warmth. Overhead the clear sky is full of twinkling stars.

Chapter 13

The Route Usually Followed

We have everything stowed by midday and all that remains is to top off the diesel tanks. This requires a wait until after half tide, as there's a four-foot spot just off the fuel dock. It's late afternoon before the tanks are full and we can steam out past the oil storage facilities and head westward to the open sea.

Before leaving home we sought advice from the Canadian Coast Guard on relevant radio frequencies and the availability of weather reports for the Labrador coast. They provided the information and encouraged us to establish a reporting schedule with them while in Canadian waters. I hesitated, concerned we might miss a report through forgetfulness or poor radio conditions and precipitate an unnecessary search. However, the Canadians were persuasive and we finally agreed. It's now time to call the station at Iqaluit (Frobisher Bay, Baffin Island) to make the necessary arrangements.

"Iqaluit, Iqaluit, Iqaluit, this is yacht *Symphony*, over."

There's no reply. Again I try and again there's no response. I try another channel: "Iqaluit, Iqaluit, Iqaluit, this is yacht *Symphony*, over."

There's another long pause with nothing but crackles and white noise. Just as it seems my reservations are vindicated even earlier than expected, a sonorous voice breaks through the static: "Vessel calling Iqaluit, this is Canadian Coast Guard Station Iqaluit, over."

I explain why I'm calling.

"*Symphony*, Iqaluit, roger . . . I'll fax you a form and you can send us the details."

"Iqaluit, *Symphony*. We're already underway and have no fax facilities. Can you take the information over the radio? Over."

After the briefest pause the operator agrees and I answer his questions about *Symphony*, the equipment on board, and our planned route. Most taxing is "What's your ETA at Nain?" I have only the most general idea of how long we will take to cover the six hundred miles to the most northerly settlement on the coast. It will depend on the weather and how much exploring we do. I say we'll be there in a couple of weeks while thinking we may beat that estimate by a day or two. We agree to report every twenty-four hours at 1600 hours universal time, which now becomes "the time to call the Coast Guard."

"We'll start a search if you're more than four hours overdue," announces the matter-of-fact voice.

"That's too short," I protest. "If we can't get through for some reason, you'll have people out unnecessarily. Please don't take action for forty-eight hours."

"Right," the operator replies, agreeing more easily than I expect. In practice the arrangement works smoothly. When we get out of range of one shore station, the call schedule automatically transfers to the next. Once we reach Groswater Bay we transfer from shortwave to VHF for the rest of the voyage. We miss our schedule twice, in each case by about four hours. The first time, we're enjoying such a fine sail I forget to call. On the second occasion, we're at anchor and our signal is blanketed by high hills.

There are just a few widely spaced bergs in the fiord. The whiteness of the ice contrasts markedly with dark rocky shores already tinged with the blue of evening. Slowly the buildings of Nuuk fade away astern and fuse together at the foot of the tall dark-gray gneiss mountains. It's rather cold. Dark clouds move in to obliterate the whole sky except for a yellow glow round the horizon. A single whale surfaces to port, leaving a cloud of gray vapor long after she's sunk back into the depths.

Most of the ice is toward the sides of the fiord, but one large berg with high vertical sides floats in the middle, its flat top densely packed with roosting gulls. As we approach, a small motor cruiser powers past *Symphony*, sending the birds into the air to form a circling mass hurling raucous protests at the intruders. Suddenly shots echo from the rock walls of the fiord, then more, and still more. After each volley, birds tumble from the sky to lie pathetically lifeless on the surface of the water. A few flap crippled wings in a futile effort to escape. Soon only solitary survivors of the flock, so numerous a few moments ago, still circle overhead. Then the sky is empty. The boat moves among the mass of floating feathers, and two swarthy men pluck the drifting corpses from the water. Tomorrow they'll be piled several deep on a table in the open market. More shots ring out from a boat by the southern shore, too distant for us to see the target or to judge the results. Right alongside *Symphony* a family of seals, two parents and four or five young, swim frantically on the surface in a mad scurry for survival. They race away from us and from the crackle of the guns, their sleek black bodies undulating rapidly as they strive to escape. We hope they make it.

At last we can no longer distinguish the buildings of Nuuk. We've left the hunting parties well astern and the fiord is silent. Several radio masts occupy the largest of a group of islands to port. Soon these too are behind us. The last rock buttress on the north side of the channel draws abeam and we emerge into the open waters of Davis Strait. The setting sun briefly finds a gap in the clouds to warm the cockpit and bathe us in a golden glow. However, the light soon fades, and the land darkens and slips slowly from view. There are no ships or bergs in sight. We have the ocean to ourselves.

The wind is light from the southwest. We set the mains'l and the genoa, and adjust the wind vane. For a while the sailing is good, but soon the wind dies away and we drift aimlessly on a smooth sea. We have occasional glimpses of a full moon, but clouds cover most of the sky. Later the wind fills in and we sail slowly westward. Then it dies. And so it is through the first night.

For three days we continue our fitful progress. Winds are variable, always forward of the beam, and most of the time we're close-hauled. In long periods of calm we catch up on maintenance. We go about many times, repeatedly adjusting the course to stay on the favored tack. The visibility too is variable, but mostly poor. Brilliant sunshine and blue skies quickly give way to patches of thick fog. In places, fog banks are widely spaced and we can see between them for a quarter or half mile. Often the top of the bank is illuminated by weak sunlight. At other times everything farther away than a hundred yards is lost behind a thick damp blanket. For a time on the second day we enjoy a brisk sail. The wind is only seven or eight knots, but the water is smooth and *Symphony* glides along checking off miles in fine style. We can see nothing beyond a tiny gray circle and we spend the day listening for any sound of approaching vessels, our eyes glued to the radar. We see and hear nothing. Eventually the wind once more dies. We motor on for a couple of hours to recharge the batteries.

Out in the strait we see none of the whales or dolphins that were our frequent companions along the Greenland coast. Just one solitary sei whale appears on the port quarter on the morning of the third day. We watch it surface, blow, and sink back below the water in a characteristic shallow dive. The only other sighting is a hefty piece of wood like a telegraph pole. Not something to run into.

Currents in Davis Strait flow generally counterclockwise. North-flowing water along the Greenland coast is warmer, while the Labrador Current to the west carries cold water and bergs all the way from north Greenland to the Newfoundland banks. It was this southerly flow that carried a Greenland berg to a fatal meeting with *RMS Titanic* in 1912. As we make our way west, I record water temperatures. Near Greenland's coast it's forty-two degrees rising to forty-five just offshore with the benefit of the warm current. It stays fairly constant until we're almost across and then begins a steady decline. Near Labrador the water is just one degree above freezing and the air is distinctly chilly.

Early afternoon on our fourth day out from Nuuk, Les first sees a long, low blue line to the southwest, the coast of North America. Almost immediately the wind dies away to leave us drifting in a flat calm. Sunshine filters through the cloud. Widely scattered bergs surround us on all sides, one minute dazzlingly white in bright sunshine, the next hidden by patches of mist. We elect to motor the three or four hours necessary to reach Bowdoin harbor rather than continue drifting so tantalizingly close to shore. As we power along, the distant blue wedge slowly resolves into mountain ranges with peaks and valleys and long ridges. It extends slowly northward to terminate in a steep headland fine on the starboard bow.

We struggle unsuccessfully to match the coastline with its depiction on the chart. Eventually the end of the peninsula breaks away from the rest and we can identify the Button Islands, lonely sentinels at the entrance to Hudson Strait. A little later we can distinguish the Cape Chidley Islands and the large rock cliff directly ahead as Cape Chidley itself. The rest of the features now fall into quickly into place.

We approach this coast with more than the usual tingle of excitement. We've always associated these waters with intrepid explorers

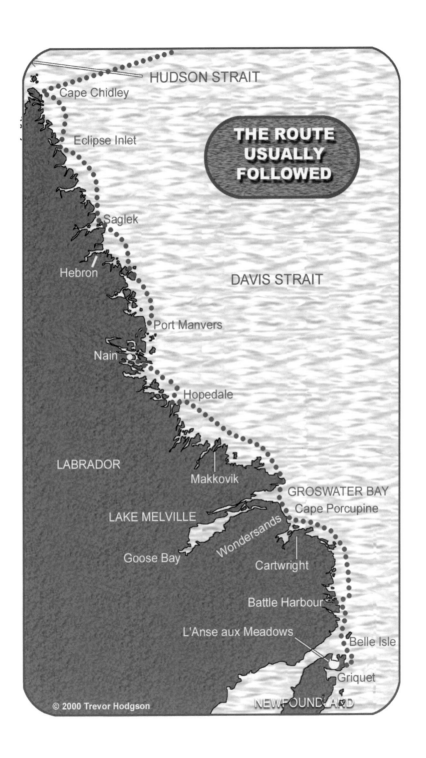

HUDSON STRAIT

Cape Chidley

Eclipse Inlet

THE ROUTE USUALLY FOLLOWED

Saglek

Hebron

DAVIS STRAIT

Port Manvers

Nain

Hopedale

LABRADOR

Makkovik

GROSWATER BAY
Cape Porcupine

LAKE MELVILLE

Wondersands

Goose Bay

Cartwright

Battle Harbour

L'Anse aux Meadows

Belle Isle

Griquet

© 2000 Trevor Hodgson

NEWFOUNDLAND

like Hudson, Frobisher, and Davis—names learned with awe from books at school. These school-day heroes have always seemed larger than life, challenging conditions that would daunt ordinary men while remaining apparently indifferent to danger. They sailed on the edge of the possible in places accessible only to those willing to endure extreme hardship. Yet here we are! It seems unreal. This cannot be where the titans of my imagination overcame the full blast of nature at its most malevolent. No impenetrable barrier blocks our way. The wind is calm. Sunshine filters through the clouds. The mountains of North America are spread before us in a magnificent but benign panorama. This landfall is desolate but splendidly beautiful.

With the nearest community three hundred miles to the south, this remote shore brings on a sense of deep isolation that seems odd after days alone at sea. On passage our world is limited to the confines of *Symphony*'s hull and deck. We look out over the waves but only to see two or three miles to the horizon. It's a small world, but one we fill. Subject only to weather, it's a world we can control. We can go where we like without interference,without anything disturbing our routine. This sparse coastline shatters our cozy world, exposing a landscape that is empty, mysterious, and unnerving. Our previous landfalls have been at established communities with docks and stores and people. Here no one waits to take our lines or to ask where we're from. We feel very alone.

The Labrador coast has never been thoroughly surveyed. The charts are unusual, some little more than black-and-white sketches. Many have no depth contours. A single dotted line labeled "The Route Usually Followed by Coastal Traffic" is the only indication of safe water. All were produced well before navigation satellites ringed the earth, and positions plotted directly from the GPS can be significantly wrong. Elsewhere, modern charts warn that positions can be in error because the chart and GPS use different datums, and often provide the necessary modest corrections. Here on Labrador the charts simply declare the datum, and hence the error is unknown!

Near shore a strong tidal current flowing from Hudson Strait pushes *Symphony* to the south. Les pulls the bow into the current and *Symphony* crabs sideways through the water. In places, the water is turbulent and swirls round as though pouring over unseen rocks. To avoid a long detour we cross a large area where the chart shows no soundings, but the depth sounder shows deep water the whole way.

The approach to Bowdoin harbor passes close to North Star Island, a small rock outcrop that's difficult to locate against the massive rock wall behind. A large iceberg appears right where we expect to see the island. We're quite close before we can see the rocks and distinguish a narrow passage between them and the ice. We squeeze through the gap between the island and the berg into the shadow of the two-thousand-foot vertical cliffs. We crane our necks to follow steep buttresses up and up until they reach the sky. We round a bluff headland and follow a curving channel into a landlocked basin. I release the anchor in thirty feet of water and let out 120 feet of chain, but as Les backs *Symphony*, it is clear the anchor's not holding. Thank goodness for the electric windlass! The anchor comes up hidden in a huge pyramid of brown weed. It takes several minutes of prodding with the boat hook to clear the anchor and scatter the weed in a slowly expanding floating carpet. We try again. Once more, Les reverses *Symphony* and we watch as the shore streams steadily forward. Again the anchor's pulled up and cleaned. Fortunately it's third time lucky. The rode tightens and *Symphony*'s bow pulls round to line up with the rode. The chain lifts from the water and comes taut. *Symphony* stops. The anchor's set. We have arrived.

I catch a special sparkle in Les's eye and we lock in a long, deep embrace. We need no words to understand the other's feelings. We've made it across the Atlantic to North America. We've completed our ocean crossing. From here we can follow the coastline all the way to Newfoundland. The realization of our ten-year dream is almost in our grasp.

It's late afternoon, but we're too excited to postpone our first steps on Canadian soil. I quickly inflate the dinghy and row the few strokes to an inlet in the shore where we land rather unsteadily on a slippery, weed-covered slab. Nearby, a small waterfall makes a final, short drop to the sea. The trudge up the hill to the south is enough to make us pant and stop for breath. The ground is rough and coarse with little vegetation. There are no trees or bushes, and no real grass, just a few small plants clinging to the ground in more sheltered spots.

We sit by the summit cairn, still savoring our arrival, absorbing

Lesley steers *Symphony* past an iceberg off the coast of Labrador

the view, and celebrating the moment. We look across the bare hill-sides, along the rocky coast, and out over ice-dotted Davis Strait. Offshore, past the steep rock cliffs, the water appears quite blue. Numerous bergs are scattered round the horizon and spread through the many inlets, adding a brilliant sparkle and a crisp, raw edge to the panorama. Inland the mountain slopes are strewn with rocks and patches of snow. It's wild. There's not even a footpath to show that anyone's been here before. The whole scene is perfectly, eerily quiet. There's no sign of animals, and no birdcalls echo from the rocky walls. Only the summit cairn betrays the visits of previous mariners.

The next day, even in our sheltered harbor, the wind reaches twenty-five knots and we're content to ride comfortably at anchor rather than venture out along the coast. We stay aboard cleaning, tidying, reading, and listening to the radio. As always when not traveling, we work on the "to do" list. I clean the cabin heater by burning a quantity of kerosene in place of the regular diesel. Les sews sail slides on the main to replace ones lost on passage.

The following morning the wind is still brisk but much less violent, and we pack and leave. We'd like to stay longer but still have a long way to go, six hundred miles to L'Anse aux Meadows and a thousand more to our home near New York. It's already September, a little late to be so far north on Labrador. From now on, winter gales can sweep the coast. We want time to appreciate the scenery and wildlife but must keep moving south whenever conditions allow. I clean one more huge stack of weed from the anchor and we retrace our route between North Star Island and the large berg. Turning southeast along "The Route Usually Followed," we try sailing with the genoa, but the wind becomes variable, then dies. We enjoy another breeze, but this soon swings round onto the bow. We give in and use the engine. The wind comes and goes throughout the day. Each time we try to sail, the wind dies away or heads us.

The coast of Northern Labrador is a feast of extraordinary scenery that has us totally captivated. The jagged backbone of the Torngat Mountains runs down the spine of the peninsula, behind dramatic rock faces soaring vertically for two thousand feet directly from the water. Long fiords separate the headlands and penetrate to the heart of the mountains, exposing shapely peaks and sharp silhouettes of serrated ridges. Everywhere, wildlife is abundant. Whales are common, usually appearing singly or in groups of three or four. At each anchorage, both morning and evening, caribou forage on sparse vegetation by the shore. We're greeted at the entrances of fiords by seals peering with mournful eyes set in small black heads. One morning an eagle circles overhead and in the evenings we sit in the cockpit, serenaded by the haunting cries of geese.

Eclipse Bay is a day's sail south of Cape Chidley. We anchor in a small bight off Miller Peninsula and spend a quiet, uneventful night. It's a pleasant morning, and before leaving we decide to stretch our legs with a walk over the peninsula. I'm below, collecting the camera and binoculars when Les exclaims, "Trev, come quick, there's a big wooly sheep."

"There's a what?"

"It's huge and white. . . . It has to be a sheep. Bring the binoculars."

I scramble to the cockpit as Les quickly revises her identification: "I think it's a bear. . . . Come and take a look."

There's no mistaking a large polar bear. The shaggy creature, its white coat tinged with yellow, ambles slowly round the bay. Periodically he stops to stare in our direction and then continues on, poking his nose into small shrubs and making short detours to rocks of particular interest. Two caribou watch from a respectful distance. Eventually the bear heads away over the top of the peninsula and out of our view. We decide to defer our shore visit to the next anchorage.

While the weather is changeable, on the whole we enjoy more sunshine than we expect. Some days are quite warm. The west wind brings the warmest days, although it's never so hot we want to discard our layers of thermal clothing. However, wind from the east or southeast, chilled by the cold Labrador Current and its parade of icebergs, feels distinctly cold. One evening we arrive for overnight anchorage at a small bay called Seaplane Cove. Colors are already fading from the hills and day will soon turn to dusk. The cloud is low over the surrounding mountains, and the valleys are covered in ice and snow. The whole setting has the somber chill of winter. The wind whips the water into whitecaps. Try as we may, our main anchor, a fifty-five-pound Delta, just plows through the bottom of soft, weedy mud. I try the Danforth, but it cannot penetrate the vegetation. By the time the

Delta sets, at the fifth attempt, we're both frozen. We hurry below, but it takes large mugs of hot chocolate and several minutes curled up in sleeping bags with hot water bottles before we feel really warm.

Our efforts to keep warm remind me of a passage in John Anderson's book *Vinland Voyage*. In 1966 Anderson led a party of six Englishmen aboard *Griffin*, a forty-foot sailboat, from England in search of Vinland. They called at Torshavn, Reykjavik and Parmiut (Greenland) from where they sailed directly to Halifax, Nova Scotia, which Anderson declared confidently was Vinland. As *Griffin* crossed the frigid Labrador Current, Anderson suffered badly from the cold. His remedy was to wear a string vest, shirt, two pullovers, short underpants, long underpants, pajama bottoms, drill or sailcloth trousers, and long socks of Norwegian wool. This was just for inside the cabin. When he went on deck, he added a second pair of socks, another pair of trousers, sometimes two more pullovers, and on top of all this his regular foul-weather gear of waterproof nylon trousers, jacket, and hood. It's surprising he could walk!

Thank goodness, getting dressed is easier for us. Our clothing is organized in three layers: thermal underclothes, a middle layer, and foul-weather suits. We carry several changes for the first two layers while on top we can have either regular foul-weather gear or survival suits. Only rarely do we resort to our warmest combinations. We're coldest when steering in the cockpit, and the chill gets mostly to hands and feet. Then we don survival suits with thick socks stuffed inside our sea boots and two pairs of gloves on our hands.

Everywhere along the coast, icebergs drift in the offing on their slow journey south. The few we find inshore add a brilliant contrast to the dark mountains, but they're widely spaced and present no difficulty. Occasionally we must pass close by a berg and we're reminded of the need for caution. Shortly after leaving one harbor I steer *Symphony* close by two bergs and again feel a chill in the air as the masses of ice slide by. Suddenly a shattering crash hits us with a thunderclap. Instinctively I duck. Astern, crashing ice has churned the sea into a foaming whirlpool. Large pieces roll over with deathly slowness while smaller bits that have been thrust violently below the water pop abruptly to the surface. Wavelets spread out from countless pieces of ice, obliterating *Symphony*'s shallow wake.

Our southward progress is steady but never spectacular. We sail whenever we can, but the wind is always variable and requires frequent changes of course and sails. We enjoy periods of downwind sailing with the genoa poled out, and some fine reaches when *Symphony* dips her shoulder to the waves and powers along like a train. However, with the wind frequently on the bow and several periods of calm, we do more motoring than usual. Motoring for long periods at a steady six knots can get tedious but here, amid such grandeur, it's impossible to be bored. The scenery is extraordinary—an ever-changing panorama of jagged mountain crests, deep mysterious fiords, and picturesque offshore islands.

We always plan to be at anchor well before nightfall. Night sailing among the rocks and islands would be trying and, in places, dangerous. It would also be a pity to miss the scenery! Evenings are generally calm with clear skies and we can enjoy a nightcap while watching magnificent displays of Northern Lights. Ever-changing curtains of light cover the sky from horizon to horizon. Jupiter is brilliant in the southern sky, while the Milky Way sparkles across the heavens. The whole panoply is duplicated in dancing patterns on the water. It's truly magical.

Late one afternoon Saglek Bay opens up to starboard. To the southwest the landscape is lower and softer than anything farther north. The cold wind that has driven *Symphony* briskly all day suddenly dies, leaving the air unusually balmy. We heave to near an island while Les tries fishing, but she has no luck.

St. John's harbor is a narrow, two-mile indentation in the south side of Saglek Bay. We motor past a small coastal vessel already at anchor, and on to the head of the bay. The water is extraordinarily clear. We watch the anchor descend through thirty feet before a puff of soft sand shows it has hit the bottom. Once the ripples subside, the anchor, with its chain lying in a gentle curve, is as visible as it would be in a swimming pool.

In the morning our neighbor weighs anchor and leaves. Les surveys the bay and surrounding hills for signs of wildlife. A flock of black-backed gulls sit on the water beside *Symphony*. Seals dive for fish around the boat and from time to time pause to watch us inquisitively. Caribou feed along a strip behind the beach and four ravens forage by the water's edge. Suddenly Les calls out excitedly, "There's a caribou swimming across the harbor!"

"Don't be silly—there can't be," I respond scornfully. "First it's wooly sheep, now swimming caribou."

"Here, take a look," she says, handing me the binoculars.

Far down the harbor I can see a small brown object, low in the water, propelled along by a light breeze. "That's no caribou," I declare definitively, "it's a tree branch with a twig sticking out."

For several minutes we watch as the log drifts toward the distant shore. Finally it bumps the shallow bottom and to my amazement a large brown torso rises unsteadily on four legs. It steps stiffly from the water and gives a rather timid shake before walking up the beach examining scraps of vegetation. Les is ecstatic. Too late I realize that while a swimming caribou may seem unlikely, on this barren coast it's the tree branch that would be really surprising.

It's a beautiful, cloudless day, perfect for exploring ashore. Leaving the dinghy hauled well above the high-water line, we set off along an unpaved road up a wide valley to the east. The derelict road-way is a relic of a time when a nearby early-warning radar site was manned. It winds along the south side of the valley. Round one corner we come face to face with a large caribou. For a second we all stand frozen in surprise. Then he turns and bounds away over the rocks. In places, the road is completely washed away, but enough remains for us to follow the line across the valley and over a rocky gorge with a small, fast-flowing stream.

Rock ledges above the gorge make a perfect rest and vantage point. For the first time on Labrador we find the ground covered with low vegetation, including dwarf birch and grass. Blueberries are all around us and we collect several sweet and juicy handfuls. Eastward, rough mountain slopes cut off the view, but to the west we look down on a panorama of inlets, fiords, and distant hills. *Symphony* lies below in a pool of turquoise water by a long strand of golden sand. It's a scene more reminiscent of Caribbean islands than the frozen north. Two wooden cabins with heavily boarded doors and windows occupy raised ground a little back from the shore, and two large open boats lie upturned nearby. Just above a line of rough vegetation marking high water, two drums of aviation fuel lie on their sides.

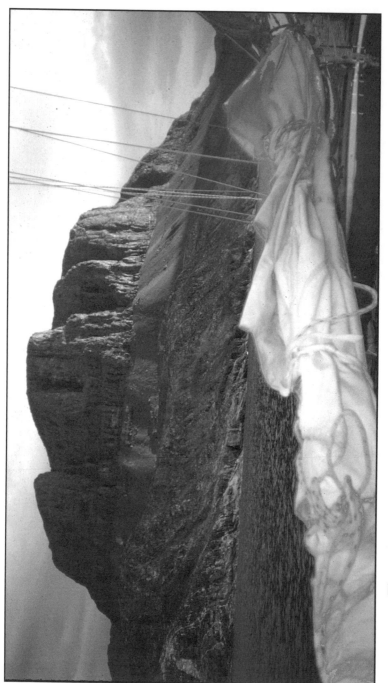

The setting sun glints on rock buttresses overlooking Three Cliff Harbor, Labrador

The evening is as perfect as the day. The sun slips from a cloudless sky behind the western mountains. Caribou reappear to graze on rough pasture behind the beach. The colors drain into twilight, and stars slowly fill the sky. Soon the heavens shimmer with millions of points of light. The Milky Way arches from horizon to horizon. Quite suddenly curtains of white light undulate and flash across the sky in ever-changing patterns. Long drapes intensify and then fade and then reappear in new positions. The sky fills with constantly changing diaphanous lights. It's the most dramatic display of Northern Lights of the voyage. We're in awe. The extraordinary spectacle is intensified by the profound isolation of the bay. It's so much to have all to ourselves, almost too much.

We leave St. John's harbor in sunshine. A starboard turn takes us past Bluebell Island and towering Cape Uivuk with its bright white-walled radar station, and back to the open sea. The sailing is good. We're close-hauled and have to make a couple of tacks, but the water is smooth, the motion pleasant, and progress quite fast. We carry the sails right to the mouth of Hebron Fiord. Here the wind heads us on the final approach and we hand the sails and start the engine.

Hebron was once a thriving Inuit settlement. It was closed by the government around 1960 and the population was forcibly resettled farther south. Several frame houses stand in various stages of decay around a derelict Moravian mission. Remains of the town wharf still project over huge boulders. Much of the bay in front of the village is foul, and we approach warily to anchor in eighteen feet of water about a third of a mile off the beach. The wind is brisk and cold, but we're well sheltered and enjoy a quiet night.

The next morning we drink our first coffee in the cockpit, watching a small whale swim round *Symphony* with a slow, undulating motion. We're just about ready to go ashore when the silence is broken by an aircraft engine, and soon a small seaplane circles overhead and lands in the bay. Passengers wave from tiny windows as it taxis to the settlement. It pulls right up to the rocks, and five occupants step down and scramble ashore.

We follow them to the landing place and tie up the dinghy. One or two houses, grouped rather haphazardly on rocky ground by the shore, have shutters of new timber over the doors and windows. A pile of lumber suggests someone has further restoration plans, maybe for use as hunting cabins. The old mission is a long rambling building perpendicular to the shore and appears to have been modified and extended many times. At the inland end a large assembly room still has a raised dais where once a choir sang and a preacher regaled his flock. Over several years the few travelers who have found their way here have left their names on scraps of paper. A tin holds a few dollars and someone's hope for future restoration. The rest of the ground floor is divided into small rooms. A giant attic runs right across the floor above.

Back in the sunlight we follow a rough path to the old cemetery, a fenced-off area on a small rise north of the buildings. Grave markers fill the small burial ground. Some are substantial stones, but in one corner simple wooden headboards mark mounds too small for anyone but infants. Nearby, outside the fence, Les finds bones projecting from a pile of loose stones and squats on the ground trying to piece them together. She identifies a human rib and arm bones that seem rather short for a modern adult.

A caribou sporting huge antlers ambles along a pathway, apparently unaware of our presence. For several minutes I stalk him, moving a little closer each time he looks away or drops his head to chew on small shrubs and grass. I stand in the open, but he's quite unable to see me as long as I'm perfectly still. Finally he wanders off round a rock outcrop, stopping occasionally to nibble the wiry turf.

One by one, three of the seaplane passengers walk over to join us. They're journalists and photographers researching an article for a travel magazine. We sit among the graves, swapping stories of the separate journeys that have brought us to Hebron. Suddenly a loud cry comes from the direction of the mission.

"Hey, quick, bring the camera, there's a bear."

"Where?"

"Over by the mission."

We all head toward the shout in a ragged line. I'm just a few yards from the mission when a huge black bear emerges round the corner of the building. He stops and stares, then with a contemptuous sniff of his nose turns and retreats in a rolling gait ahead of the straggling group of humans. He pauses dramatically on a projecting rock, his impressive form outlined against the sky, and then drops down and disappears behind the boulder. We all return to the landing together.

The photographers ask to use *Symphony* as foreground in an aerial view of the settlement. We agree to be photographed sailing in the bay in return for a copy of the picture. We're quite excited as it's difficult to photograph our own boat under sail. While the journalists board the plane, we raise the anchor and set the mains'l and genoa. *Symphony* reaches across the bay in front of the buildings and the plane makes a low pass overhead before disappearing from view between the mountains. It's the last we see of them and we never do get our picture.

Port Manvers Run lies behind offshore islands, providing a sheltered route for the final forty miles to Nain. We're north of the passage, sailing fitfully in a light and variable wind. It's misty, with patches of fog and a thick ceiling that blocks out everything over two hundred feet away. With ten miles to go, the wind rises and sailing becomes boisterous as we approach on a close reach on the starboard tack.

The entrance to the run requires a couple of turns between rock outcrops, first to starboard round Willis Rocks, the most prominent in the entrance, and then to port to avoid more rocks unseen below the water. The southeast breeze provides a fair wind for the whole maneuver and we decide to enter under sail. Being cautious, I roll a few more turns in the genoa. Les steers while I match the visible rocks with those on the chart. We jibe round the first island and leave it just two boat lengths to starboard. We're right where we planned, but the jagged rocks seem awfully close. With many reefs nearby, some below water, others lashed by the waves and shrouded in sheets of spray, our adrenaline flows freely. When the end of the island comes abeam, we turn toward Thalia Point, which forms the north side of the entrance. Another turn just short of the point brings us mid-channel into a large bay at the start of the run. Immediately the tension eases.

In the bay we're sheltered completely from wind and waves, and soon *Symphony* is drifting without steerage.

"Time to start the engine," I call to Les.

"How about catching a fish for dinner?" she responds.

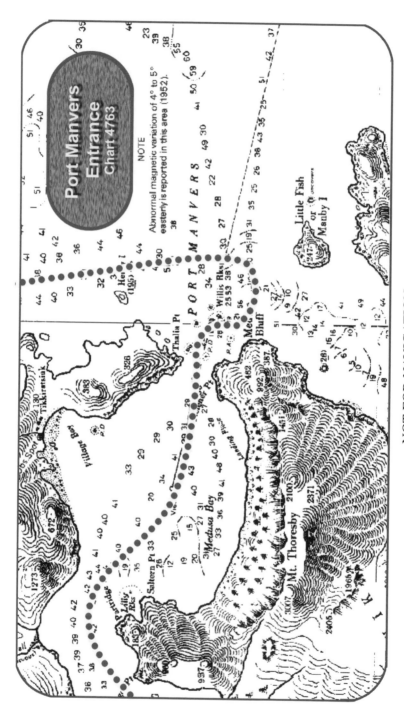

NOT FOR NAVIGATION

"Okay." Fresh fish sounds appetizing and I'm content to enjoy the tranquility of the bay a little longer before destroying it with the noise of the engine.

Les casts her line over the side but again fails to catch her first Canadian fish. The low cloud cuts off the mountains at mid-height and the general aspect is gray and colorless. However, below the overcast we can see a sandy beach to the north. To the south, on the lower slopes of Mount Thoresby, we find the first real trees we've seen since leaving Norway. They're evergreen and rather small, but they mark a significant step on our journey from bare arctic tundra to more temperate and fertile lands. A couple of miles inside the run we find a tiny cove only eight feet deep that makes an excellent overnight refuge.

After a good night's sleep we continue south through the run and on through broad channels between several islands. Early afternoon we pass a low headland to starboard and see Nain, straggling along the northern side of an open bay. *Northern Ranger*, a large blue-hulled freighter that is the lifeline of Labrador's coastal villages, occupies the whole of the single wharf. People are bustling about on the decks and a few tourists, evident by their cameras, descend a gangplank and stroll off to explore the village. Hoping the freighter's stay may be short, we anchor a little way off to watch and wait. On *Ranger*, youths race unchecked along the decks and climb noisily over the superstructure while the crew work to transfer various freight items to the wharf, using a derrick on the foredeck. One item that we can't identify seems to be especially troublesome and occupies the men for a considerable time. There are few items for the return and they're soon aboard. The derrick appears difficult to stow, requiring four or five crewmen to direct the operator in his cab high over the ship. Eventually the derrick is secured, a deep siren booms across the water, and a few passengers make their way along the wharf and up the gangway. With another loud wail *Ranger* reverses into the fiord before steaming down the inlet and out of sight. Soon we have *Symphony* tied up alongside the wharf and we're ready to explore.

Our first task is to find the RCMP (Royal Canadian Mounted Police) post to complete Canadian entry formalities. The main street is unpaved, uneven, and pot-holed. We pass several people, all small and dark-haired. Each one calls out "hello" or "hi"—quite different from the more reticent Greenlanders. A large station wagon with soft suspension lurches from side to side as it slowly negotiates large dips in the road surface.

The RCMP post is a log building at the end of the road. As we enter, a middle-aged woman looks up from her desk. "Can I help you?" she asks.

"We've arrived by boat from Greenland. We want to enter Canada formally," I declare.

"Err . . . ," she hesitates, "you want to do that here?"

"Yes, the Coast Guard said you're the people to contact."

It's clear she's unsure what to do and huddles with a couple of male colleagues. One officer comes over to the desk and we repeat our story in answer to his questions.

"We can't help you," says the woman we saw first. "Here's the number for Customs. You should call them." She hands me a slip of paper and invites me to use the phone in a rear office.

I suspect Canadian Customs receives few calls from Nain. I explain to the operator that I wish to report our arrival in Canada. There's a long pause and I'm put on hold. Eventually a young-sounding female voice inquires, "Can I help you?" I explain once more.

"Where are you?" she asks. "Are you at a port of entry?"

"I'm in Nain, Labrador," I reply.

"Maine? In the USA?"

"No. Nain, not Maine. It's in northern Labrador," I explain, enunciating the names slowly.

"Is that a port of entry?"

"I'm afraid I don't know. The coast guard advised me to contact the RCMP. They've referred me to you."

"Are you at the marina?"

I'm tempted to say "You haven't been to Nain, have you?", but a smart remark could only be unhelpful, so I simply explain, "There's no marina at Nain—we're moored at the town wharf."

"Wait a minute." The line is quiet and I assume she's consulting a superior. The voice returns. "You should really go to a port of entry, but I'll take your report over the phone."

I try to sound appreciative and respond to familiar questions about *Symphony* and ourselves. I'm given an entry number, and one final admonition: "If you come this way again, please come to an official port of entry. The ones nearest to Nain are Goose Bay and St. Anthony."

I promise to try. It's not worth explaining that Goose Bay is at least five days out of our way and we won't be near St. Anthony, Newfoundland, for another three weeks.

While I negotiate with Customs, Les describes our voyage to a group of RCMP officers. She finishes by complaining about the relatively poor fishing off Labrador: "In Iceland and Greenland it's easy to catch good fish. I've tried lots of times here," she complains, "and never got a bite."

"Just as well," chides one policeman gently. "Round here, fishing's against the law."

We know fish stocks are seriously depleted along the Canadian coast, but the severity of the decline is a complete shock. That fishing with a simple pole and line could be prohibited never occurred to us. We've read accounts of the early explorers hauling in cod as fast as they could heave the line, and that seems consistent with our own experience in Iceland. How could such abundance be so completely eliminated?

One officer expresses interest in our navigation and radio equipment and visits *Symphony* for a brief tour. In return, he invites us to his home for a shower. We readily accept.

Now officially in Canada we head for a grocery for the first time in a couple of weeks. There are two food stores in Nain, one run by the Hudson Bay Company and the other by the government. Neither one is as good as the stores in Greenland, but we find pork chops and potatoes and replenish our stock of paper towels. Fortunately they accept credit cards, as we have no Canadian money.

The Bank of Montreal has a branch in a wooden shed perched on a rock overlooking the main street. It has an uneven floor. Encouraged by a Visa sign in a window, we join the line at the counter. The line is short but moves with funereal slowness. The teller is quite unfamiliar with bank procedures and telephones someone for help with every customer. When it's finally our turn, it's apparent our quest for cash is hopeless. The complexities of the system, strangeness of the computer, and mysteries of English and French all confuse the teller beyond her ability or understanding. We thank her and leave. Our best find in the village is at the fish factory where we buy both smoked and frozen arctic char.

It's a couple of weeks since we called home and we want to reassure our family that all's well. There are, we're told, three pay phones in Nain, one at each grocery (both out of order) and a third at the hotel. We wait until evening when our daughter will be at home and make our way to the hotel. The door opens into a large but very plain bar. The air is thick with smoke. The phone is on the wall of a side room where people are seated on chairs watching a game of pool. Opposite are several electronic arcade games. The phone rings regularly and is answered each time by the same woman, who calls over the appropriate person to respond. The conversations are all quite short. When the phone falls silent, we make our call home. Happily all seems well. After a brief conversation we head for the door. "How about a beer?" I ask Les.

"Okay. Why not?"

"Two beers please," I say to the barman, expecting he'll ask, What sort?

"We don't have beer," the barman states flatly.

"What do you have?"

"Just spirits and mixes," he replies, as though it's obvious.

We decline and make our way back along the rough streets. Several people pass, each calling out a greeting as though we're long-time residents. We find the wharf busy, clearly a gathering place for the youth of Nain. Here they're much more aggressive than our young friends in Iceland and Greenland. They hustle around as they follow us along the wharf. Questions and demands fly at us, with several, usually the girls, talking at once.

"Is that your boat?"

"Where are you from?"

"Can you give me something?"

"Have you got a tooney (a two-dollar coin)?"

"Can I have a dollar?"

Two girls follow us uninvited when we step aboard *Symphony* and we have to direct them firmly back to the wharf. A restful night free of intruders seems unlikely at the dock, so we slip away and anchor fifty yards to the east on the edge of a shallow shelf.

The next morning a gale warning spurs us to find better shelter and we head for Kauk harbor, a land-locked anchorage just a few miles south. We spend a quiet day aboard as the wind twists and bends small shrubs and bushes on the hillside above.

As we continue farther south, the mainland is still mountainous, but hills are more rounded and less forbidding. Dramatic cliffs still sweep skyward from the water, but they're interspersed with more gentle slopes. Islands off the coast are rocky, but these too are lower and less rugged than those farther north.

Sailing is generally uneventful, but on our approach to one narrow and shallow passage the engine suddenly splutters and stops. I rush to the bow and set the anchor before we can drift toward nearby islands. The problem is easy to find: The fuel filter is blocked. We took fuel from a tanker at the wharf in Nain. We were warned the fuel might be dirty, and since then we've done quite a bit of motoring. It's a simple matter to change the filter and we're soon on our way.

As daylight fades on a pleasant evening, we anchor a quarter-mile southwest of a fish-processing plant in the harbor at Hopedale. Today we're fortunate—it takes just two tries to set the anchor! We have a spaghetti supper and a quiet night.

The following morning dawns cloudy with fog patches. Soon the sun breaks spasmodically through the overcast and eventually drives away any lingering cloud. After a leisurely breakfast we motor to the wharf at the plant. The fishing season is over and two workmen are decommissioning and winterizing the plant. They spend the day coiling hoses, washing everything, and generally tidying up. Behind the plant the town itself has a wild, frontier quality. A derelict wooden pier stands adjacent to the fish plant, and next to that a dead seal lies on a rock slab. Several sealskins are drying, stretched out on wooden racks behind a small frame house. A black bear skin lies discarded by the roadside. Two chained huskies toss a few desultory barks in our direction before flopping down to return to their rest. Long, straight wooden poles, the trunks and branches of straggly trees, are stored on end in stacks resembling Indian tepees. Locals call them sticks. They're cut in the fall, towed to town behind skidoos, and stacked for use as winter fuel. Two women riding ATVs overtake us as we walk on the rutted road. Regular street signs, like the octagonal red-and-white "STOP" sign and the black-and-white "Speed Limit 25 KM/H," seem incongruous.

Hopedale is a strange place to meet an archivist. However, as we continue our walk, we find Connie standing in the middle of the street talking to Don, who leans from the window of a large station wagon. Both Don and Connie are employed by Parks Canada, Connie to catalog artifacts at the local museum and Don to renovate the museum buildings. We talk for several minutes about life in Hopedale, the work they're doing, and sailing. Connie describes the museum collection as large, disorganized, and worth seeing. We accept her offer to arrange a guide for us to visit the museum later in the day.

Julius, a physical education student and summer guide, meets us at the door of the museum. He's an engaging young man with a broad toothy smile and a baseball cap set at a jaunty angle. His polarized glasses glint in the sunlight. He leads us through the mission assembly hall, along tortuous passages full of the smell of history, and into the museum building. This museum is like no other we've seen. There are no neat display cases with carefully labeled artifacts. There's no order. It appears that people left hurriedly with no time to care for belongings. We walk into rooms that are apparently just as they were when the residents walked out. We can see why a guide is needed to accompany visitors. It's a treasure house we cannot begin to appreciate. One room packed with books includes antique volumes from the eighteenth and early nineteenth centuries. Another is an early-twentieth-century dentist's office complete with chair and implements in an untidy pile. Others have comprehensive sets of nineteenth-century woodworking tools, household items, or agricultural implements. Few items are labeled. There's much work here for Connie to do.

Julius answers a stream of questions as we move from room to room. We ask him about life in Hopedale: "It's so beautiful here, but it must get pretty cold in winter."

"It does, but it's not difficult to keep warm; you just have to wrap up well."

"But the days must be so short and the nights long and dark."

"True," concedes Julius. "The summer's nice, but most people prefer the winter."

"Really? Whatever for?"

"In winter you can go places," he replies. "Everywhere's frozen over so you climb on a skidoo and go where you want. You can head into the mountains, gather wood, and visit relatives in other communities. It doesn't matter that there are no roads."

His words change my whole view of life in the north. We've seen many communities without roads and dependent on boats for transportation. We thought of ice obstructing navigation and visualized the winter months as a time for hunkering down and keeping warm. That the ice could facilitate travel rather than obstruct it is a whole new idea. That winter is the time to be out and about while the summer restricts mobility had not occurred to us.

We finally bid farewell to Julius and emerge from the museum to a beautiful day. Sunlight shimmers on the water. It's too nice to stay in town and we decide to find a quiet anchorage among offshore islands. From the chart I select a bay that appears well protected from all directions and we set off for an easy sail in light winds.

A group of huskies howl from the low summit of one island. As we approach, they race down to a low point that appears to be a landing place. Julius explained that huskies are left on isolated islands for the summer. Just once a week the owner approaches in a boat and tosses food ashore, often the carcass of a seal. Otherwise the dogs fend for themselves. Julius was emphatic that we should not land or get too close. "These are not pets," he warned sternly. "They're sled dogs." We're very happy to follow his advice and stay well clear.

The evening turns into one of classical beauty as the sun sinks behind the islands and the colors slowly drain away, first from the land and then from the sky. Mussels collected along the shore make a delicious pasta sauce. On one promontory we find hundreds of broken sea urchin shells where they've been dropped by gulls. The howls of more huskies on an island a mile away cross the still water with extraordinary clarity. I watch a small boat approach the island. As it draws closer, the howling grows in a powerful crescendo, then suddenly stops. I'm too far away to see, but it's plain that food has been tossed ashore and is being torn apart by hungry dogs.

We continue our journey southward, now among lower and softer, less dramatic scenery. There are still cliffs, but they no longer soar in single sweeps from sea to sky. The inland hills are lower and more rounded, while offshore islands are rocky and low-lying. Just ahead are some of the best-known landmarks in the Viking sagas and we look forward to the next step in our Viking odyssey.

In our enthusiasm to press on, we stretch one day until well after sunset. Faced with a night entry to an unfamiliar harbor, I choose a bay called Sloop harbor that appears easy to enter, with no hidden dangers and with steep rocky sides to provide good radar images. We enter at little more than bare steerage, checking the position by GPS and keeping midway between radar plots of the cliffs on each side. It feels good when the chain rattles through the fairlead and we are safely set for the night. The next morning it is reassuring to find we are indeed in the middle of the anchorage—right where we planned to be.

Chapter 14

Land of Forests

After three week of total immersion in Labrador's natural wonders, we're returning to the Viking trail. We're approaching the place described most precisely in the Vinland sagas. As Leif and his companions headed south:

> The country was flat and wooded, with white sandy beaches wherever they went; and the land sloped gently down to the sea. Leif said, "This land shall be named after its natural resources; it shall be called Markland (Wood Land)."
>
> *The Greenlanders' Saga*

We leave Sloop harbor and the inter-island channels for the open water of Groswater Bay. The land falls away on each side and vanishes into thick haze. Patches of mist and gray overhead cast a dull pall over the water, but a faint yellow glow suggests we may later see the sun. Somewhere to starboard, Hamilton Inlet leads for one-hundred-fifty miles through Lake Melville to Goose Bay. I set a southwesterly course across the mouth of the inlet to rejoin the coast farther south. The wind is astern and we sail gently wing and wing. A freighter steams out of the mist, passes our stern, and disappears toward the inlet.

Soon a dark horizontal line stretches through the mist ahead. As we draw closer, it thickens into a mass of trees stretching back from the shore to cover the low coastal hills and the flanks of the mountains behind. We gaze in wonder at a sight remarkable to eyes now accustomed to barren slopes and bare rock summits. We saw trees as far north as Port Manvers Run, but those were isolated saplings compared with the mature forest now before us. Here the trees don't huddle for shelter in protected hollows but spread out to cover the whole landscape. Not since Norway have we seen land covered by such a dark green carpet. Startling as this sight is for us, it must have amazed and excited Viking explorers. Their Greenland colonies lacked timber needed for buildings and ships and here's a limitless

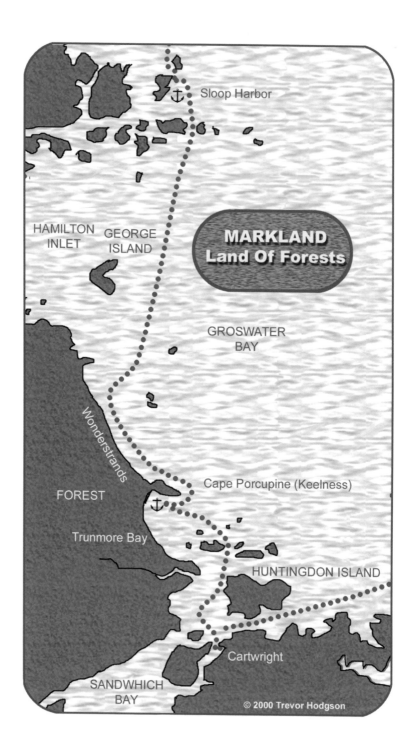

MARKLAND
Land Of Forests

Sloop Harbor

HAMILTON
INLET

GEORGE
ISLAND

GROSWATER
BAY

Wonderstrands

FOREST

Cape Porcupine (Keelness)

Trunmore Bay

HUNTINGDON ISLAND

Cartwright

SANDWHICH
BAY

© 2000 Trevor Hodgson

supply much closer and more accessible than Norway and apparently here for taking.

As we get closer, we see a light wedge that separates the forest
from the water. Slowly this broadens into a beach of white sand curving gently north and south as far as we can see. Almost anywhere else
such a magnificent strand would be packed with sun worshipers and
backed by tall hotels. Here the only inhabitants are small creatures
that forage the tidal strip, and the only background the leafy forest
canopy.

A quarter-mile from the surf we turn south to follow the shoreline, and in half an hour a shadow appears ahead that slowly becomes
a long promontory with a distinctive profile. It rises steeply from the
beach to a long, curving summit ridge before falling in a concave
curve to the sea. Its symmetrical form is a convincing silhouette of the
keel of an upturned boat. Viking explorers naturally called it
Keelness. It's called Cape Porcupine on modern charts where it
appears rather small, but from our position by the shore it's prominent, stretching across our course and almost three miles out to sea.

The wind is light and we make slow progress round the cape into
Trunmore Bay to its south. North of the cape the beach extends
twelve miles and here it continues another six before joining extensive shoals on the approach to the village of Cartwright. Trunmore
Bay is very shallow and we pick our way carefully to an anchorage in
eleven feet opposite the highest point of the promontory. The wind is
northwesterly and the cape provides an effective lee.

What a remarkable place! It's quite unlike anywhere else we've
seen. No other beach approaches the extraordinary extent of this gently curving strand and nowhere else does a huge forest sweep to the
very edge of the sea. While many headlands are more dramatic than
Cape Porcupine, the curving mound of Keelness is distinctive, its profile so different from the towering cliffs farther north that it's readily
identified. Together the features are unmistakable. This is clearly
Leif's Markland.

Five hundred years after Leif Eriksson's exploration, and five
hundred years ago, the English captain John Davis, on his second
voyage in search of the Northwest Passage, anchored his bark
Mooneshine close to where *Symphony* now lies. It was not a happy

visit. The native North Americans were hostile, ambushing five crew-men who were ashore fishing. The ship's guns fired to support the landing party, but before the natives were driven off, two sailors were dead and two seriously wounded. Davis decided not to pursue the attackers and instead to sail for England, but before they could leave, the weather changed, threatening the ship and the lives of the whole company.

> This present evening it pleased God to further increase our sorrows with a mighty tempestuous storm. . . . We unrigged our ship, and purposed to cut down our masts, the cable of our shut anchor broke, so that we only expected to be driven on shore among these cannibals for their prey. Yet in this deep distress the mighty mercy of God, when hope was past, gave us succour, and sent us a fair lee, so as we recovered our anchor again, and new moored our ship.

Mooneshine survived the storm and returned safely to England.

Fortunately our own stay is peaceful. The night remains calm and we wake to a morning of complete stillness. We're late preparing to leave. As we sip our coffee, we watch a distant small dot grow into an open wooden boat powered by a large outboard engine. There are two men aboard and we're soon in conversation with Herb and Dave as they hold their boat away from *Symphony*'s topsides. Herb, a small man of about forty, sits by the engine smoking a cigarette. Dave is noticeably younger, with a generous black beard. He wears a worn float coat and woolen cap. A small cooler and two guns lie in the bottom of the boat.

"Hi," calls Herb. "Are you all right?"

"We're just fine, thanks. What a beautiful morning."

"Yeah. We're from Cartwright just over there," he nods to the south. "We're hunting ducks."

"We've not got any today," adds Dave.

"We thought you must have a problem," Herb continues. "We don't reckon to see boats anchored out here in the open. It can get rough when the wind whips up."

"Oh, we've been lucky. It's calm and the winds have been in the northwest. Thanks for checking, though."

"I like your boat. She looks real sturdy," adds Les.

"The boat's Herb's—I'm just along for the ride. I pulled these old clothes from Herb's shed," Dave volunteers, tugging at his worn float coat.

"Dave's a schoolteacher," interjects Herb, in a tone with a certain deference.

"We plan to call at Cartwright later. Is there a store there?" I ask.

"Oh, yes, you can get pretty much what you want," Dave says.

"I hope it sells beer."

"Oh, you can get beer all right," says Herb reassuringly. "Anyway, we should be on our way. We'll see you when you get in." They push their boat away from *Symphony*. Herb pulls at the starting rope. The engine bursts into life at the third try, and they motor off southeast in a cloud of spray. We clear away our coffee cups and finish packing. Before long we set off after them.

The approach to Cartwright follows a rather narrow and irregular channel through a vast sandy shoal. There's still no wind and we motor. Les steers while I keep an eye on the chart, take sights on small islands and headlands, check the GPS, and suggest minor adjustments to the course. The route appears awkward on the chart, but we pass easily and the depth sounder never shows less than fourteen feet. We lead a small fishing boat along the entrance channel before rounding a low headland on the port side and heading toward a collection of boats and harbor buildings.

Most space at the short commercial wharf is occupied by fishing boats, but we find just enough room to squeeze in on the end of the pier. Before we're alongside, two familiar figures tumble from a blue truck, and Dave and Herb are calling out in welcome. We toss them the dock lines and soon have *Symphony* secured. Our new friends prove to be even better than their words as they climb down the bulkhead ladder carrying cans of beer. We spend a happy hour chatting and showing off *Symphony*. It's dark when the party breaks up and we climb into Dave's truck to go first to the store, then on to Dave's home where we're welcomed by his wife, Ola, and their five-year-old daughter, Victoria. We're treated to genuine Canadian hospitality with wonderful hot showers followed by dinner of pork and potatoes, pasta salad and rice. While we enjoy ourselves, our laundry is whirling round in the washing machine.

We talk well into the evening. We relate the highlights of our voyage and bombard our hosts with questions about life in Cartwright. There are fewer than seven hundred in the community, which supports itself through fishing, now mostly shrimp. There's no resident police force; the nearest RCMP post is at Mary's harbor, a hundred miles away over inhospitable mountains and much farther by sea. Everything arrives here by ship except a few items carried aboard a small plane on a daily service that uses the grass runway on the west side of the harbor. Dave and Ola have lived in Newfoundland ("on the Island"), where Dave was born and raised. Ola still has relatives in her hometown of Makkovik, a small coastal settlement a hundred and forty miles north.

"It is so beautiful here now, but how do you manage in winter?" asks Les.

"Well, everybody gets on their skidoo," chorus Dave and Herb, echoing Julius in Hopedale.

"How far do you go?" I ask, expecting to hear of short expeditions in the vicinity of the village.

Herb surprises us with his description of his annual trip to Goose Bay, a hundred and fifty miles through uninhabited backcountry in the middle of winter.

"It's all right. I know the trails. There's two or three ways to go," he says.

"But how long does it take?" asks Les.

"A couple of days. I sleep out overnight."

"Wow, that sounds really cold."

"Not really. I have thick sealskin clothes, a jacket, trousers, and really thick gloves. I sleep in the *komatik* (a covered box on a sled behind the snowmobile). It's not bad at all," explains Herb as though describing the way to the grocery store.

Suddenly I see Herb in a new light, but now Dave surprises us with an even more astounding tale of winter travel.

"We went up to Ola's folks in Makkovik last Christmas," he says casually.

"You mean, you and Ola? What about Victoria?"

"She was in the *komatik* with me," says Ola.

"So how far is it?" I ask.

"I'm not sure. It took about twelve hours. We stopped once on the way."

"You didn't just stop on the ice!" exclaims Les with evident disbelief.

"Sure," says Dave. "We got all wrapped up in furs in the *komatik*—it was fine. We didn't tell my parents, however. They wouldn't have been pleased."

Time slips by quickly. We're fascinated by the lives of these generous people whose world includes the familiar televisions, washing machines, and personal computers, but whose natural environment is so different from our own. All too soon it is time to leave. Ola runs us back to the harbor in the truck about 1:00 A.M.

The next morning we have our first look at Cartwright, a straggling village with buildings of various ages and architectural styles strung along unsurfaced roads. The school where Dave teaches is a simple, modern two-story building. Nearby we find a credit union, and encouraged by a Visa sign in the window, we join a short line of people waiting to be served by a single woman assistant. However, the customers are restless, as no transactions are possible because "the phones are down." We continue our walk round the settlement, and when we check back later, the problem is still not fixed. The community grocery occupies a warehouse building where the harbor pier meets the shore. It's very similar to the stores in Nain. Fresh meat in particular is in short supply and the selection in the chest freezer is limited. However, it does accept Visa, and the phones here are working so we buy a few essentials. At the checkout I pick up a small printed leaflet that is as near to a tourist brochure as anything we have found on Labrador. The list of visitors' attractions includes many we expect, such as fishing and hunting, but it's the first place we've found that lists berry picking as a major activity.

Around midday Dave collects us in his truck for a drive to a nearby radar station. He arrives with our laundry, all dried and folded! We follow an unsurfaced road round the bay and past a small hotel and grass airstrip. The road continues through coniferous forest with occasional views into broad valleys where rivers meander through grassy clearings. The land looks fertile, the trees healthy and the grass green. We look for signs of agriculture in the sheltered valleys, but Dave explains the climate is too harsh and the growing season too short. Eventually a steep hill takes us up into the clouds, and round a couple of sharp bends we find modern buildings with antennae, workshops, and office facilities. We pull in briefly at a small parking lot, but the fog gives no sign of clearing and we head back to Cartwright. We pass several vehicles, many with families enjoying a drive on the only road outside the village. Dave acknowledges waves from several other drivers.

The weather forecast has the wind freshening to twenty-five knots and backing to the southeast. *Symphony* is exposed at her unprotected berth and we must find a more sheltered mooring. First we need diesel fuel and propane. Both are available at the hotel but needless to say, when we try to call, the phones are down. With help from the dock office we finally get through and before too long a truck appears at the wharf. We fill the fuel tanks and exchange our depleted propane tank for a full one. We decide to make one more call at the grocery for a few items of fresh food. I wait on the wharf while Les scrambles up the side of the dock to join me. However, as she reaches out to grab the top, her foot slips and she crashes backward to the deck, landing heavily on the point of a lifeline stanchion. She lies prostrate on the deck. I scramble down and try to comfort her. She's very slow getting up. When she's ready, I help her down to the saloon and into her bunk. She's clearly in considerable pain.

Despite Les's injuries we still need to move *Symphony*. I make Les as comfortable as possible and head to the store. However, when I get to the checkout with my few purchases, the phone lines are once more down and there's no way to process my credit card. I leave the items behind in the wire basket and return to *Symphony* empty-handed. We'll have to survive on ship's stores until our next port of call.

For shelter we've selected Grady Tickle, a narrow inlet twenty miles east. Les struggles to the cockpit to take the helm while I recover the dock lines. It's apparent she's in severe distress, and as soon as we clear the dock she returns to her bunk. Apart from my concern for Les, the sail to Grady Tickle is a delight. We hold a close reach with the full genoa for the whole twenty miles. I hand the sails for the final approach and motor through a rocky entrance into a small inlet between two islands. It was once used by a fishing community, and many small wooden shacks line the sides of the bay, some on stilts overhanging the water. All are in advanced decay. There's plenty of swinging room in the inlet and soon I have the anchor down and set.

Instead of recovering as I expect, Les appears to go into shock. When she tries to get up, she collapses on the bunk, dizzy and nauseous. I help her back into bed and do what I can to make her comfortable. Now I'm worried. I don't know how to help her except to have her lie still and give her time to recuperate. It's several hours since she fell, and she seems to be getting worse. Maybe we should have stayed at Cartwright. It has only meager medical facilities, but maybe there's someone who could offer advice and encouragement. I search a medical book for help but find no treatment other than what we're already doing. Its emphasis on the seriousness of shock and the need for hospitalization does nothing to ease my anxiety. Should I call the Coast Guard? The nearest station is three hundred miles away. I decide they can do little to help over the radio, so a call is tantamount to a request for an emergency evacuation. I think about it long and hard but decide to wait, all the time hoping for some sign of recovery. I cook mince with rice for dinner, and Les eats a small helping from a bowl as she lies in her bunk. I doze fitfully through the night. Les seems to sleep quite soundly. We both wake several times. By the early morning hours the shock seems to be lessening. Les succeeds in visiting the head and returning to her bunk without falling over.

The day is overcast, breezy, and wet. The forecast is poor. It's obvious we'll stay where we are and give Les more chance to get over her ordeal. During the morning the winds increase and *Symphony* stretches back on the anchor chain, but the inlet proves a good haven and we feel quite secure. Les still feels ill and spends the whole day in her bunk, but by evening she's well enough to come to the table for dinner. Unfortunately I manage to burn the chops.

Before the dishes are cleared away, the wind backs to the northwest and rises to a full gale. The Tickle is open to the sea at both ends, but the north end is strewn with rocks that break up the waves. The seas pound the rocks, sending cascades of spray high in the air. A strong current flows right through the anchorage, pulling *Symphony* across the line of the wind. I consider setting a second anchor to hold the bow into the wind, but she seems secure and I decide against the extra complication. Les keeps anchor watch, snuggled in her sleeping bag by the radar while I sleep. The next day is much the same and it's late evening before the wind starts to decrease.

We leave Grady Tickle after our three-day stay in much better shape than when we arrived. Les will be sore for several days and her whole thigh is one ugly black bruise, but all symptoms of shock have disappeared. We're both ready to be on our way. The wind is light on the bow, but a long swell sweeps in from the east. Whenever we leave the shelter of islands, *Symphony* rolls uncomfortably so we take an inside route through Indian Tickle. The wind freshens. Blowing from the southeast across the cold Labrador Current, it brings a distinct chill. Near Domino Point we leave the inside passages and begin the run southward down the coast. Rollers sweep beneath *Symphony* and crash against the rocks, sending spray tens of feet in the air.

Our destination for the night is Batteau harbor, another abandoned fishing station. The approach is truly impressive, through a slender cut between rocky islands swept continuously by huge breakers. The wind drives the swell up onto rocks, where it explodes with a deafening boom into millions of tiny droplets. A passage between two especially noisy and violent plumes gives us some moments of tension. Waves crash onto rocks on both sides and white water swirls around unseen dangers before we slip through the constricted passage and into the smooth water of the harbor.

Groswater Bay is now well astern and we've left behind the beaches and forest. However, we've not returned to the barren rock cliffs that we saw north of the bay. The coast and offshore islands are low-lying but covered with profuse vegetation. There are no real trees, but a thick green carpet of moss and lichens covers the ground while low shrubs add countless variations of form and shade. Squasho Run, another inland passage, is particularly beautiful. We pass through on a fine, bright day with the brisk southeast wind bringing its customary chill. Open waters are rough and uncomfortable, but in the sheltered channel it's warm and pleasant. The sides of the run form huge natural rock gardens with every imaginable shade of green set among warm tones of red granite.

The weather remains variable. We enjoy days when bright sunshine illuminates every indentation of the rocks and highlights the profusion of color in the minerals and plants. However, the long-feared gales are now quite frequent. It's approaching the end of September. We've been lucky with the weather so far, but it's starting to turn. We press on southward, not really hurrying—the cruising is too good for that—but mindful we must soon be clear of the coast. South of Squasho Run we spend a day sheltering at anchor in Eagle Cove. Again we keep anchor watch through the night, fearful *Symphony* might drag and be cast on the rocks. It's a beautiful place to be confined. Multiple shades of green mix with scattered deciduous trees already showing yellow leaves. The cove is landlocked, so secure among surrounding hills that it takes several attempts to complete our check-in with the Coast Guard. Even when we eventually make weak contact, the operator has difficulty copying our position, but we manage to avoid having anyone turning out to look for us.

On September 22, one week after leaving Cartwright, we round Cape St. Lewis into St. Lewis Sound. It's late in the afternoon and we motor to Lewisberg to find a berth for the night. We tie up near a couple of fishing boats at a fish plant on the east side of the harbor. The crew of one boat is busy enclosing the stern section with a wooden structure. We're told she's preparing to head to Nain for scallops. We find a faucet and fill the water tank.

We still have no Canadian coins and no one at the wharf knows where to find an ATM. From a phone at the rear of the fish plant we call the local store only to find it does not accept cards. By now thousands of mosquitoes are making their presence felt painfully. We were warned bugs could be troublesome on Labrador, but this is the first time we have found them—or they us. Now they hunt in droves and bite voraciously, compensating for any previously lost time and making our lives truly miserable.

Although dusk is falling, we head across the bay to Mary's harbor, hoping to leave behind the pesky insects. We have a pleasant, uneventful sail. A crowd of men and boys on the dock at the harbor entrance call out directions as we approach in the dark. A large tug occupies the outer end of the dock. As we pull alongside, her skipper

Untrimmed during our voyage, my beard is quite long
by the time we reach North America

pokes his head from the cabin doorway: "Hey, tie up alongside if you
like," he says. "It'll save adjusting your lines."

"When are you leaving?" I ask.

"Not till seven in the morning."

"Okay, I'll just pull in ahead of you. . . . We might be late in the
morning. . . . I'd hate to hold you up."

Two men catch our lines and fasten them to large cleats. With the
engine stopped, we clamber to the wharf. There are no mosquitoes!
One man introduces himself as John, the operations manager of the
fish plant.

"How far's the nearest store?" we inquire.

"Oh, about a mile and a half. I can give you a ride if you like," offers John unhesitatingly.

"Is there somewhere still open?"

"Sure. You've got an hour or more yet."

The selection at the small grocery is not extensive. We get a six-pack of Canadian beer and select some chicken from a chest freezer. The following day we cross the harbor by dinghy, find a bank, and finally, after almost four weeks in the country, manage to get Canadian money.

Our last stop on Labrador is Battle harbor. It's on the southern extremity of St. Lewis Bay. A strong stern wind drives *Symphony* on and we cover the six miles from Mary's harbor at a brisk pace. The entrance seems strewn with rocks and very narrow, so we hand the sails and start the engine. We suffer the usual anxiety when passing close to water swirling round hazardous rocks, but the entrance proves much easier than it appears. Helped by two men, we tie up to a substantial and new-looking wooden wharf. The wind is blowing strongly, directly into the harbor, and *Symphony* strains on her lines. A colleague joins our two helpers, and together we turn *Symphony* and warp her round into an effective lee on the side of the wharf.

Battle harbor was established as a fishing station in 1775. It became the British headquarters on the Labrador coast, north of the region dominated by the French. We're impressed that a harbor with such an intimidating entrance could achieve such importance. Perhaps the obstructions were an advantage in days when visitors might well turn out to be hostile. The harbor is a narrow channel between the mainland and a rocky island. The buildings, formerly houses, churches and warehouses, spread up the side of the island.

The settlement has been thoroughly restored as a museum and tourist destination. It opened for the first time just four months ago. It's an ambitious project with a store, hotel, and showers, and with good dockage at newly constructed wharves complete with shore power. It's now the end of the season and workmen are closing the buildings and preparing for winter. We have the place to ourselves as we wander through the old settlement buildings and examine the museum displays. In one first-floor gallery we find a long, curved wooden rudder labeled as the spare rudder of *Gaia*. Apparently her builders were not completely confident with her steering oar. On her

Vinland Revisited voyage, *Gaia* called at Lewisberg before going on to L'Anse aux Meadows. Confident the rudder wouldn't be needed, it was left there and subsequently sent over to the museum. The inscription, signed by skipper Ragnar Thorseth and twelve crewmembers, reads: "This is the spare rudder from the Viking ship *Gaia* which crossed the Atlantic from Norway to Labrador as part of the Vinland Revisited expedition July 1991 (It was never used)."

We feel a strange satisfaction at finding this rudder. We're about to make the final leg of our voyage to L'Anse aux Meadows, and here's a small part of another expedition inspired by the same heroes and exploits as our own. We return to *Symphony*. Tomorrow we'll follow Ragnar and his companions across the Strait of Belle Isle to Newfoundland.

Chapter 15

L'Anse aux Meadows

We're underway early for our crossing of the Strait of Belle Isle. The museum buildings are dark, silent shadows against the hillside. A solitary light in a hotel window is the only sign of staff preparing for another day of packing up. Gulls call imperiously overhead as we cast off, but they quickly move on. Three agitated dogs bound frantically across a rocky island at the harbor entrance and shatter the morning quiet with excited barks.

Inside the protective islands the water is barely rippled, but as we pass through to the ocean, long swells collide with the rocks, sending spray flying into the air. Despite the agitated water the wind is light. We set the main, roll out the genoa, and head for the indistinct, dark-blue smudge of Belle Isle. We search the horizon for Newfoundland, but nothing interrupts the long thin line between sea and sky. The coast of Labrador slowly falls away to starboard and becomes the north shore of the Strait of Belle Isle. *Symphony* moves quickly with the wind vane steering and there's little to do but keep watch.

A strong current carries us westward into the strait and I adjust the course to compensate. It's the first time we've noticed a strong current since *Symphony* was pushed southward on our approach to Cape Chidley. This caught the attention of the exploring Vikings as they recorded their approach:

> The expedition sailed on until they reached a fjord. They steered their ships into it. At its mouth lay an island around which there flowed very strong currents, and so named it Straum Island.
>
> *The Saga of Erik the Red*

Before long the wind backs to the southwest and freshens. Soon a vigorous breeze, opposing the tidal stream, produces short, choppy and uncomfortable waves. We roll in part of the genoa, then reef the main. *Symphony* dips her bow into the waves and shoulders her way

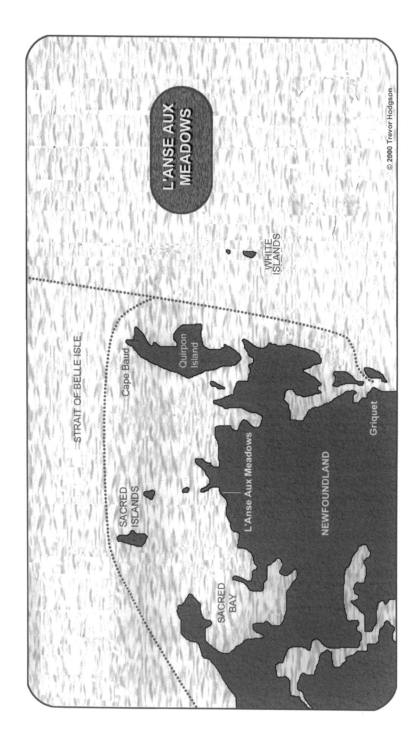

L'ANSE AUX MEADOWS

STRAIT OF BELLE ISLE

SACRED ISLANDS

SACRED BAY

Cape Baud

Quirpon Island

WHITE ISLANDS

L'Anse Aux Meadows

NEWFOUNDLAND

Griquet

© 2000 Trevor Hodgson

forward on a close reach—her best point of sail. Progress is fast, but the motion soon has me feeling distinctly unwell. I take an antihistamine pill (usually quite effective) and rest quietly while Les keeps watch.

Our course lies west of Belle Isle that we now see is a high grassy plateau atop a wall of steep cliffs. We can see no buildings or obvious landing places, and the island has a private and unwelcoming aspect. Our attention goes ahead where at last a small dark cone appears on the horizon. Soon a second, lower triangle appears to the right. A thin line links the two and gradually spreads out to the west. The easterly cone is Cape Baud, the most northerly point of Newfoundland. It grows steadily into a rock headland and soon we can distinguish a lighthouse and its associated buildings.

We plan to anchor at Griquet where a landlocked bay promises good protection close to the Viking houses at L'Anse aux Meadows. It's on the east side of the northern Newfoundland Peninsula and we pass a half-mile off the high, precipitous cliffs that buttress Cape Baud. By the time we're near Griquet, daylight is failing. A passage between the mainland and a small island leads to a picturesque bay surrounded by low hills dotted with a few white houses. Fishing boats occupy all the spaces at a small wharf and we decide to raft against one of them. As we get closer we see a man of about thirty years old with an older fellow climb down to the boat. With a wave of his arm, the young man motions us to draw alongside. As Les brings *Symphony* to a halt, he takes the bow line and ties it to a cleat high up on the superstructure. I scramble up the topsides and fix another line to a large cleat on the aft deck.

Returning midships, I extend a hand to the younger man. "Hi. I'm Trevor."

We're greeted in a voice remarkably soft for such a big man. "Hello. My name's Barry Bridger; this is my father, John."

"Is it all right to stay a day or two?" I inquire.

"That's fine. You'll have no bother here," replies Barry.

"Will this red boat be moving?"

"Oh, no. He's away down in St. John's. He'll not be back till the middle of the week."

"Do we need to check with anyone?" I ask.

Barry's voice stiffens just perceptibly. "No, you're all right. I'm the harbor administrator."

Everything has worked out more easily than expected.

"What brings you to Griquet?" asks Barry.

When we describe our Viking odyssey, John immediately recalls another ship on a similar voyage.

"Just like Tom and Roz. . . ," he confides to Barry who nods in agreement. "They were here twelve years ago," he continues, as though we should know who they are. (In fact we do. We've read Tom Cunliffe's *Topsails and Battleaxe*, in which the English sailor describes his family's journey from Norway to Newfoundland aboard their pilot cutter *Hirta*.) "They were here for a week or so. We used to join them for a game of cards and a drink. Their daughter was nine. She had her birthday party at our house; we had a few kids round. We still get a card at Christmas."

We explain our own plans to visit L'Anse aux Meadows.

Barry and John exclaim together: "You've passed it; you've come right by there." A long conversation ensues over the location of L'Anse aux Meadows and its distance from Griquet. Barry leads me to another boat where he elaborates over a well-used chart on the pilothouse table. When he's sure I understand where we are, we rejoin the others.

"Would we be better to stay somewhere else?" I ask.

"Oh, no. The north side's all foul," explains John. "This is the best harbor you'll find."

"I thought we might get as close as possible by dinghy, and then walk," I suggest.

"You don't want to do that," says John. "That's too far."

"Maybe we can get a bus?"

"I'll be happy to take you," says John. "I have to take my wife to work first thing, but then we can go." We accept John's kind offer and arrange to meet at half past nine.

Right on time, John's dark-blue car pulls up on the quay and we climb over the deck of our neighbor to join him. Soon we're driving along a series of narrow but well-surfaced roads that turn and undulate through a varied landscape. Thick woodland gives way to areas of open heath. We pass lakes and green pastures. Well-separated houses stand by the roadside and across the valleys. We make a long, gradual descent toward the coast overlooking a rock-strewn bay with two small islands in the background before we head uphill once more. A group of small modern houses cluster round a tiny inlet.

To someone arriving in Newfoundland from almost anywhere but Labrador it must seem wild and undeveloped. For us it's another step in our gradual return to civilization. Farther north, nature is ascendant, allowing only a few tough souls a hard living on the edge of the wilderness. Here the balance is more equal. Much of the land is still untamed, but the effect of human presence is unmistakable. The summer season is longer and it is possible to grow potatoes and beets. Cows graze in green pasture. Roads link neighboring communities. No one is isolated.

From a small parking lot a path leads down to a modern building tucked low into the hillside. Inside double glass doors a spacious reception area is empty except for three or four staff talking in a group, all young women looking very official in Parks Canada uniforms. It's the end of the season and in five days the visitor center will close for the winter. The few tourists who will come here today have yet to arrive. A short film explains how Danish archeologists Helge and Anne Stine Ingstad first discovered Viking remains here and describes the subsequent excavation. A small exhibition displays the crucial artifacts which confirm that Vikings actually made it to North America: soapstone whorls, a cloak pin, and lumps of slag from a smithy where nails were forged to repair the boats.

A long pathway winds downhill behind the center to where remains of Viking buildings lie in a shallow arc a few feet above the water. Raised footings projecting from the close-cropped grass reveal the usual rectilinear shape of Viking longhouses. A separate building, safely away from the others, was the smithy. This small settlement is typical of those we've seen all across the North Atlantic. We recall similar ones by the shores of Hafrsfjord in Norway, overlooking the fiord at Kirkjubør in the Faroes, at Stöng in Iceland, and at Brattahlid in Greenland. This site is more exposed than others and appears vulnerable to gales blowing across the Strait of Belle Isle. However, those following the pioneers along the coast of Labrador guided only by oral directions would find it relatively easily.

Lesley explores the Viking houses at L'Anse aux Meadows

Away from the shore the land rises gradually through a large open area of rough pasture, unremarkable perhaps unless you've just come from the barren, rocky valleys of Greenland and Labrador. Vikings searching for grazing land would be drawn irresistibly to such a place.

> The country seemed to them so kind that no winter fodder would be needed for livestock; there was never any frost all winter and the grass hardly withered at all.
>
> *The Greenlanders' Saga*

This is the first low-lying meadow we've seen since Greenland, as striking to us as it obviously was to French explorers who rediscovered the site and coincidentally included "Aux Meadows" in its name.

Next to the historic buildings, Parks Canada has reconstructed two Viking houses, with walls and roofs of grass. The interiors have the usual benches along the sides, central fireplaces, and roof openings to vent the smoke. We could still be at Hafrsfjord or Stöng. Outside, two small boats, upturned on trestles, could well be one of the *Gokstad* boats in Oslo. Their curving prows echo those in Shetland and the Faroes and their keels remind us of Cape Porcupine. We sit in the sunshine on a small mound. There's no wind; the air feels warm. Haze cuts off the view short of the Labrador coast, and Belle Isle is barely visible. The landscape here bears few modern scars. Returning Vikings could perhaps still recognize where they camped a thousand years ago. For a time the site must have seen vigorous activity, with boats hauled up on the stony beach as explorers prepared shelter for their first winter in a strange land. Maybe it was here Gudrid, the wife of Thorfinn Karlsevni, gave birth to Snorri, the first European child born in the New World.

However, the Vikings' stay in North America was fraught with difficulties. Ships were lost on passage between here and Greenland, and eventually the settlers confronted native people in a conflict even fearsome Viking warriors could never win. They were hopelessly outnumbered and far from home. They suffered casualties they could ill afford. Thorvald, Leif's brother and son of Erik the Red, was one of several to be killed. Disagreements among the Vikings themselves compounded their problems. Despite the attraction of plentiful pasture and timber, they were eventually forced back aboard their ships for the return to Greenland.

On the drive back to Griquet, we pause at a viewpoint where we admire a panorama of lakes and forests, and John takes us to visit his small local church. Like Barry, John talks with the gentle lilt that we come to associate with Newfoundlanders and accents the final syllable in the island's name. When he wants to emphasize a point to Les, he interjects with "I'm telling you, my dear" and greets her observations with "You got that right, my dear."

John and his wife, Stella, raised a large family of "boys and maids," all now grown and, except for Barry, away from home. John was harbor manager before Barry, and his father held the post before him. John is retired now after forty-seven years at sea fishing and sealing in the harsh waters surrounding his native island. He describes the bitter sub-arctic cold of winter sealing and explains his role as the winch-man, hauling the kill back to the ship. On one offshore voyage John collapsed with a heart attack. "After a day or so I was okay," he said, "but the skipper, he said I had to get checked." The ship docked at Cartwright and John was airlifted first to St. Anthony and then on to St. John's where he underwent extensive heart surgery.

Some years ago, before decent roads linked the towns and villages, John kept a team of sled dogs. He talks with obvious pride of his team of huskies and his special relationship with the lead dog. One night in deep winter a woman neighbor was taken ill. With no other way to get her to medical help, John carried her on his sled through a storm the fifteen miles to St. Anthony.

For five days weather forecasts foretell gale-force winds, and like the fishing boats, we stay in port. John and Stella are most hospitable. We enjoy supper at their home where we're introduced to bottled caribou and moose, and jams from the berries that grow profusely on the hills. John takes us to the store in his car. Barry takes us to St. Anthony where we tour the home of Wilfred Grenfell, who founded missions all along the Labrador coast and first brought medical care to the remote communities.

Life here is driven by the annual cycle of seasons, and it's time to prepare for winter. Huge stacks of wood stand drying by the roadside waiting to be hauled back to the houses. The heath land is a riot of blueberries, partridge berries, and bakeapples. The berries are collected by the gallon and made into jam. The hunters are out, seeking the single moose allowed each household. Remarkably absent from these preparations is fishing. Even here in the home of the cod fishery it's illegal to cast with a pole and line.

Five days pass quickly and it's time to say goodbye to the generous Newfoundlanders. When we call at John's house, a young neighbor stands inside by the door. He has the look of a man who's been up all night.

"He just got his moose," explains John.

"Where was that?" we ask. "Just around here?" We don't recognize the name of the place he identifies but understand it's about five miles away.

"It came up real close, a three-hundred-pounder," says the neighbor. "He just stood at the side of the trail."

"That's the best," says John. "I've seen 'em up to six hundred pounds, but that's too much. Those big'uns can be tough; three hundred pounds is about right."

We take our leave. With mixed emotions we untie from the red fishing boat. We'll miss our new friends who have opened their home to us and been so kind.

We're at the end of our six-month Viking odyssey. We've followed the entire chain of Norse settlements across the North Atlantic and visited many houses and churches marking the settlers' route. The scenery and wildlife have been extraordinary. We have also met warm-hearted people who welcomed us to their homes and were generous with their time and hospitality. They've left us with indelible memories and a wish to return.

The end of our voyage leaves us not with exhilaration—no doubt that will come later when we see our families and have time to reflect on our journey—but with a sense of deep satisfaction. We're content with our adventure. We set out with high hopes and one by one they've been fulfilled. We've traced the Viking route from island to island, seen extraordinary landscapes and wildlife, and met many generous people with lives so different from our own. It will take a little time for it all to sink in. However, we are still eight hundred miles from New York. It's October and we've already seen the fury of early winter gales. We need to head east as expeditiously as possible.

The wind is southwesterly, and as soon as we clear the cliffs at the harbor entrance we set the genoa and make good time on a broad reach. We round Cape Baud and sail close-hauled, still with just the genoa, outside the islands along the north shore. We can just see the dark green rectangles of the reconstructed houses at L'Anse aux Meadows, low down by the shore at the foot of a long, rising pasture. As we continue to the west they merge into the landscape. We're on our way home.

Appendix

Reflections on the Vinland Sagas

The Vikings' exploration of the American East Coast was the magnificent culmination of their extraordinary Atlantic voyages. It is described in two Icelandic sagas, *The Saga of Erik the Red* and *The Greenlanders' Saga,* both of which, like others of their genre, are colorful tapestries woven with threads of history and fantasy. The stories of returning pioneers were passed orally from generation to generation for two hundred years before they were inscribed on vellum. Founded on accounts of historical events they were molded by repeated telling and then embellished by the scribes who finally recorded them.

Scholars have devoted considerable research to understanding these tales and locating the places they describe. Analyses of the texts have been supplemented with theories of Viking navigation, astronomy, climatology, geography, and other areas of knowledge and special interest. However, the texts are sufficiently general that even after considerable analysis a variety of interpretations are possible. While the Viking camp at L'Anse aux Meadows is generally accepted as authentic, whether it formed the primary settlement or just a staging post on voyages farther south is more controversial.

Without expertise in any of these learned fields I'm reluctant to join this discussion. However, our journey has given us a perspective shared by few others. The fiords and mountains of Labrador have changed little in a thousand years and the sights that impressed us are those that impressed the Viking pioneers. From the decks of *Symphony* we've gazed with awe at the same mountain ranges, sailed round the same towering rock buttresses, and shared astonishment at the discovery of sandy beaches and extensive forest. The panorama unfolded for us just as it did for the Vikings, with similar relationships of time and space. Although most analysis begins with the saga texts, we start where the Vikings did—with the landscape they sought to describe. Places appear different when approached in different ways. You cannot drive to L'Anse aux Meadows through thick woodlands and acres of green grass and view it as the explorers did. If you sail from the north, your eyes become accustomed to bare rocks and barren valleys and you can appreciate the extraordinary pasture at L'Anse aux Meadows.

As a result of our up-close view of the Vikings' route, we've come to question three elements of the most commonly accepted scenario for the voyages:
- •The route across Davis Strait
- •The location of Helluland
- •The relative importance of grapes and pasture in Vinland

At the core of both sagas are simple sailing directions prepared by pioneers to guide those who followed. Unable to write, their directions were necessarily pictorial and concise. They identify only the critical landmarks along six hundred miles of coastline, but these proved adequate to guide subsequent explorers to their destinations. The sagas describe just a few physical features including a useless area of flat stones called Helluland, a fiord with fast-flowing currents, extensive beaches and forests, and a promontory shaped like a ship's keel. Scholars relying on precise analysis of the saga language (surely questionable, with their dependence on oral tradition) have located these landmarks all along the American East Coast. Straumfjord may be identified with Hudson Strait, or the Strait of Belle Isle, or the Hudson River; the Wonderstrands are at Cape Cod, Long Island, or the New Jersey shore; and the forests of Markland are everywhere from Labrador to Carolina.

From the deck of a small boat, limited in speed and subject to wind and weather, the pieces fall more naturally into place. Perhaps the most distinctive features are at Trunmore Bay. No voyager from Greenland, having coasted along four hundred miles of magnificent but barren north Labrador, could gaze at the beaches of white sand backed by a carpet of green forests and reasonably doubt he'd found Markland. From there the sagas lead consistently and convincingly south to Straumfjord, the Strait of Belle Isle, and on to Leif's booths at L'Anse aux Meadows where archeology has confirmed a Norse camp.

The location of Helluland has always been more elusive. Its description seems vague compared with the clear delineation of features farther south, and many writers place it somewhere on Baffin

Island to the north of Hudson Strait. It's as though no one knows where it is and Baffin is sufficiently vague and far off to bother no one. This issue is related to the Vikings' route from the Greenland settlements. In many interpretations they first sail north, cross Davis Strait at its narrowest point and then proceed south, following the Baffin coast, crossing the mouth of Hudson Strait, and continuing on down the coast of Labrador. This route is based on a saga reference to Leif heading north from the eastern settlement and a view of Vikings as coastal sailors who kept ocean crossings as short as possible. It has also been suggested they took advantage of the generally counterclockwise currents in Davis Strait, but these are insignificant compared with the extra distance involved.

We considered this northern track for our own voyage. We eventually rejected it because it makes no sense. It almost doubles the five-hundred-mile voyage and extends the travel time significantly, important considerations when subject to the whims of the wind, whether aboard a Viking knarr or modern sailboat.

The long detour was as unnecessary for Leif Eriksson and Thorfinn Karlsevni as it was for us. Vikings understood latitude. They sailed routinely to and from Greenland, Iceland, and Norway. Leif's voyage was inspired by the adventure of Bjarni Herjoldsson who was driven from his course between Iceland and Greenland by northeast gales. When he ended up off an unknown shore well south of Greenland, he knew his latitude well enough to find his way there (though he'd not been to Greenland before) and to provide sailing directions for Leif and his companions. All the Vikings who explored the American coast were seasoned mariners with at least one ocean passage to their credit. Karlsevni sailed to Greenland from Iceland and reportedly completed a voyage to Norway. Leif himself sailed to Norway and back. It seems unlikely such experienced sailors would set off northward for a destination they knew full well was to the south.

We wonder too about Hudson Strait. If the Viking route crossed the turbulent waters between Baffin Island and Labrador, its omission from their accounts is surprising. As we discovered, it has strong tidal currents. It would be impossible to miss, and therefore, one would think, worth mentioning to those coming later. It may of course have featured in early repetitions of the accounts and been dropped over time. Equally possible may be the conclusion that the Vikings never used this route for their voyages to Vinland.

The sagas are clear that Helluland lies north of Markland. We never saw the "many flat stones, so big that a pair of men could easily clap sole to sole on them," but south of the Torngats the coast, while still rocky and barren, is relatively low and flat. I like the idea that this area, roughly between Hopedale and the north shore of Groswater Bay, is Helluland. It provides a useful landmark, the first low-lying land on the way south. When a sailor recognizes these rocky, low-lying islands, he knows he's closing in on Markland. In contrast it's difficult to see value in a waypoint on Baffin, even if anyone went that way. Whether or not the coast there is mountainous adds nothing to the mariner's route finding or understanding of his progress.

No element in the sagas has caused more controversy than the tales of wild grapes. While grapes grow on the American East Coast, none have ever been found as far north as Newfoundland. For some writers this eliminates L'Anse aux Meadows as Vinland and they postulate other settlements farther south. Others argue that Vinland really means "The Land of Pasture" and that the issue of grapes is irrelevant.

Whatever Leif intended, it's clear the thirteenth-century saga writers wanted to promote Vinland as Wine Land. Perhaps wine sounds more exotic than grass, but does this reflect what the explorers found? Maybe we can look beyond the scribes and establish what was in the minds of the pioneers: What did they see when they first gazed at the new lands? What were they seeking? What features of the new lands would persuade colonists to settle? Iceland, Greenland, Helluland and Markland are all broad descriptions of the landscape. The icecaps of Iceland and the green slopes of Greenland's mountains are there to be seen and there's still no shortage of trees in Markland. We can look at the terrain, nod wisely, and say "Oh, yes, this is so-and-so-land." We felt much the same as we stood by the houses at L'Anse aux Meadows, our eyes surveying the broad expanse of rough pasture spreading back from the shore. We had seen no other place like it and nothing comparable since Greenland. Leif learned from his father that an attractive name could encourage settlement. The promise of Vinland was strong enough to launch several expeditions, including at least one well-organized attempt at settlement. Which, grapes or pasture, was the stronger lure? What motivated such endeavor and what would the settlers have to find in their new land to make the venture a success?

Besides timber for homes and shipping, Vikings needed pasture for the cows they took with them on their settlement voyages. Pasture meant a viable home site and maybe life itself. On the other hand, grapes were not part of their culture, cannot sustain life, and would provide little incentive to move family and home overseas. Leif's announcement that he found grapes would provoke astonishment but not emigration. Wood and pasture would move men. He found the first at Markland and the other at Vinland two days' sailing to the south. As we stood at L'Anse aux Meadows it all seemed so obvious.

When the sagas were finally written, they had to accommodate the world view of their authors and patrons. Starting with oral stories and sailing directions (or what remained after two hundred years) the scribes didn't hesitate to add imaginative creations to improve the tale or please their sponsors. Key participants must appear favorably and surprising facts explained and authenticated. Vikings were proud people to whom honor was all important. No Viking could be killed by a *scraeling*, the contemptuous term the Vikings used for an Inuit or Native American. There was no denying the death of Erik the Red's son on one of the expeditions, but his reputation, his honor, could be salvaged. He was slain, therefore, not by the arrow of a despised scraeling but by a fantastic "uniped." The scribes showed similar creativity regarding wine. They were clearly aware that reports of wild grapes in Vinland would amaze their readers. To authenticate the idea, they have grapes discovered by a German (a retainer of Leif) who declares in self-justification, "I was born where wine and grapes are no rarity." On another occasion, a Viking is intoxicated from eating too many grapes.

Whether Leif advertised his new land as Wine Land or Pasture Land, the saga writers' promotion of grapes has been successful. Helped by ambiguity in the Viking language and perhaps by the abundance of berries all along the Labrador coast, they've convinced most readers that Vinland means "Wine Land." Quite likely the Vikings did find wild grapes in greater Vinland as they explored southward from their Newfoundland camp. However, in choosing a home, their primary motivation was probably like our own. They needed food for their families, which meant pasture for their cows. This they found at Vinland. They liked what they saw there and tried to claim it, but the natives were hostile and numerous. With no clear superiority in weaponry they had no alternative but to return to Greenland.

Glossary

Abandon Ship Bag. Container of essential items to be used in a life raft.

abeam. To the side of a boat, perpendicular to the heading.

aft. Toward the rear of a boat.

amidships. Halfway between the front and back of a boat.

anchor rode. Line connecting an anchor to a boat.

anchor watch. Watch kept in case anchor drags.

antifouling paint. Paint that deters growth of barnacles and other organisms on the bottom of a boat.

autopilot. Electronic device to maintain a boat's course without manual steering.

back. Wind direction, changing counterclockwise (clockwise in southern hemisphere).

backstay. Wire running from the masthead to the stern of a boat to support the mast.

ballast. Additional weight low down in a boat to improve stability.

bare steerage. Minimum speed needed to maintain steering control.

beam reach. Sailing with the wind abeam.

beam wind. Wind at right angles to a boat's heading.

belay. To attach a line to a cleat, bollard, or other fixture.

bight. Loop of line.

bilge. Interior bottom of a boat where any water collects.

bollard. Post for securing mooring lines.

boom. Aluminum pole securing the foot (bottom) of the mainsail.

bow roller. Roller on the bow used to store and deploy the anchor.

bowsprit. Spar projecting forward from the bow, often used to support the headstay.

broad reach. Sailing with the wind on a quarter.

butterfly hatch. Ventilation hatch with openings on both sides of a central support.

cap rail. Wooden rail along the top of the topsides.

chandlery. Store that sells items for ships.

channel sixteen. VHF frequency used to communicate with
  other boats and shore stations, and to call for assistance
  in emergencies.

chart plotter. Device showing the position of a boat on a
  video display.

chronometer. Accurate timepiece for use at sea.

cleats. Pieces of metal or wood with projecting ends on
  which a rope can be tied.

clew. Corner of a sail; on a yacht, the aft bottom corner.

clinker. Hull built of overlapping planks.

close-hauled. Sailing as close as possible to the wind.

companionway. Steps leading below decks from the cockpit.

Danforth. Anchor with flat flukes (triangular blades) suitable
for soft mud and sand.

day mark. Post or other sign marking a channel or
  obstruction.

Delta. Plow type of anchor suitable for harder bottoms.

dismast. To lose a mast, especially in bad weather.

dock lines. Lines (ropes) to secure a boat at a dock or wharf.

dodger. Fabric cover to protect the companionway.

dorade. Device allowing ventilation below decks without
  admitting water.

double-reefed. Sails made smaller than with
  a single reef.

double ender. Boat pointed or rounded at the stern as well
  as at the bow.

dress ship. To set signal flags along the mainstay and
  backstay.

dry out. To strand a boat deliberately on a falling tide so
  that the hull, rudder, and propeller can be inspected or
  repaired.

fair wind. Wind that allows a boat to make the course
  desired.

fall off. To change course so that the wind is farther from the bow.

fender board. Plank laid outside the fenders to protect a boat from rough wharfs.

following seas. Waves approaching from astern.

force 3. A wind between eight and twelve miles per hour; based on Beaufort Scale that assigns numbers (from 0 [calm] to 12 [hurricane]) to wind velocities.

forecabin. See forepeak.

foredeck. Deck forward of the mast.

forepeak. Forward cabin, just aft of the chain locker.

freeboard. Distance from the water line to the upper edge of the topsides.

gale. Sustained wind of at least 40 miles per hour.

genoa. Large headsail set on the headstay.

ghost. To glide along in smooth water with a minimum of wind.

gooseneck. Device connecting the boom to the mast, allow ing the boom to angle up, down, and sideways.

GPS (Global Positioning System). An electronic instrument displaying a boat's position.

gunwale. The junction of the deck and topsides.

gybe. To change direction such that the stern passes through wind.

halyard. Line (rope) used to haul a sail up the mast or up the stay.

headsail. The sail set on the headstay.

headstay. The forwardmost stay.

headstay roller. Device to roll the headsail around the head-stay, for reefing or storage.

heave to, be hove to. To set the sails so that the boat makes no headway but drifts slowly sideways, allowing the crew to rest, especially in severe weather.

heeling. Natural tipping of a sailboat under way.

height of the sun. Angle seen between a line to the sun and a line to the horizon, usually measured with a sextant.

jibe. See gybe.

keel. Part of a boat projecting downward from the hull that balances the boat against the force of the wind on the sails.

knot. Speed of one nautical mile per hour.

latitude sailing. Route-finding method before modern navigation aids were available.

lazarette. Storage locker in the cockpit.

lazy bundle. Part of the sail not used when the sail is reefed.

leech. Aft edge of a sail.

lifelines. Wire lines around the edge of the deck to prevent crew from falling overboard.

lines. Ropes used on board a boat.

longship. Fast and light Viking fighting ship.

luff. Forward edge of a sail; also, to bring the bow of a boat into the wind, causing it to lose speed or stop.

main, mains'l. Mainsail.

monkey fist. Weighted ball used to throw a light messenger line.

nautical mile. One minute of the earth's latitude, 6078 meters.

offing. Offshore, away from the land.

painter. Line to secure the dinghy.

parachute sea anchor. Device to hold the bow of a boat toward the oncoming seas in a storm.

plow. Anchor suitable for hard bottoms.

pole star. Polaris or the North Star, stationary in the northern night sky, showing the approximate direction, north.

port. Left side of a boat facing forward.

port tack. Sailing with the wind on the port side.

Q flag. Yellow flag used to call customs and immigration officials on arrival in a country.

quarter. Between the beam and the stern.

raft. Boats lashed together while moored or at anchor.

range, range marks. Marks that are lined up to define a safe passage between obstructions.

reach. To sail with the wind forward of the beam but not close-hauled.

red duster. Red ensign flown on most British vessels.

reef. Method of reducing the effective size of a sail in high winds when the full sail would overpower the boat.

reef points. Lines to tie up the unused part of the sail when reefed.

rode. See anchor rode.

rolling hitch. Knot used to attach one line to the middle of another.

rhumb line. Direct course to the destination.

sail slides. Hooks used to attach a sail to a wire stay.

scope. Measure of the amount of rode deployed.

scud. To sail fast with a following wind.

sextant. Navigational instrument used to determine longitude and latitude by measuring altitudes of celestial bodies.

shaft zinc. Zinc used on the propeller shaft.

sheet. Line used to control a sail.

sixareen. An open Shetland boat accommodating six men.

slack water. Period between incoming and outgoing tides.

slip. Berth for a boat, usually in a marina.

sloop. Sailboat with one mast.

snubber. Nylon line tying the anchor chain to a cleat on a boat.

sounding. Reading of water depth.

soundings. Area where the depth of the water is relatively shallow.

spar. Pole used for supporting sails and rigging.

spring lines. Lines used to stop forward and backward movement of a boat when tied up at a quay.

square sail. Sail set on long poles (yards), used on traditional large sailing ships.

SSB (Single Side Band) radio. Radio used for long distance communications; can be linked to a computer to receive and send e-mail.

stanchion. Metal pole supporting lifelines.

starboard. Right side of a boat when facing forward.

stay. Wire supporting a mast.

staysail, stays'l. Sail set on a stay aft of the headstay.

steering oar. Steering device used on Viking boats.

stem, stemhead. The front of a boat.

stern arch. Arch at the stern to support radar and other antennae.

stoppers. Short lines used to tie off a rode to cleats.

stuffing box. Waterproof seal where the propeller shaft passes through the hull.

storm board. Piece of wood used to secure companionway in stormy weather.

strake. A line of planking running from stem to stern.

tack. To change direction so that wind crosses the bow of a boat.

tackle. System of rope and blocks used to apply leverage.

tender. Small boat used to go ashore; a dinghy.

topping lift. Line supporting the boom when it is not supported by the sail.

topsides. Sides of a boat above the water line.

transom. Stern of a boat.

trip (tripping) line. Line that releases the anchor from the sea bed.

trysail. Small sail that replaces the mainsail during storms.

veer. Wind direction changing clockwise (counterclockwise in southern hemisphere).

VHF (Very High Frequency). Radio for short-range communications between ships and shore stations.

warp. To move a boat by hauling on lines.

white horses. Caps on tops of waves.

winch. Mechanical device for hauling lines.

wind vane. Device to keep a boat at a constant angle to the wind without the need for manual steering.

windlass. Device for hauling the anchor.

wing and wing. Sailing downwind with the mainsail set to one side of the boat and the genoa to the other.

yole. Traditional, open Shetland boat.

zinc. Sacrifical block on exterior metal items to reduce electrolysis.

Bibliography

The full bibliography of the Vikings and their voyages is extensive. Included here is a small selection of books that are particularly relevant to the North Atlantic crossing and the places we visited.

Anderson, J. R. L. *Vinland Voyage*. London: Eyre and Spottiswood, 1967.

Armitage, John, and Mark Brackenbury. *Norwegian Cruising Guide*. London: Adlard Coles, 1996.

Cunliffe, Tom. *Topsails and Battleaxe*. London: David and Charles, 1988.

Dufferin, Lord. *Letters From High Latitudes*. London: Merlin Press, 1989.

Haywood, John. *The Penguin Historical Atlas of the Vikings*. London: Penguin Books, 1995.

Ingstad, Helge. *The Land Under The Pole Star*. New York: St. Martin's, 1966.

Jones, Gwyn. *A History of the Vikings*. London: Oxford University Press, 1984.

Jones, Gwyn. *The Norse Atlantic Saga*. London: Oxford University Press, 1986.

Larson, Laurence Marcellus, trans. *The King's Mirror*. New York: Twayne Publishers, 1917.

Magnusson, Magnus. *Iceland Saga*. London: Bodley Head, 1987.